TEJANO WEST TEXAS

Tejano West Texas

ARNOLDO DE LEÓN

Texas A&M University Press
College Station

First edition

This paper meets the requirements of ANSI/NISO Z39.48-1992 (Permanence of Paper).
Binding materials have been chosen for durability.
Manufactured in the United States of America

LIBRARY OF CONGRESS CATALOGING-IN-PUBLICATION DATA

De León, Arnoldo, 1945– author.
Tejano West Texas / Arnoldo De León. — First edition.
pages cm
Includes bibliographical references and index.
ISBN 978-1-62349-290-8 (cloth: alk. paper) —
ISBN 978-1-62349-305-9 (ebook)
1. Mexican Americans—Texas, West—History. I. Title.
F395.M5D415 2015
973'.046872—dc23

2014046007

Contents

Maps and Tables

Introduction: Investigating West Texas Tejano History

West Texas stretches from approximately the 100th meridian and extends westward to far west Hudspeth County. Physiographically, West Texas encompasses the southernmost part of the High Plains, and more precisely the expanses known geographically and historically as the Edwards Plateau and the Trans-Pecos. Rocky terrains typify this area, as do brush, range grass, mesquite trees, cacti, and desert vegetation. Mountain ranges (especially within the Big Bend) distinguish the Trans-Pecos particularly.

Environmentally, West Texas holds certain commonalities. Its arid nature discourages agriculture, although pockets of the region do lend themselves to irrigated farming (cotton, melons, and grain sorghum). Landowners thus opt for ranching and fare well raising cattle, sheep, and goats.[1]

Both the Edwards Plateau belt and the Trans-Pecos remain somewhat disconnected from the rest of the state; residents at times must travel lengthy distances to the big cities, the ones situated along present-day I-35 or east of it (or perhaps to El Paso for those in Far West Texas). The largest urban concentrations in this lightly populated, mainly rural West Texas range include San Angelo, Del Rio, Midland, and Odessa; Fort Stockton, Alpine, Pecos, Sonora, and Ozona fall under the classification of medium-size communities.

People of Spanish-Mexican descent entered this West Texas region sometime around the 1770s and during the 1850s became coagents with Anglo-Americans in advancing its development. Yet works by scholars writing from points east of I-35 attribute almost no credit to Mexican-descent people for the settlement and growth of West Texas; instead, they mark the area's process of modernization as beginning with the large-scale movement of Anglo-Americans and their industrious spirit. Thus publications dealing specifically with nineteenth-century Tejanos leave the impression that Mexicans played hardly any role in the history of the western region, for those works fix upon the central and southern sections of the state.

Insufficient archival sources in part account for this scholarly imbalance. Even as migration from both the United States and Mexico into West Texas accelerated after 1865, bringing an end to the state's last frontier, contemporaries did not leave many accounts. The few existing diaries, journals, and travel narratives by whites then entering the region neglected to address the Mexican presence; those few Anglos that did encounter Mexicans portrayed them in an unflattering manner. Because the state of Texas only began organizing many of the counties in those parts during the 1870s, and others of them later, not until 1880 did the federal government take the US census therein. Neither the Mexican nor US governments assigned consuls to that vast area, thus depriving researchers of on-the-field reports. Newspapers (of any language) appeared late in West Texas; firsthand accounts about the area came from observers and journalists working for post–Civil War newspapers such as the San Antonio *Express*, Austin *Statesman*, or the El Paso *Times*.

Researchers also encounter problems having to work with the size of the Mexican-descent population and the vastness of the region these Mexican *pobladores* (founders) inhabited. A relatively small aggregate of people constituted the Mexican American community beyond the 100th longitude. In the latter decades of the nineteenth century, moreover, West Texas remained sparsely settled. Most Mexicans lived in Trans-Pecos counties (indeed, what little secondary literature exists on nineteenth-century Mexicans have Pecos and Presidio Counties as its center point). Historians of necessity must confine themselves to scattered areas: only Tom Green, Sutton, Val Verde, and Kinney Counties had an observable Mexican American population between the 100th meridian and the Pecos River. Because of this reality, the early pobladores and their role in the development of West Texas has almost been forgotten.

Works on twentieth- and twenty-first-century Tejano history similarly overlook the presence of Mexican Americans west of the 100th meridian. Inattention to West Texas Tejanos may be due to the scholars' preference for studying the communities of South Texas and of the larger metropolitan sites of San Antonio, Houston, Dallas–Fort Worth, and El Paso with their greater concentrations of "Hispanic/Latino" residents. Certainly, Mexican Americans in the above-listed geographic loci overshadow the 266,000 Hispanic-background people who resided in this West Texas area as of 2010.[2] Despite their respectable numbers, West Texas Tejanos constituted only 1 percent of the entire Texas population (24,664,211) and 2.86 percent of the combined Hispanic Texas population (9,295,349).[3] Even Tejano historians have thus supposed that Mexican American life in West Texas history is peripheral to the broader Tejano narrative. What presently attempts to demonstrate the salience of twentieth-century West Texas Tejano history exists mainly in a sprinkling of articles published in regional journals.

This collection of chapters expands upon the existing knowledge on West Texas Tejanos. The articles, written over the span of my career as a professor of history at Angelo State University, touch upon different events and study subjects in the Edwards Plateau and Trans-Pecos region (the chapters in some instances do venture outside these parameters; one focuses specifically on Northwest Texas) covering the time period from circa the 1770s—when the first Mexican pobladores established themselves at La Junta de los Ríos—to the recent past. As a collection, it serves as a modest step in an effort to illustrate that much Mexican American history exists west of the 100th meridian. Hopefully, the work will spark enough interest to stimulate further writings on the too-long-neglected story of West Texas Tejanos.

Throughout these chapters, I apply various terms to identify those Mexican-descent residents of Texas, whether they were native or foreign-born. I rely on the word *Tejano* chiefly, but I similarly use *Mexican Americans*, *Texas Mexicans*, *Hispanics*, *ethnic Mexicans*, *Chicanos*, *Mexicanos*, and even *Mexicans* to label Mexican-origin people. In particular places, I do select the word "Mexican" to designate people from Mexico—hopefully the context therein will make the connotation clear. In referencing Euro-Americans, I have chosen commonly used names such as *whites*, *Anglos*, and *Anglo-Americans*.

Many individuals helped this product reach fruition. Foremost would be those who granted me permission to reprint old publications, among them the Texas State Historical Association, Davis Brothers Publishing Company, Ltd., the McGraw-Hill Companies, the West Texas Historical Association, the Center for Big Bend Studies, and the University of Oklahoma Press. Sincere thanks to Mary Lenn Dixon, former editor-in-chief of Texas A&M University Press, who immediately saw value in the compilation and welcomed my proposal. She had always been receptive to works on Mexican American history and probably deserves as much credit for advancing the condition of the field (through Texas A&M University Press) as any other person in the state. Angela Howell, our very efficient office coordinator in the Department of History at Angelo State University (from 2010 to 2015), never once refused to lend me a hand with any assistance

I requested; at the same time, she enthusiastically supported the project. Gratitude and appreciation goes also to María De León (no relation), our extremely competent work-study student (2013–14) who, in between her commitment to the business of the department, managed to do copying, typing, and scanning for me. She scanned from journals and flawlessly corrected copy of the oldest essays, some of which I had written on yellow pads (before modern electronic technology!) or saved on floppies now incompatible with the competencies of today's processors.

Notes

1. Ronnie C. Tyler, *The Big Bend: A History of the Last Texas Frontier* (Washington, DC: National Park Service, 1975), 5–10; Paul H. Carlson, *Texas Woollybacks: The Range Sheep and Goat Industry* (College Station: Texas A&M University Press, 1982), 101–2, 152–54; Rupert N. Richardson et al., *Texas: The Lone Star State*, 8th ed. (New York: Prentice-Hall, 2001), 5; Ron Tyler, ed., "Edwards Plateau," *The New Handbook of Texas*, 6 vols. (Austin: Texas State Historical Association, 1996): 2: 802–3; and "Trans-Pecos," in ibid., 6: 548–49.

2. *Texas Tribune*, Census 2010 Interactive Map: Texas Population by Race, Hispanic Origin, accessed November 20, 2013.

3. Ibid.

TEJANO WEST TEXAS

Forgotten *Pobladores*: Blazing Frontiers in West Texas, circa 1770s to 1890s

The first people from Mexico to establish a permanent settlement in West Texas crossed from modern-day Ojinaga (at La Junta de los Ríos) into today's Presidio, Texas. From La Junta de los Ríos during the 1770s and after, these pobladores *(settlers) explored many West Texas sites and founded a small number of settlements therein. After the war with Mexico (1846–48), Anglo-Americans began to join them. Until the early 1880s, the two peoples cooperated in colonizing West Texas; some Tejanos served as political officeholders and others became successful entrepreneurs. These early Mexicans who helped develop West Texas have, for the most part, became "forgotten pobladores."*

Long before Anglo-American settlers appeared en masse in West Texas, people of Mexican descent had explored, charted, and sank roots in portions of the region. In the decades between the late 1620s and the 1680s, Spanish missionaries and soldiers from New Mexico and from El Paso del Norte made brief forays into the Concho River country and the Big Bend in response to pleas by Jumano Indians asking for Christian instruction and for protection from Apaches.[1]

The first permanent colony founded by Mexicans in what would become West Texas resulted in the 1770s when the Spanish government ordered an *entrada* to establish an outpost at a confluence of rivers known as La Junta de los Ríos. The expedition produced the beginnings of a community of settlers, missionaries, and soldiers and took on the name of Presidio del Norte. The settlement, established for the purpose of Christianizing Indians and developing the area economically, spanned both sides of the Rio Grande and embraced modern-day Ojinaga, Chihuahua, and Presidio, Texas. When in 1821 Mexico won its independence from Spain, the new government closed the presidio and the outpost continued as a civilian settlement. Officials separated the two villages with their respective names around 1865.[2]

The pobladores at La Junta de los Ríos found living conditions harsh. They faced isolation in their remote land so far from established townships, farmsteads, and ranches in the interior of Mexico. But the colonists represented typical Mexican pioneers. The majority of the settlers were Mexican due to their *mestizo* lineage (they carried Spanish and Indian blood), and they continued mixing with the local Native American population. Most would be considered seasoned settlers familiar with the travails of life in the hinterlands and thus experienced in the ways of survival. They made subsistence their priority and honed skills such as determining locations of water sources, building living quarters (usually one-room *adobes* or *jacales*) with whatever materials the environment granted, using farm lands with a shortage (if not lack) of proper work implements, raising stock amid rugged range lands, and fighting Indians.[3]

In addition to dealing with material discomforts, villagers at Presidio del Norte contended with hunger, supply scarcities, hostility from indigenous Indian nations, epidemics of smallpox and cholera, and inevitable death. Yet they counted on their resourcefulness and will. For foods, they relied on the local flora (cacti, mesquite and fruit trees, shrubs bearing berries or nuts, for instance), on small-scale farming and gardening (which yielded them beans, squash, watermelons, and corn), and on stock raising (which supplied them with beef, pork, and veal). They might have found benefit in commerce along the Chihuahua Trail as wagons passed through Presidio and Ojinaga during the 1850s.[4] Their community and social activities on the frontier revolved around the church and some schooling, on the celebration of births, marriages, and birthdays, and on the observance of religious and secular holidays.[5] No census count exists disclosing the number of people living at La Junta de los Ríos. For the decade of the 1840s, historians suppose the figure ranged somewhere from eight hundred to two thousand.[6]

Expectedly, life's difficulties forced the pobladores into devising means to ameliorate local conditions. Possibilities for such improvement could be found to the north, across the Rio Grande. But too many barriers impeded movement in that direction, among them the scarcity of settlements in northern Chihuahua (and consequently, the fear of moving even farther away from the heartland), the shortage of settlers in Presidio del Norte (the colony could hardly afford to be further diluted by depopulation), definite Indian (Apache) danger, uncertainty as to what lay in any wilderness land, and naturally, the inhospitable climate and topography that typified West

Texas. Anyone entering that terrain (either from Mexico or from Texas proper) struggled (and still do) with weather—namely, limited rainfall.

By the early decades of the nineteenth century, pobladores from Presidio del Norte and other parts of northern Chihuahua periodically ventured into what came to be called the Big Bend region of West Texas. An abundance of wild game, open ranges for grazing livestock, fertile (albeit isolated) lands for farming, and trade with Indians who hunted buffalo farther to the north lured Mexicans into that frontier space. Out of these excursions into the Trans-Pecos occurred the mapping and identification of geographical locations, especially ones in (although not limited to) the Big Bend.[7] The names of many sites—such as Pilares, Lajitas, Porvenir, and Presidio—and waterways (Concho River, Pecos River, Alamito Creek, and Cíbolo Creek) in West Texas testify to Spanish-Mexican activity there, as well as landmarks such as Santa Elena Canyon and the Agua Fría Mountains.[8]

Chihuahuan officials apparently endorsed expansion across the Rio Grande as a practical policy; by the early 1830s some individuals (among them a person named Juana Pedraza from Chihuahua) had acquired parcels of land in the general proximity of today's Presidio, Texas.[9] With general administrative assent, Mexicans from Presidio del Norte and northern Mexico trekked north, pioneering several places across the Río Bravo. After 1845, they would have entered the state of Texas as the Lone Star Republic had by then been annexed into the United States and any ownership Mexico had previously claimed to regions in its far north had been renounced by the Treaty of Guadalupe Hidalgo of 1848. Trailblazers to found fledgling Mexican settlements included the families of Manuel Múzquiz, Gregorio Carrasco, and Darío Rodríguez. Manuel Múzquiz, a political figure fleeing turmoil in his native Mexico, in the 1850s helped launch the cattle industry in the Big Bend hinterland. Múzquiz, who established his holding near to Fort Davis (first built in 1854) in the canyon named after him, brought Mexican longhorns across the Rio Grande from Presidio del Norte and turned his investment into a paying concern. With the help of his family and of loyal *vaqueros*, Múzquiz supplemented his earnings by furnishing beef to the post at Fort Davis. But then the federal government closed the garrison at the opening of the Civil War, and repeated Indian raids on Múzquiz's holdings forced the *don* to return to Mexico by 1865 (his estate functioned as a Texas Ranger station sporadically during the 1880s).[10] Close to Fort Davis also lived Gregorio Carrasco and family, immigrants from Mexico, who (father Gregorio and son Lauriano) managed a prosperous farm enterprise by 1860.[11] North of today's Candelaria, Darío Rodríguez, whom the 1860 census listed as worth $20,000 in personal wealth, managed a successful sheep ranch.[12]

By 1860, then, when the federal government took the first census for Presidio and El Paso Counties (both established by 1850), people from Mexico constituted a fair portion of the population to have sunk roots in West Texas. Of a total population of about nine hundred, almost 60 percent were of Hispanic descent. These pobladores lived in communities that extended from the settlements of Bosque Carmelo and Fort Quitman, presently in Hudspeth County but in those frontier days a part of El Paso County. In what the state of Texas then delineated as Presidio County existed the villages of Wild Rose Pass (wherein the Gregorio Carrasco family farmed), Las Limpias, Fort Davis, Presidio del Norte, Fort Leaton, Fort Stockton, and Comanche. Almost all in 1860 were immigrants from Mexico—the exception being the very young born in Texas—and for the most part unable to read and write. As would be expected of the circumstances under which they lived, some of the settlers worked out extended family arrangements, although this was not necessarily the norm. In this harsh land, the pobladores earned their living as farmhands, herders, servants, laborers, and teamsters for West Texas military stations.[13]

The region of Texas extending from San Antonio to the El Paso area was very much a frontier wilderness when Anglos began moving into it during the 1850s and was even when their influx escalated following the Civil War. Settlers always saw prospects in making a go of cattle and sheep raising in that frontier, but not until the 1870s did ranching become a profitable enterprise for stockmen; farmers had encountered similar obstacles, as only select sections of West Texas had proven adequate for cultivation. Despite a military presence to calm fears, not until January 1881 did Indian threats to West Texas end when Texas Rangers north of Van Horn eliminated what remained of the Apache chief Victorio's surviving band.[14]

Newcomers faced further frontier menaces from gangs of outlaws. During the 1870s, for instance, brigands attacked freight wagons crossing the Pecos River carrying goods and groceries west from San Antonio toward Presidio or El Paso, accosting teamsters and confiscating cargoes.[15] A weak police presence encouraged desperadoes and road agents to wreak havoc on West Texas, especially after the western counties had been organized during the 1870s and 1880s; state officials now left it to local authorities (who had small budgets) to preserve local order.[16] Then, West Texas into the 1890s still harbored (as did frontier areas in other parts of the western

United States) dangerous men who threatened, abused, and killed people regardless of class, race, or color.[17]

Forays by horse thieves, cattle rustlers, and other outlaws (which included attacks by both Mexican Americans and Mexican nationals) added to a state of danger and disorder. Ruffians struck ranches throughout the region, including ones in Brackettville, Sonora, Alpine, Fort Davis, and Van Horn, up until the 1890s.[18] What some called the "Bloody Peninsula," a sixty-mile stretch of harsh land across lower Presidio County, turned into a particularly active scene of outrages. There, ranchmen during the 1890s organized for self-protection against attacks by rustlers crossing into Texas.[19] Border gunmen also hit US silver ore mines in Presidio and Shafter during the 1890s. To be sure, mining towns such as Shafter faced their own troubles. The concentration of miners invited to Shafter an assortment of characters, among them saloonkeepers, prostitutes, and opportunists who sought to meet the miners' wants. The mix of this element and a presence of ne'er-do-wells made for a combustible environment that inevitably produced murders, brawls, killings, and lynching.[20]

Ethnic Mexicans themselves abetted conditions on the frontier. They engaged in disputes (and at times committed murder) over grazing rights, over sheep that trespassed into private lands, or over sheep unintentionally mixing with another rancher's flock.[21] They tangled with white men over women or over insults. They could attack servicemen, such as black troopers stationed at Fort Davis, with whom they at times fraternized.[22] Mexican on Mexican violence occurred as well.[23]

Mexicans already inhabited segments of West Texas decades before the 1860s. Research indicates that ethnic Mexicans then joined the march into the region alongside whites during the 1860s and continued doing so through subsequent decades. Many came from Mexico, and especially from border states such as Chihuahua, while others arrived from the Texas interior, from places like San Antonio. Generally, the new arrivals spread throughout West Texas (according to the federal census taken in 1880 of the several newly organized counties), and they constituted a majority population in the larger Trans-Pecos counties of Presidio and Pecos, as well they did for the following decades (they also held a numerical superiority in Val Verde County, created in 1885).[24]

An accord between Mexicans and Anglos prevailed in the years immediately following the Civil War. Such an accommodation developed for several reasons, among them frontier reality. Cooperation pressed upon

Anglo newcomers since, as noted above, Mexicans in some parts of the region outnumbered whites until the last decades of the nineteenth century.[25] Anglos relied on Mexicans to tackle problems unique to the West Texas frontier, such as tapping into its particular ecological environment. More immediate was learning how to defend themselves effectively from the local Indian population: which ways worked best when fortifying themselves, what supplies needed to be stored if under siege, or what battle techniques worked best? Whites saw wisdom in depending on Mexicans to acquire knowledge of range management techniques (herding horses, cattle, and sheep) appropriate to the West Texas environs.[26] Founding successful ranches but also establishing rural and urban communities and laying out an infrastructure demanded working amicably.

Both groups, then, sought common ground in an effort to secure adequate political, economic, and social tranquility. Such an exigency permitted Anglo men to marry Mexican women. Cases of such arrangements existed even before the Civil War, among the best known being those of Ben Leaton, who married the aforementioned Juana Pedraza of Chihuahua, and Milton Faver, who married Francisca Ramírez (also of Chihuahua). Leaton had arrived in the Big Bend during the 1840s, acquired property there, and laid out a settlement just south of today's Presidio, Texas, with his wife (following Leaton's death in 1851, Juana Pedraza married one Edward Hall, a local customs official).[27] Milton Faver established his own landed estate close to present-day Shafter (and some twenty-five miles away from Leaton's place) around 1857 after moving from Ojinaga with his wife Francisca and one son named Juan.[28] Intermarriage, at least until about the 1880s, became a fact of life tolerated in certain places of West Texas.

Such cases of intermarriage might have been expected, for even as many as fifteen years after the Civil War ended, a sparse number of white women lived in West Texas for white men to marry.[29] In remote settings such as the Fort Davis community—where few white women resided before the 1880s—white men there considered young Mexican women (*señoritas*) particularly sensuous and seductive.[30] During the 1870s and into the 1880s, indeed, a number of white men took as wives Mexican women living around Fort Davis. According to one scholar, "In 1880, no fewer than half of married Anglo males in Fort Davis had wives of Mexican ancestry."[31] In fact, some of the more prominent white officials in the town had Mexican spouses (the pattern of interracial marriages in Fort Davis declined by the latter decades of the nineteenth century with the closing of the post and an increase in the number of Anglo ranch families arriving in the region).[32]

Similar cases of Anglo men and Mexican women bonding could be found in Presidio, Fort Stockton, San Angelo, and Del Rio.[33] Aside from the human instinct for sexual companionship, of course, other factors entered into these cross-cultural couplings, among them love, the desire to raise a family, and the possibility of developing social networks that might produce economic power or political influence.[34]

Because of population disparities, Anglos in West Texas recognized the need to have Mexicans participate politically (though not necessarily in influential positions) in order to establish some semblance of order. This arrangement seemed especially crucial in the decade following the Civil War when whites pushed westward into counties then in the process of being organized. Thus, Juan José Acosta occupied the post of the Presidio County commissioners' court when the Texas government formally organized Presidio County in 1875.[35] Continuously from 1875 to the early 1880s, Spanish-surnamed persons appeared on the list of Presidio County justices of the peace, grand jurors, and jurors.[36] At the same time (1875), Pablo Alderette held office as county commissioner in Tom Green County and as a justice of the peace in the precinct, while several Mexican Americans made up part of both the grand and petit juries formed that year.[37] Cesario Torres participated in the three-man commission assigned to organize Pecos County in 1871 and when the county gained official status in 1875 won election (along with Hipólito Carrasco, a local rancher) as justice of the peace—subsequently Cesario Torres officiated as a county commissioner (1875–86). Bernardo Torres (brother of Cesario) served as foreman of the first grand jury assembled in Pecos County in 1875.[38] The need to have a stable constabulary opened opportunities for Mexican Americans, and some found work as deputies or as constables during these years.[39]

Reasons resembling those swaying Anglos to league politically with Tejanos to assist in conquering the West Texas range, to establish settlements between San Antonio and El Paso, and to connect the region through a functional road system produced economic arrangements with Mexicans. On their own, therefore, Mexicans found ranch spreads, as in the case of the aforementioned San Antonio native Cesario Torres who (with his brothers Bernardo and Juan and family relative Félix Garza) pioneered the Pecos County area in the early 1870s. A short distance from today's Fort Stockton, Cesario acquired government land with scrip and, using the tradition of squatter claims, erected the Seven-D cattle ranch. Under the name of Torres Irrigation Company, Cesario and family built in the mid-1870s an irrigation system on the Pecos River to help area farmers; the state compensated them with land certificates for their work (the contract called for the company to keep up repairs on the canals for ten years before receiving its certificates). Cesario Torres's own holdings as of 1870 included real estate in the amount of $1,000 and personal worth of $4,000, and his settlement included several Mexican families and laborers whom Torres supported. Torres continued expanding his landholdings throughout the 1870s so that by the end of the decade his acreage included much livestock and croplands in which, with the help of resident Mexican families, he harvested an assortment of grains and vegetables. Beginning around 1882, unfortunately, Cesario began facing financial disappointments. His brother and company partner Bernardo passed away that year, leaving Cesario with obligations (among them maintaining the canals in working form) the Torres Irrigation Company still had to the state. Then Cesario defaulted on bonds he and his brother had pledged certifying the integrity of several county officials whom they considered friends. His predicament forced him to sell first his Seven-D ranch in 1886 and then in 1887 the Torres Irrigation Company; he moved out of the Fort Stockton area and relocated to San Antonio.[40]

To be included among Torres family members who contributed to the development of West Texas and Pecos County would be his brother Bernardo. Before his death, Bernardo had almost equaled Cesario's gains, leaving to his family an estate valued some $8,700. Also to be credited would be Félix Garza, a family member by marriage (it is unclear whether Félix was Cesario's brother-in-law or his father-in-law). Garza had accompanied the Torres family to Pecos County and through his own Garza Irrigation Company advanced the development of farming in the region. During the mid-1870s, he served Pecos County as a constable and justice of the peace.[41]

The contributions of the Torres family to the development of West Texas included even others in Cesario's own family. From compensation the state had given Cesario, Bernardo, and Juan for having built the abovementioned irrigation system in the mid-1870s, Bernardo Torres acquired property located in what would become Langtry, Texas. When Bernardo passed away Cesario bought the land from Bernardo's widow. To handle the ranching operations around Langtry, Cesario sent his well-educated bilingual son Jesús Pablo, who in 1882 began having problems with a newcomer named Roy Bean. Troubles revolved around the fact that Roy Bean ran a competing beer business in Langtry and that Bean, in the capacity of a Pecos County justice of the peace (appointed in August 1882), wielded much influence in Torres's own town.[42] For almost two decades Torres and Bean (the self-styled "Law West of the Pecos") carried on a personal rivalry, and in 1896, Torres defeated Bean as justice of the peace in Langtry (which since 1885 had been reassigned to newly created Val Verde County). The two competed again in 1898 and 1900, with Torres winning consecutive terms until losing to Bean in 1900.[43]

Further succeeding in the Trans-Pecos region were several Mexican rancheros in neighboring Presidio County, the best known among them being Victoriano Hernández, founder of Alamo Ranch (situated some sixty miles from present Marfa). Hernández arrived from Mexico in 1874 and homesteaded along the Alamito Creek. He promptly erected a large adobe home and auxiliary buildings, transporting needed building supplies from Mexico. Over the years, Hernández enhanced his ranch by planting fruit trees, cultivating a garden, and increasing his animal stock. The ranch served as a setting for festivities that his large family, his workers, and many visitors enjoyed. He passed away in 1903, leaving his landholdings to heirs.[44] Other active ranchers—judging from the cattle brands they registered with the county as of the year 1875—included Jesús Rodríguez, Cleto Esida, Josibio Flores, Abateo Carrasco, Máximo Acosta, and Lino Baeza.[45]

Also successfully raising livestock in West Texas was Pablo Alderette, who arrived in San Angelo and the "Concho Country" around 1869 or 1870, planted lands along the North Concho River, and by 1880 had improved the claim of about four hundred farm acres to a worth of $6,000; additionally, don Pablo ranched a few cattle and horses. His son Guillermo Alderette had earned notice (along with another local landowner named Jesús María Para) by the 1870s as among the most prominent Concho Country ranchers as well as a land investor, and upon inheriting his father's property (Pablo died in 1882), Guillermo diversified into other ventures, including the saloon business. The 1890 tax rolls showed his taxable property at approximately $4,000. His widow ultimately sold their real estate possessions to a local Anglo entrepreneur in the late 1890s.[46]

Farming also enticed those willing to take risks, work hard, and improve on untilled lands. Most prominent among such enterprising individuals was Secundino Luján, a resident of Ojinaga who in the 1870s colonized part of Presidio County. According to one account, Texas state officials persuaded Luján to undertake the establishment of farms on the Texas side of the Rio Grande; in compensation the Luján colonists would be given the right to work on Texas soil, receive 160 acres, and ultimately become US citizens. With four other organizers, Luján started the project by first preparing the grant for farming; then in 1871–72 the land developers transported their families to what the settlers named San José del Polvo (abbreviated as Polvo, modern-day Redford). The farming families built a canal upon their arrival but launched in 1876 a larger operation authorized by the legislature (this project followed the lines of the agreement made with the Torres family in Pecos County). About the same time, Governor Richard Coke recognized the settlers' farm rights. By then (February 1876), Luján (and the other organizers) had accepted US citizenship. Luján subsequently served in such Presidio County capacities as precinct commissioner.[47] Fabricio Granado of Fort Davis also farmed early in Presidio County and according to the 1880 census had stocked his 160-acre estate (valued at $1,300) with horses, mules, donkeys, sheep, and cattle.[48]

Around Fort Stockton in Pecos County, many Mexicans had earned prominence as farmers by 1870, according to the federal census; like the Torres families in the same county, they also had under cultivation a variety of vegetables and fruits. Some of these farmers also pursued ranching and registered their cattle brands with county officials.[49]

In Val Verde County, Paula Losoya Taylor established herself as a successful farmer after cofounding Del Rio in the 1860s with her husband James Taylor (both arrived from Uvalde, in Uvalde County). Acquiring land from the state, husband and wife went about developing their farm acquisition with laboring help from locals living in a struggling district known popularly as "Las Sapas" (so-called because settlers lived in improvised housing set underground and covered with brushwood for protection from the elements; *sapas* referred to these excavations). Although losing her husband soon after arriving in the region, Señora Losoya (who was bilingual) expanded upon her (and her husband's) land purchases and by the early 1880s had almost three thousand acres under cultivation. She watered her gardens (which included corn plants, fruit trees, sugar canes, and vines) through *acequias* (irrigation ditches) connected to the San Felipe Springs and powered her two mills with water from these same canals. She contributed to life in Del Rio further by investing in town enterprises (she built a candy factory) and also by donating monies to support border Catholic churches and local educational establishments.[50]

Demand for services essential to sustaining life in the hinterland opened up possibilities for some Mexican Americans to launch independent businesses. Thus did Cesario Torres (the same of Fort Stockton) negotiate during the 1870s a contract with the US government to furnish wood for troops at Fort Davis and Fort Stockton.[51] As well, Carmen Ramírez, Milton Faver's brother-in-law, during the 1870s and until his death in 1875 supplied beef and mutton to military forces assigned to the Big Bend area.[52]

Tranquility, it seemed, presided over the era of early contact between Mexican pobladores and the initial wave of Anglo colonists settling in

West Texas. Together, the two groups had acted as "builders of the frontier," fending off menacing outlaws and Indians, establishing political and economic order, implanting settlements, and initiating the modernization of the region. By the 1880s, however, this peaceful accommodation began to evaporate.

Notes

1. Donald E. Chipman, *Spanish Texas, 1519–1821* (Austin: University of Texas Press, 1992), 61–62, 69–70.

2. Israel Mendoza de Levario, *A Brief Chronicle of Presidio del Norte: Homeland of the Jumano* (Austin: La Junta Press, 2012), 13, 17; Oakah L. Jones, "Settlements and Settlers at La Junta de los Ríos, 1759–1822," *Journal of Big Bend Studies* 3 (January 1991): 52.

3. Jones, "Settlements and Settlers at La Junta de los Ríos," 53–54.

4. Howard G. Applegate and C. Wayne Hanselka, *La Junta de los Rios del Norte y Conchos*, Southwestern Studies 41 (El Paso: Texas Western Press, 1974), 36–37.

5. Mendoza de Levario, *Brief Chronicle of Presidio del Norte*, 16, 18, 21, 67.

6. Carlysle Graham Raht, *The Romance of the Davis Mountains and Big Bend Country* (El Paso: Raht Books, 1919), 119; and Roy L. Swift and Leavitt Corning Jr., *Three Roads to Chihuahua: The Great Wagon Roads That Opened the Southwest, 1823–1883* (Austin: Eakin Press, 1988), 37.

7. Mendoza de Levario, *Brief Chronicle of Presidio del Norte*, 16, 17. The journal by Don Francisco Colomo (in Mendoza's book) contains numerous notations of travels made toward the Pecos area, some of them going back to the 1820s.

8. Virginia Madison and Hallie Stillwell, *How Come It's Called That?* rev. ed. (New York: October House, 1968), 16, 44, 51, 53, 54, 81, 102, 104–5, 108; as well as entries specific to these sites found in Ron Tyler, ed., *The New Handbook of Texas*, 6 vols. (Austin: Texas State Historical Association, 1996).

9. Leavitt Corning, *Baronial Forts of the Big Bend: Ben Leaton, Milton Faver, and Their Private Forts in Presidio County* (San Antonio: Trinity University Press, 1969), 21–22.

10. Arthur R. Gómez, *A Most Singular Country: A History of Occupation in the Big Bend* (Salt Lake City, UT: Signature Books; Provo, UT: Charles Redd Center for Western Studies, Brigham Young University, 1990), 96–97, 146; Helen Simons and Cathryn A. Hoyt, eds., *Hispanic Texas: A Historical Guide* (Austin: University of Texas Press, 1992), 300; "Múzquiz Creek," in Tyler, ed., *New Handbook of Texas*, 4: 911–12.

11. Robert Wooster, *Frontier Crossroads: Fort Davis and the West* (College Station: Texas A&M University Press, 2006), 41.

12. Raht, *The Romance of the Davis Mountains and Big Bend Country*, 194; Paul Wright, "Population Patterns in Presidio County in 1880: Evidence from the Census," *Journal of Big Bend Studies* 7 (January 1995): 186, 194.

13. *Population Schedules of the Eighth Census of the United States, 1860* (Washington, DC), Roll 1293, Presidio County and El Paso County, 77–80, 82–84, 66–76, 85–88; Wooster, *Frontier Crossroads*, 40–41.

14. Clayton W. Williams, *Texas' Last Frontier: Fort Stockton and the Trans-Pecos, 1861–1895*, ed. Ernest Wallace (College Station: Texas A&M University Press, 1982), 246; Robert M. Utley, *Lone Star Justice: The First Century of the Texas Rangers* (Oxford: Oxford University Press, 2002), 215–16.

15. San Antonio *Express*, November 10, 1873, 3; January 22, 1884, 4; Patrick Dearen, *Crossing Rio Pecos* (Fort Worth: Texas Christian University Press, 1996), 18–19.

16. San Antonio *Express*, April 15, 1887, 2.

17. An example would be Andrew Jackson Royal, of the Fort Stockton area. Williams, *Texas' Last Frontier.*

18. San Antonio *Express*, August 26, 1881, 1; August 27, 1881, 1; April 15, 1887, 2; October 1, 1896, 6; Austin *American*, May 4, 1886, 6; Raht, *The Romance of the Davis Mountains and Big Bend Country*, 310–12; Sutton County Historical Society, *Bad Old Days in and around Sutton County, 1889–1939: Murder, Mischief, Misery, and Mayhem* (Sonora: Sutton County Historical Society, 199?), 1.

19. New York *Times*, July 2, 1892, 1; San Antonio *Express*, August 16, 1891, 3.

20. Austin *Statesman*, January 15, 1892, 1. On these mines in the Big Bend, see Gómez, *A Most Singular Country*, 156–57, 113, 116; Cecilia Thompson, *History of Marfa and Presidio County, Texas, 1535–1946*, 2 vols. (Austin: Nortex Press, 1985), 1: 290; Bob Alexander, *Riding Lucifer's Line: Ranger Deaths along the Texas-Mexico Border* (Denton: University of North Texas Press, 2013), 111–12, 114.

21. San Antonio *Express*, October 19, 1890, 2.

22. Ibid., January 16, 1884, 2.

23. Ibid., August 16, 1891, 3; Sutton County Historical Society, *Bad Old Days in and around Sutton County*, 3, 4, 12, 18.

24. Glen Sample Ely, *Where the West Begins: Debating Texas Identity* (Lubbock: Texas Tech University Press, 2011), 77; Arnoldo De León and Kenneth L. Stewart, *Tejanos and the Numbers Game: A Socio-Historical Interpretation from the Federal Censuses, 1859–1900* (Albuquerque: University of New Mexico Press, 1989), 12; Arnoldo De León and Kenneth L. Stewart, "Tejano Demographic Patterns and Socio-Economic Development," *Borderlands Journal* 7, no. 1 (1983): 8, table 1. On ethnic Mexicans living in Presidio County between 1860 and 1880, see Wright, "Population Patterns in Presidio County in 1880," 188, 196. For Mexicans living in Fort Davis in 1860, 1870, and 1880, see Wooster, *Frontier Crossroads*, 40–41, 125, as well as Paul Wright, "Residential Segregation in Two Early West Texas Towns," *Southwestern Historical Quarterly* 102 (January 1999): 306. For Tejanos living in Fort Stockton in 1870 and 1880, see Williams, *Texas' Last Frontier*, 135–36, 261–62, and María Eva Flores, CDP, "The Good Life the Hard Way: The Mexican American Community of Fort Stockton, Texas, 1930–1945" (PhD diss., Arizona State University, 2000), 31, 34. For Tejanos living in Marfa, Alpine, and Marathon as of 1900, see Gómez, *A Most Singular Country*, 99. For Alpine, see Clifford B. Casey, *Alpine, Texas: Then and Now* (Seagraves, TX: Pioneer Book Publishers, 1981), 23, and Wright, "Residential Segregation in Two Early West Texas Towns," 306. For San Angelo, see Arnoldo De León, *San Angeleños: Mexican Americans in San Angelo, Texas* (San Angelo: Fort Concho Museum Press, 1985), 18, 33.

25. Some observers make this point, among them Wright, "Population Patterns in Presidio County in 1880," 198; and Ely, *Where the West Begins*, 77.

26. Mendoza de Levario, *Brief Chronicle of Presidio del Norte*, 67, 68.

27. Corning, *Baronial Forts of the Big Bend*, 22–23, 33.

28. Ibid., 43–45, 52. Juan Faver himself married Mexican women. Ibid., 58–59, 64.

29. Wright, "Residential Segregation in Two Early West Texas Towns," 300, and Wright, "Population Patterns in Presidio County in 1880," 189. Compared to pre–Civil War San Antonio and post–Mexican War South Texas a Tejano landed elite did not have roots in West Texas. Presumably, then, partners in these cross-cultural marriages came from poor, pioneer families. I. J. Bush, a medical doctor stationed in Fort Davis during the early 1890s, noted, "practically the only women in West Texas were Mexicans of the lower class." I. J. Bush, *Gringo Doctor* (Caldwell, ID: Caxton Printers, 1939), 37. A few women, however, might have held some social standing in Mexican towns such as Ojinaga, but not many. On South Texas marriages between Anglos and Mexican women belonging to the elite class, see David Montejano, *Anglos and Mexicans in the Making of Texas, 1836–1986* (Austin: University of Texas Press, 1987), 34–37.

30. San Antonio *Herald*, May 25, 1868, 2.

31. Wright, "Residential Segregation in Two Early West Texas Towns," 305.

32. Wooster, *Frontier Crossroads*, 125–28; Wright, "Residential Segregation in Two Early West Texas Towns," 305.

33. For the extent of intermarriage throughout Presidio County in 1880, see Wright, "Population Patterns in Presidio County in 1880," 190–91. For Fort Stockton, Flores, "The Good Life the Hard Way," 3, 65. On San Angelo, De León, *San Angeleños*, 23, 151. Alpine was not established until 1881–82, about the time that white men entered West Texas with their families. Consequently, little intermarriage occurred there. See Wright, "Residential Segregation in Two Early West Texas Towns," 305.

34. Wooster, *Frontier Crossroads*, 126.

35. Barry Scobee, *Fort Davis, Texas: 1583–1965* (Fort Davis: Barry Scobee, 1963), 97–99; Lucy Miller Jacobson and Mildred Bloys Nored, *Jeff Davis County, Texas* (Fort Davis: Fort Davis Historical Society, 1993), 94–95, 135. Ely, *Where the West Begins*, 79. According to Wright, Mexican Americans did not hold any political offices at Fort Davis or at Alpine after 1880. Wright, "Residential Segregation in Two Early West Texas Towns," 308–9.

36. Thompson, *History of Marfa and Presidio County*, 1: 132–34, 140, 143, 151, 175, 177; Jacobson and Nored, *Jeff Davis County, Texas*, 94–95.

37. Grace Bitner, "Early History of the Concho Country and Tom Green County," *West Texas Historical Association Yearbook* 9 (October 1933): 105, 108.

38. Raht, *The Romance of the Davis Mountains and Big Bend Country*, 175, 215–16; Williams, *Texas' Last Frontier*, 147, 192, 195, 200, 291. Other county commissioners in Pecos County during this period included Emilio Lavedra (1875–80) and Rosario Ureta (1891–?), ibid., 220, 272, 343. Joe C. Primera, "Los Hermanos Torres: Early Settlers of Pecos County," *Permian Historical Annual* 20 (1980): 90. See further Ely, *Where the West Begins*, 79.

39. Wright, "Population Patterns in Presidio County in 1880," 193; Thompson, *History of Marfa and Presidio County, Texas*, 1: 132.

40. Raht, *The Romance of the Davis Mountains and Big Bend Country*, 175–76; Williams, *Texas' Last Frontier*, 120, 126, 135, 195, 205, 207, 220–21, 260, 262; Primera, "Los Hermanos Torres," 89, 91–94; Doug Braudaway, "Torres Founders of Langtry," online publication for Val Verde County Historical Commission, accessed November 28, 2013; Marsha Lea Daggett, *Pecos County History*, 2 vols. (Canyon, TX: Staked Plains Press, 1984), 1: 128, 132, 222; Dearen, *Crossing Rio Pecos*, 64–66; Jack Skiles, *Judge Roy Bean Country* (Lubbock: Texas Tech University Press, 1996), 54.

41. Williams, *Texas' Last Frontier*, 205, 207; Primera, "Los Hermanos Torres," 89, 91–92; Daggett, *Pecos County History*, 2: 184–85.

42. Primera, "Los Hermanos Torres," 90, 91; Braudaway, "Torres Founders of Langtry"; Skiles, *Judge Roy Bean Country*, 10, 115, 154; Doug Braudaway, "Bracketing Bean: The Other Two Leaders of Langtry, Texas," *Journal of Big Bend Studies* 20 (2008): 62–67; C. L. Sonnichsen, *Roy Bean: Law West of the Pecos* (New York: Devin-Adair, 1958), 97.

43. Braudaway, "Torres Founders of Langtry"; Sonnichsen, *Roy Bean*, 100, 106, 110–11.

44. Madison and Stillwell, *How Come It's Called That?*, 112–14.

45. Thompson, *History of Marfa and Presidio County, Texas*, 1: 351.

46. De León, *San Angeleños*, 140; San Angelo *Standard*, October 4, 1884, 5; October 9, 1886, 3; August 20, 1887, 3; September 15, 1888, 7.

47. Thompson, *History of Marfa and Presidio County, Texas*, 1: 119, 133–34, 141, 200; Jacobson and Nored, *Jeff Davis County, Texas*, 124; Jack Richard Chappell, "El Polvo" (A Paper Presented to Dr. Clifford B. Casey in Partial Fulfillment of the Requirements for the Course History 432, Sul Ross State College, 1964), 9–12, 15. Earl H. Elam, "Acculturation on the Rio Grande Frontier: The Founding of San José del Polvo and the Family of Lucía Rede Madrid," *Journal of Big Bend Studies* 5 (January 1993): 82–87.

48. Wooster, *Frontier Crossroads*, 41, 127.

49. Daggett, *Pecos County History*, 1: 101, 128, 152–57, 162–70.

50. San Antonio *Express*, January 24, 1883, 2; "Paula Losoya Taylor," in Tyler, ed., *New Handbook*

of Texas, 4: 297; Whitehead Memorial Museum, *La Hacienda: An Official Bicentennial Publication* (Del Rio: The Museum, 1976), 3, 5, 369. Also, Steven W. Prewitt, "'We Didn't Ask to Come to This Party': Self Determination Collides with the Federal Government in the Public Schools of Del Rio, Texas, 1890–1971" (PhD diss., University of Houston, 2000), 31, 33–34.

51. Raht, *The Romance of the Davis Mountains and Big Bend Country*, 217; John Ernest Gregg, "The History of Presidio County" (master's thesis, University of Texas, Austin, 1933), 55.

52. Gómez, *A Most Singular Country*, 98. "Morita, Texas," in Tyler, ed., *New Handbook of Texas*, 4: 839.

2

Reversals: Racial Conflict and Tejano Adaptation, 1880 to 1890s

Up to around 1880 *Anglos and Mexicans had generally worked together to bring order, progress, and modernization to West Texas, but sometime around that year good relations began to erode. As a greater number of Anglos entered the region, the need for Mexican cooperation in "conquering the frontier" lessened. Friction, violence, and segregation now replaced cordial associations. To cope with these difficulties, Tejanos adapted. They improvised at developing mechanisms for survival, retained cultural forms* (lo mexicano) *that provided a degree of assurance in a threatening world, accepted the Americanization around them, and pressed on in founding new settlements.*

Peaceful coexistence between Anglos and Mexicans seemingly reigned in the region of the Edwards Plateau and Trans-Pecos when Anglos met Mexicans. But this calm relationship clouded a darker dimension of group relations. Racial antagonism and distrust had always simmered and in the last decades of the nineteenth century burst openly to reverse the previous state of racial coexistence. Having by then evened out demographically with the *pobladores* and having become increasingly confident of their claim to West Texas, Anglos turned to intimidation and violence to uphold their ascendancy.

Antipathy toward Tejanos rested on attitudes whites held toward Mexicans. Prominent Anglo-American citizens of the region, plain folks, travelers, and newspaper reporters (among others) commonly considered Mexicans (and referred to them unabashedly) as "greasers."[1] They might have conveniently made an exception of some, but otherwise, Anglos viewed the Mexican population as being mongrels of Mexican-Indian blood, dark skinned, dirty-looking, and physically inferior.[2] Whites would probably have been, as a community correspondent to a Coke County newspaper confessed in 1898, "a happy people [if] Negroes or Mexicans" did not live locally.[3] Indolence and passivity appeared to Anglos to be congenital Mexican traits, but also gambling and drinking.[4] To observers, Mexicans lacked schooling and civility. They built their homes in the most primitive ways ("wretched cabins as the lowliest Tennessee negro would not put his pig in," one southern traveler judged) and worked land acquisitions with the most primitive farm implements, said tools devised in the crudest manner.[5] Anglos stereotyped Mexicans further as an immoral people; some critics judged them as being promiscuous and indifferent toward adultery.[6]

Among the most common stereotypical traits Anglos imputed to Mexicans was that of being inherently violent. Anglos imagined Mexicans as being villainous, bloodthirsty, and sadistic cutthroats. According to accounts by Anglo settlers and reports disseminated in newspaper stories, Mexicans possessed uncontrollable impulses. One West Texas (Anglo) ranch hand in the 1880s thought Mexican range hands in the San Angelo area to be fine when sober, "but when they got drunk they'd fight over almost anything—horses, saddles and gear, money or señoritas. They were quick on the draw and had red hot tempers."[7] Mexicans could cause the most fiendish atrocities, such as massacring and then stabbing, slashing, and butchering people (both white men and Mexicans).[8] In May 1891, a San Antonio newspaper published an incredible story (of "a diabolical murder") that had occurred in Del Rio. The fantastic details of the crime had the perpetrator killing his lover, hacking her body, and before skipping town, writing in blood: "fresh meat for sale."[9]

Relationships between Anglos and those deemed undeserving of a place in West Texas—due to their mongrel status, their backwardness, and their propensity for violence—had always been precarious. During the last two decades of the nineteenth century following the period of Indian pacification, conflict seemed to have escalated (at the same time, the political and economic status of ethnic Mexicans appeared to have declined—discussed below). In part, clashes between the two peoples resulted from a Wild West culture that endorsed the ending of quarrels and disagreements with firearms and through vigilante justice. But engagements with racial overtones became a salient indication of racial discord in West Texas. Newspapers disseminated stories of race wars, as in the case of a confrontation that occurred between Mexicans and whites in Murphyville. Newspapers reported the incident as a "riot," purportedly started because Mexicans resented the presence of Anglos in the new town (modern-day Alpine, established in 1882) and sought to oust them. Then on April 18, 1886, Mexicans attacked the Cattle Exchange Saloon, ostensibly a popular drinking place for whites. According to a news dispatch, Anglos regrouped after the encounter and then "cleared the town and surrounding country of Mexicans."[10] Fights (brawls) between males of the two races erupted over Mexican women, as whites—much to the chagrin of resentful Mexican males—sought female companionship at weekly *fandangos* (festive affairs assembled either in the open air or a hall, and with music provided by a violin, guitar, or harps), held in remote settlements such as Valentine.[11]

In a region with ever-present racial tension, feuds seemed inevitable and indeed erupted. Some of these engagements might have their origins in grudges between an Anglo and Mexican family and could escalate to involve an entire community. In one such case that took place in Del Rio, the Albino Pérez Sr. family allied itself with the Indalicia Rivera family against Samuel Griner and his brothers. According to newspaper reports, Indalicia and Louis Rivera had in 1880 killed Samuel Griner. Although the sources do not reveal motive, ill feelings might have arisen from domestic problems between Jones Griner and his wife, the daughter of Indalicia Rivera. There then entered into the picture Albino Pérez Jr., a known desperado under indictment for murder, who apparently wished to avenge the death of his father (Albino Pérez Sr.) killed in December 1883 at the hands of Anglos (nothing attached the Griners to the crime). By the spring of 1884, therefore, great bitterness determined race relations in Del Rio, so much so that according to details residents provided to Mexico's government, a secret society of Anglos existed in Del Rio with designs of inflicting violence upon local Mexicans.

Then, in May 1884, Albino Pérez Jr. and "a band of Mexicans armed with Winchesters and revolvers" exacerbated matters when they attacked a dance hall where Henry Griner and friends had gathered for an evening's pleasure (Anglo witnesses called it a planned attack, as the Mexican revelers left the place at a predetermined time around 11:00 p.m. knowing of the raid in advance) and killed Griner. The incident provoked hatred on both sides, and in what newspapers depicted as a "riot," each camp (Mexicans and Anglos) threatened violence and swore to destroy Del Rio. Indeed, whites set aflame some houses in the town. The murder of Henry Griner (by the Pérez-Rivera faction), according to one source, had simply awakened long-standing ill feelings between the races. But others noted that the Mexicans who had rallied behind the Pérez and Rivera band belonged to a "bad" element within the Mexican community in the city, with the law-abiding Mexicans condemning the action of the wrongdoers. Troops from the Eighth Cavalry brought order to the town with street patrols, but racial distrust did not ease with the establishment of peace. Some Mexican laborers in Del Rio believed their lives were endangered and sought to leave for their home country. Mexico's minister in Washington called upon authorities to investigate matters, but the district attorney in Kinney County answered that Mexican Americans need not fear threats to their safety and that they should rest at ease. Thus the matter ended.[12]

Other feuds stemmed from issues of racial chauvinism. In 1897, at the Four Sixes Ranch in Presidio County, Anglo cowboys and Mexican sheepherders (apparently both working at the Four Sixes) clashed when the cowboys with pistol fire disrupted the sheepherders' festive observance of Cinco de Mayo (Fifth of May, commemorating the Battle of Puebla in Mexico, May 5, 1862). The Mexicans counterattacked later, setting fire to one of the cowboys' tents; the cowboys in turn vowed to kill the Mexicans. Ugly tensions simmered between the two sides for some time thereafter, but the ranch owner apparently resolved this localized feud, as newspapers did not report anything further on the episode.[13]

Suspicion based on racial stereotypes (of the "blood-lusting Mexican") in one instance (and probably many others) produced in 1886 the threat of death if Mexicans did not leave a community in McCulloch County. The Mexican consul in San Antonio called for an investigation of the case for the expulsion, but according to the response from the county clerk, a "Mexican Greaser" had callously slain a policeman and therefore suspected accomplices in the crime (and in sundry other criminal activities around the area) had been told to leave as they had caused local disorder by their gambling, drinking, and undisciplined behavior. But law-abiding Mexicans, the county clerk assured the consul, still possessed the freedom to work in the county. The answer did not satisfy the consul, but no further action appears to have been taken to ensure the protection of members of the Mexican community in McCulloch County.[14]

Racial hatred often spurred atrocious acts against Mexicans; murders and other violent outrages inflicted on Tejanos rested on two assumptions: that perpetrators would suffer no penalty for crimes committed against Mexicans and that no law prevented the killing of a Mexican.[15] Some Anglos regarded Mexicans as devoid of human stature anyway. One West Texas sheep rancher remarked casually that white folks looked upon the killing of a Mexican with cold indifference. On one occasion, he remarked, riders came upon the body of a Mexican lifeless on the road, but passed it by, as "it was nobody's business to bury him."[16]

Whites felt licensed, therefore, to take extralegal measures against Mexicans who defied white power. Fierce retaliation, in the form of vigilante justice and lynching,[17] certainly, occurred against any Mexican accused of committing any number of transgressions. In the Fort Davis area in 1883, citizens resorted to a lynching campaign to cope with local lawlessness, hoping that the offensive would end in peace and order.[18] Another lynching incident occurred in Shafter in 1890. According to details, authorities arrested a Mexican troublemaker, and while in police custody (chained to a tree), the Mexican fell victim to a party of white miners who forcibly abducted the prisoner and shot him. Suspecting whites of complicity in the execution, some in the local Mexican population advised Anglos to best leave the region. More physical encounters in Shafter between the Mexican community and Anglo miners followed the killing until a unit of Texas Rangers arrived in Presidio County to keep the Anglo mine workers from harm's way.[19]

Lynch law could be ruthlessly applied to Mexicans committing the loathsome infraction of raping a white woman. Sometime in the early 1890s, citizens in Junction City immediately called for a lynch law upon learning the particulars of a case surrounding a Mexican accused of attempting to ravish a rancher's wife. According to one contemporary (circa 1890–91),

> Had he been a Texan, it would probably have fared very differently with him from the first; but it is difficult to convince these people that a Mexican is a human being. He seems to be the Texans' natural enemy; he is treated like a dog, or, perhaps, not so well.[20]

In still another lynching instance, unidentified parties waylaid (motive unknown) Jesús Salceda near Knickerbocker (a small village some twenty miles from San Angelo) and hanged him from a live oak tree in 1894.[21]

In parts of West Texas, a select group of Mexican-origin pioneers in the years following the Civil War succeeded in obtaining a niche politically and economically. Among them were the families of the brothers Torres, of Secundino Luján and Fabricio Granado of Presidio County, of the Alderettes of Tom Green County, and of women like Paula Losoya of Val Verde County. In their heyday these families commanded respect and esteem and enjoyed some level of community influence. They had achieved a degree of prosperity through sacrifice, indomitable effort, and personal fortitude.

Yet by the later years of the nineteenth century, the fortunes of these early *pobladores* waned and opportunities that previously might have been available to Mexicans plunged. Officeholding by Tejanos, even in counties such as Pecos and Presidio where Spanish-surnamed people dominated, dropped after about 1880 (until it resurged many decades later in the twentieth century). In San Angelo, a parallel reversal took place. Pablo Alderette died in 1882, representation at the county level ceased, and no longer did San Angeleños receive appointments to jury duty as they had in the 1870s.[22]

Economically, a like regression of standing occurred. The old lands of the Tejano pioneers slipped into the hands of Anglo-Americans. Land loss among Mexican Americans in the United States occurred for several reasons, according to those who have studied the topic, and a combination of circumstances probably account for similar West Texas experiences. Anglo opportunism and fraud invariably rank among causes producing land dispossession, but scholars also find fault with Tejanos. Many Mexicans considered their ranches and farms as means of supporting their families; consequently, they neglected to invest in their operations or they otherwise failed to adopt innovations needed for enhancing property values. During times of economic distress, therefore, they confronted difficulties in meeting tax obligations, repaying loans, or finding funds to sustain their herds or crops. Droughts forced many to sell their stock or property to Anglos having access to financial resources. All these forces certainly played upon West Texas Tejanos, but so did their language difficulties (which impeded their ability to conduct transactions), their problems in verifying the legality of their titles, their helplessness in knowing the steps needed to defend their claims, and their superficial grasp of the US legal system.[23]

Several other factors might explain the slump that befell the broader Hispanic population.[24] First, the general dislike many Anglos held toward Mexican "greasers" impeded Tejano upward mobility. Violence and lynching continued in some parts of West Texas even into the twentieth century.[25] The freighting and transportation business that Mexicans had once dominated, as another example to be attributed to their dislocation, by the 1880s had become the domain of Anglo capitalists able to develop the region's infrastructure through better roads and the new railroad network. The Texas and Pacific Railroad cut through modern-day Pecos (Reeves County) while the Galveston, Harrisburg, and San Antonio Railroad passed through Alpine, both connecting with the Southern Pacific (and into El Paso) at Sierra Blanca by 1882. The tracks linked West Texas with the rest of the state (and the country), bringing more ranchers and new farmers, ailing people seeking health cures, common citizens eager for fresh starts, and the accoutrements of civilization (urban life, schools, churches, and the expansion of the telegraph).[26] The population explosion abetted the Tejanos' decline. Whereas Mexican Americans had enjoyed a population advantage in broader West Texas before the 1880s, the disparity now vanished. With so many Anglo newcomers in the region, the two races evened out in numbers by 1900, and earlier prospects for opportunities for achievement dissipated.[27] Then, individual issues could exacerbate matters for some people, as in the case of Cesario Torres. As described earlier, he faced financial problems following Bernardo's death. Once the military began leaving the area, furthermore, personnel in army wagon trains no longer needed Cesario's produce.[28]

Politically, Mexicans became expendable, although useful for political opportunists. For the general working-class Tejano population of the region, political standing had always been subject to consent by ranchers, farmers, and businessmen of good standing. Anglos had never readily countenanced a people largely considered "greasers" and ones ignorant of democratic rule to share full political participation. Indeed, power brokers had manipulated, at least since the 1870s, the Mexican vote for personal aggrandizement. Emboldened by advantages rapidly accruing to them, Anglo leaders after 1880 continued the practice of rounding up voters from the local working population before an election, treating them with liquids and other benefits (perhaps a dance), holding them hostage for the night and in the morning instructing them for whom to vote, and then escorting them by foot or in wagons to the polling stations.[29] Were Mexicans to bid for a voice in politics, whites employed other strategies to hamstring the challengers' efforts. In July 1886, for instance, Tom Green County Democrats refused to recognize the Mexican delegation wishing to participate in the convention's work, approving a resolution that stated that "no party be allowed to vote in this convention who cannot speak the United States language."[30]

Factors particular to their circumstances further contributed to a weakening of the Mexicans' standing. The West Texas frontier had no old towns (such as San Antonio, Laredo, and Brownsville) with an existing Mexican American political or economic structure upon which new arrivals might build (in some of the border towns of South Texas old families held political and economic ground into the early twentieth century). Presidio represented the oldest of these towns, but its population grew haltingly (as late as 1925, it had fewer than one hundred residents).[31] San Angelo, Fort Davis, and Fort Stockton sprouted from the establishment of frontier forts in their vicinities in 1867, and Del Rio's origin began in 1871 while Alpine emerged from the arrival of the railroad in 1882; these all struggled as fledgling towns with poor laboring Mexican Americans inhabiting them. Isolated villages and farms/ranches were too hardscrabble for people to be attentive to little else than life hardships. Further, very few Mexicans in the late nineteenth century possessed professional skills and political experience. As recent arrivals from Mexico, most knew US institutions only vaguely (in South Texas, many Mexican Americans had been born in Texas or had been in the state for several years and thus had become familiar with US institutions). Lost dreams thus became a harsh reality for Mexicans in West Texas due to debilitating forces emanating from inside and outside their communities.

The hardening of segregated town neighborhoods accompanied the post-1880s downturn. San Angelo stood visibly segregated by 1900: Mexicans lived in a section adjacent to the downtown district (but were rapidly being pushed out of there) and the Santa Fe *barrio* (neighborhood) from where many walked to work at the nearby Santa Fe Railroad line.[32] So too did Fort Stockton grow into a racialized community; Anglos referred to one particular segregated barrio as "Little Mexico."[33] Del Rio by the 1880s also featured at least two identifiable barrios: Chihuahua and San Felipe (the latter referenced as "the Mexican portion of town").[34] Similar segregation occurred in Murphyville (Alpine), beginning with the settlement of Mexican American family members of men constructing railroad lines through the area in the early 1880s. Initially, Mexicans erected temporary tents south of the Southern Pacific Railroad tracks so as to be close to husbands and fathers, but as Murphyville prospered, the Mexicans converted their tents into more permanent adobe homes in an area of town that came to be called "Old Mexico."[35] Racial segmentation at Fort Davis never reached the degree it did in Alpine, but one section of that town (home for many Mexicans) went by the popular designation of Chihuahua.[36] The majority of Mexicans in West Texas daily grappled with uncertainty in these segregated enclaves (as well as rural hamlets), which generally amounted to no more than squalid sites with inhabitants living in run-down hovels.[37]

Such hurdles as they faced during the 1880s and 1890s did not discourage Tejanos' will to challenge adversity. As other Texans, Mexicans used their home quarters (in their case racially segmented neighborhoods) to ferret out job prospects. Where possible, some entered the workforce as blacksmiths, gunsmiths, shoemakers, tailors, butchers, and brick masons. Around the army posts of Fort Concho, Fort Davis, and Fort Stockton, Mexicans had managed (since the military's arrival in West Texas during the 1850s) to secure employment as teamsters, gardeners, hay contractors, buffalo hunters, fence builders, masons, and adobe-house carpenters; women living close to these posts labored as cooks, laundresses, housekeepers, or did other types of "women's work." As the military returned following the Civil War, Mexicans once again became a reliable civilian complement to the soldiers.[38] But they eked out a livelihood by any other means possible; as late as 1900, they constituted nearly 50 percent of hired help in the agricultural sector of the West Texas economy, working for whatever wages they could acquire.[39] In the farmlands of Tom Green County—and wherever else husbandry became a going enterprise—Mexicans picked cotton for dismal pay, seldom knowing what they would do once the harvest season ended.[40] In primarily range country, they took jobs as ranch hands, most times without guarantee of year-round employment.[41] This uncertainty, undoubtedly, extended to sheepshearers and *pastores* (sheep herders) who worked the woollyback ranches around Del Rio, the "Concho Country," the Devil's River area, and the ones west to the Pecos valley.[42] Nevertheless, Mexicans coped, at times with the assistance of Mexican American labor contractors in towns such as San Angelo.[43]

To persevere, Mexican Americans relied on a cultural compass they trusted (simultaneously, they counted on their capacity to adjust their lifestyle to the American social order in the region). Many still maintained an interest in Mexico's domestic affairs and even loyalty to the homeland. Some excitement in West Texas occurred during the Catarino Garza episode (a movement actually centered in South Texas) which in 1891–92 aimed to overthrow the Porfirio Díaz government. Rumors had Garza passing through Del Rio, San Angelo, and Marathon in the Big Bend. According to some of these reports, numerous Mexican ranch hands (fifty, by one account) from around the San Angelo area were responding to Garza agents recruiting locally and readied to march off—armed with Winchesters and handguns—to join his forces. Such claims proved to be largely erroneous, but the rumors might have originated from loose talk Anglos picked up from Mexicans continuing to harbor an interest in the politics of Mexico. Or, it could have been the imagination of paranoid whites fearing a sinister plot grounded in knowledge that Mexicans still nourished bonds to old Mexico.[44]

Certainly, Tejanos maintained fealty to "lo mexicano," that is, to a Mexican ethnicity. They gave deference, for instance, to distinguished members of the community, as was the case in San Angelo where common people extended due respect to the city's first Hispanic families.[45] As in other parts of the state, Mexican Americans in West Texas remained true to their mother tongue, ate foods common in their native country, and attended Catholic church services (although Protestant sects, among them the Methodists, catered to Spanish speakers) in segregated Mexican quarters.[46] Where possible, Mexican Americans established (and financed) small Spanish-language schools (known popularly as *escuelitas*), perhaps in one of the children's parents' home.[47]

In family arrangements, Tejanos abided by a patriarchal structure common in Mexico and in so doing prescribed certain roles to women: culture dictated that wives and daughters be good homemakers and mothers and that they set the example for morality and religious devotion and teach the young about proper respect and manners. To women sometimes fell the task of establishing kin networks, perhaps by selecting friends or neighbors to sponsor their children as *padrinos* (godparents) at baptism, confirmation, or marriage.[48] To certain women fell also the role of *parteras* (midwives) or *curanderas* (folk healers). But in violation of male expectations, some women exercised leadership roles, as had Paula Losoya Taylor.

In their neighborhoods, barrio leaders established benevolent societies (with names such as the Sociedad Fraternal Unión, active in San Angelo in 1880s and 1890s) in efforts to assist their fellow neighbors during stressful periods or at times of family emergencies. These *mutualistas* (mutual aid societies) also joined community organizers in observing national secular dates, like Diez y Seis de Septiembre (Mexico's day of independence) and Cinco de Mayo, celebrating them with marches, patriotic speechmaking, foods, and various types of merriment.[49] Community groups, where feasible, promoted artistic performances; in San Angelo, the Mexican Dramatic Company in 1896 staged a Spanish-language drama titled "In the Hilt of the Sword."[50] Tejanos remembered respectfully and observed solemnly private occasions celebrating family birthdays, baptisms, weddings, or anniversaries. But other affairs, such as the *fandango*, tolerated unrestrained frolic, although these occasions could also be "civil."[51]

Oral tradition constituted a primary element of Mexican American ethnic life, and Tejanos relied on folktales and other folkloric forms as a means of passing on life lessons, imparting survival strategies to the young, explaining geographic formations, or providing particulars believed to be behind the labeling of landscapes. The people of Presidio, for instance, turned to folklore to unravel one particular geological mystery: a nook in what they called the Mountain of the Holy Cross located on the Mexican side of the Rio Grande. The shaping of the spot that perplexed them, they believed, had resulted from a climactic struggle between the devil and an early Spanish missionary; to stop the devil's mischief upon the valley, the priest, armed only with a holy cross, forced the devil into the Mexican side and into taking refuge in a cave. Thus did the den, according to this legend, come to be called "the devil's grotto."[52] A reputed master storyteller, one Natividad Luján from the Big Bend region, offered his own account for the naming of Santiago Peak, located in today's Brewster County. According to Luján's folkloric rendition, the peak acquired its name from the fact that Apaches had killed his uncle Santiago sometime in the nineteenth century.[53]

Notwithstanding their preference for "lo mexicano," Mexican Americans understood the need to modify their cultural ways. Parents thus sent their children off to school wherever communities opened their doors to Mexican students, as in towns like San Angelo, Fort Davis, Fort Stockton, Del Rio, and even remote rural villages such as El Polvo in the Big Bend.[54] Mexican Americans exhibited assimilative change in their integration of US national holidays such as the Fourth of July and even the African American observation of Juneteenth,[55] and also in an interest taken in politics. Despite the cold shoulder they had encountered from the Tom Green County Democrats, some San Angeleños still maintained loyalty to the Democratic Party, for as of the 1890s, they held membership in the Tom Green County Democratic Club.[56]

Overcoming adversity required more than finding affirmation in a comforting way of life while adjusting culture to the increased Anglo transformation unfolding in the region. It also necessitated devising creative means to contend with the many hardships that dogged West Texas pioneers. In coping with frontier difficulties, Tejanos fell back on old yet reliable methods. For their lodging needs, as an example, Mexicans counted on ancestral construction designs. Since pioneering West Texas, Mexicans had turned to the traditional built structure called the *jacal*, a makeshift dwelling framed with walls of mesquite posts (then daubed with mud or clay) and covered by a straw-thatch roof. In areas such as Fort Davis and Fort Stockton, Mexicans continued relying on the jacal, but equally on adobe homes, trusting the well-accepted theory that earth brick kept quarters cool in the summer and warm during cold weather.[57] So functional did Anglos consider the adobe model that they copied it freely as they penetrated the West Texas region. The blueprint served them practically in building stage stations, posts at military garrisons such as the ones at Fort Davis, jails, schools, and municipal structures (like the Fort Stockton courthouse).[58]

In tilling the soil and range work, Tejanos also harked back to time-tested practices. In farming corn, beans, grapes, cotton, and other crops on land belonging either to them or to Anglos, Mexicans used time-proven Mexican ways or they devised techniques necessary to accomplishing a job. Anglo witnesses described Mexican approaches as primitive, but they actually observed native adaptability. Given the lack of proper equipment and the state of frontier underdevelopment, Mexicans tilling Big Bend lands perforce used wooden plows hitched to oxen. When shelling ear corn, Mexican farmhands around Fort Stockton in the 1880s built a trapezelike apparatus equipped with a braided sheet of leather that permitted the seeds to drop (following a hard pounding) onto a tarp on the ground. Workers then took the canvas full of kernels and in a team effort flipped them onto an elevated platform, allowing the wind to blow away the chaff and other debris (that done, they sacked the corn for later use). Similar improvisation separated oats and wheat from the straws. To feed draft animals, Mexicans put to use the grama grass that grew in abundance in this same area. Cutting the grass with hand scythes, they bunched it into bundles, tied the clumps with twine derived from the leaves of the indigenous Spanish dagger, and hauled them off to the farm or ranch.[59]

In West Texas, Mexicans had helped (as Anglo ranchers entered the eastern edges of the Edwards Plateau) herd sheep and goats with routines long the standard in Mexico.[60] As the sheep industry became a mainstay on the range, Mexican *pastores* (many of whom migrated from Mexico into the Trans-Pecos) managed anywhere between one and two thousand sheep, caring for them (unaided) in isolated grazing fields, and facing monotony and the task of finding new feeding grounds and water for the flock. For this duty (which went on endlessly), an Anglo rancher in the last decades of the century paid a Mexican shepherd about $12 a month and provided him with needed supplies.[61]

Sheepshearers also abided by work patterns prevalent in Mexico. Ones who worked the several sheep ranches in Terrell County during the last decades of the century at times traveled to the campsites in family units. Women did the cooking and performed other domestic chores while boys helped with some of the lighter tasks of shearing, such as picking up the shorn wool. The arrangement made for a work rhythm that allowed crew members to unwind and socialize under familiar surroundings at the end of a hard workday. Pay to individual shearers rounded out to about 1.5 cents per sheep clipped.[62]

To coax nature into collaborating with them—as in diverting water flow, for instance—Tejanos resourcefully employed adroit schemes while using the most rudimentary equipment. In digging some of the early *acequias* for irrigating fields, Mexicans had done so armed only with picks and wooden shovels.[63] At Polvo, residents working on the local six-mile-long canal (finished in 1878) improvised explosives to blast for a tunnel through granite rock. Secundino Luján, one of the colony's organizers, made dynamite by utilizing fertilizer available at a bat cave, relying on the residue of burned mesquite, and by sojourning to Mexico to obtain sulfur.[64] Concerning irrigation projects built by border Mexicans, among them the one at Polvo, historian John Ernest Gregg wrote with wonder:

> The ingenuity shown by the Mexicans [on both sides of the border] in this

> work was remarkable. The mouth of the ditch was of necessity some distance upstream from the land to be irrigated. So the ditches were run along the higher benches of land than that on which the land to be irrigated lay. A small brush or rock dam was constructed so that it extended at an angle out into the river stream. This directed the water into the mouth of the ditch. While it is true that a rise in the river would wash out such a dam, it could be cheaply and easily replaced. These early gravity ditches were constructed without the aid of surveying instruments. A point would be selected from which to begin the construction of the ditch, and the water would be allowed to flow into the mouth of the ditch and the proper fall would be secured by digging in such a way that the water would continue to flow. These early people seemed to have a sense of knowing where the proper leads would run.[65]

Of the job done by the Torres Irrigation Company in the mid-1870s a contemporary observer (identified as H. C. K.) similarly marveled: "primitive engineering, backed by perseverance, has constructed a dam by dumping between three and four thousand wagons loads of rock into the stream, thus raising the water several feet, and causing it to flow into a ditch nine feet wide."[66] Such feats of ingenuity served Mexicans well past the transformation West Texas underwent by the 1880s.

Although the fate of Tejanos in West Texas took an unfortunate dive after the 1880s, the downturn did not blunt their impact on the region—which proved to be long term. Through hard labor, they not only advanced ranching and farming and railroad building, but toward century's end became the manpower to undergird mining operations. After Juan Acosta "discovered" cinnabar in 1884 in the Terlingua area, the industry boomed, and by the late 1890s, Mexicans made up much of the mining and hauling crews, facing grueling conditions while earning pitifully low wages. They served as freighters (and contractors), and under the most punishing demands handled the wagons and mules that moved equipment, supplies, foods, and personnel from the railheads to the mining camps and then brought back the cinnabar on the return trip.[67]

Through a pioneering spirit, Tejanos also helped stabilize West Texas: they fulfilled colonization impulses, as had their forebears. Despite not being welcomed in the region, Mexican Americans planted roots in open spaces, primarily in those areas not as yet claimed by Anglo-Americans. In the Big Bend, for one, they occupied lands through preemption (squatters' rights) and gave birth to self-sustaining hamlets. Pobladores "made do" by raising a few animals and engaging in small-scale farming close to auspicious environs, such as those privileged with natural springs. As Anglo-Americans encroached on the squatters' land, they did not readily contest the Mexicans' right of settlement; instead, they came to depend upon the Mexicans for the vegetables they harvested and the vaquero skills they offered.[68] Some of these semiautonomous villages did not survive too deeply into the twentieth century.

Other new settlements, however, went on to endure a longer life span. One case was Saragosa, Texas (Reeves County), founded when several Mexican families settled in its vicinity in 1880; Antonio Matta established a ranch at Saragosa that came to anchor the community.[69] As well, Brogado (also in Reeves County) grew from the arrival of Mexicans in the 1870s who began farming in the area blessed with spring water.[70] In Presidio County, one Domenicio Mata established a campsite in 1883 that came to be known as Casa Piedra, so-called because of the rock home he built on his property. Resident families there lived (as did others in lower Presidio County) on corn and beans and by harvesting cotton and hay.[71] Late in the century, the Molinar family started farming near the Terlingua mining district and named their budding village after the family—"Molinar."[72] About the same time (1895), Inez Sánchez arrived in modern-day Brewster County from Mexico and as the head of eighteen families founded San Vicente.[73]

Foremost, Tejanos persisted in enhancing the cultural richness of the area. Notwithstanding Americanization processes, "lo mexicano" remained in various forms—certainly in the Spanish language, religious observations, folklore, and in various other expressions. More publicly, "lo mexicano" came to be evident in Mexican foods that became staples in people's daily fares and the observations of patriotic Mexican holidays (which drew the local citizenry and even city officials into the festivities). A century later, this syncretic way of life had permeated the broader West Texas culture and thrust it into the wave being dubbed the "browning of America."

Notes

1. Waterman Lilly Ormsby, *The Butterfield Overland Mail*, ed. Lyle H. Wright and Josephine M. Bynum (San Marino, CA: Huntington Library, 1942), 64, 68; Sam Woolford, ed., "The Burr G. Duval Diary," *Southwestern Historical Quarterly* 65 (April 1962): 490, 493; San Angelo *Standard*, September 21, 1889, 1.

2. San Angelo *Standard*, September 21, 1889, 1; Marcos E. Kinevan, *Frontier Cavalryman: Lieutenant John Bigelow with the Buffalo Soldiers in Texas* (El Paso: Texas Western Press, 1998), 108.

3. *The Coke County Rustler*, Robert Lee, Coke County, December 16, 1898, 1.

4. Colonel Nathaniel Alston Taylor, *The Coming Empire; or, Two Thousand Miles in Texas on Horseback* (New York: A. S. Barnes, 1877), 265, 357; San Angelo *Standard*, September 21, 1889, 1;

Robert Wooster, *Frontier Crossroads: Fort Davis and the West* (College Station: Texas A&M University Press, 2006), 125.

5. San Angelo *Standard*, September 21, 1889, 1; Marsha Lea Daggett, *Pecos County History*, 2 vols. (Canyon, TX: Staked Plains Press, 1984), 1: 134; Taylor, *The Coming Empire*, 360.

6. Arnoldo De León, *San Angeleños: Mexican Americans in San Angelo Texas* (San Angelo: Fort Concho Museum Press, 1985), 27; San Angelo *Standard*, September 21, 1889, 1; Winifred Kupper, ed., *Texas Sheepman: The Reminiscences of Robert Maudslay* (Austin: University of Texas Press, 1951), 123.

7. Ramon F. Adams, *From the Pecos to the Powder: A Cowboy's Autobiography* (Norman: University of Oklahoma Press, 1965), 30.

8. San Angelo *Standard*, August 2, 1890, 2.

9. San Antonio *Express*, May 1, 1891, 3.

10. Austin *Statesman*, April 20, 1886, 1; San Antonio *Daily Express*, April 20, 1886, 4.

11. San Antonio *Daily Express*, November 5, 1894, 2.

12. Austin *Daily Statesman*, May 8, 1884, 1; May 10, 1884, 1; May 11, 1884, 2; September 6, 1884, 1; Austin *Democratic Statesman*, July 26, 1884, 3; Austin *Statesman*, November 8, 1886, 1; Mario T. García, "Porfirian Diplomacy and the Administration of Justice in Texas, 1877–1900," *Aztlán: International Journal of Chicano Studies Research* 16 (1985): 5–7.

13. San Antonio *Express*, July 26, 1897, 8.

14. García, "Porfirian Diplomacy and the Administration of Justice in Texas," 17–19.

15. The story of Judge Roy Bean holding to this consideration is told in J. Marvin Hunter, *The Trail Drivers of Texas*, 2 vols. (New York: Argosy-Antiquarian, 1963), 2: 664. Bean's views appear incredible as he was married to a Mexican woman!

16. Kupper, *Texas Sheepman*, 63.

17. Some historians, among them Glen Sample Ely, *Where the West Begins: Debating Texas Identity* (Lubbock: Texas Tech University Press, 2011), 87 passim, argue that a distinguishing feature of West Texas race relations was the infrequent application of southern-style lynching (characterized by torture of victims, public-burning spectacles, and various barbarous practices) to Mexican Americans. But particular situations could well spur West Texas Anglos into taking extralegal measures, among them lynching, to control Mexicans.

18. San Antonio *Express*, December 7, 1883, 4; December 12, 1883, 1.

19. Carlysle Graham Raht, *The Romance of the Davis Mountains and Big Bend Country* (El Paso: Raht Books, 1919), 304–5; Cecilia Thompson, *History of Marfa and Presidio County, Texas, 1535–1946*, 2 vols. (Austin: Nortex Press, 1985), 1: 297.

20. Mary Jaques, *Texan Ranch Life* (London: Horace Cox, 1894), 360–63. See also, San Angelo *Standard*, November 24, 1894, 2.

21. Austin *Statesman*, February 7, 1891, 1; David L. Chapman, "Lynching in Texas" (master's thesis, Texas Tech University, 1973), 98, appendix B.

22. De León, *San Angeleños*, 28, 16–17.

23. Ely, *Where the West Begins*, 80; Arnoldo De León, *Mexican Americans in Texas: A Brief History*, 3rd ed. (Wheeling, IL: Harlan Davidson, 2009), 45–46, 49.

24. Others who note a decline in Mexican American political and economic presence in West Texas include Ely, *Where the West Begins*, 79–80, and Paul Wright, "Population Patterns in Presidio County in 1880: Evidence from the Census," *The Journal of Big Bend Studies* 7 (January 1995): 193, 198.

25. Monica Muñoz Martínez, "'Inherited Loss': Tejanas and Tejanos Contesting State Violence and Revising Public Memory, 1910-Present" (PhD diss., Yale University, 2012), investigates racial violence in the early twentieth century in West Texas. See further, Nicholas Villanueva Jr., "'Sincerely Yours for Dignified Manhood': Lynching, Violence, and American Masculinity during the Early Years of the Mexican Revolution, 1910–1914," *Journal of the West* 49 (Winter 2010); and Nicholas Villanueva Jr., "Decade of Disorder: The Execution of León Martínez, Jr. and Mexican/

Anglo Race Relations in Texas during the First Four Years of the Mexican Revolution," in *The Mexican Revolution: Conflict and Consolidation, 1910–1940*, ed. Douglas W. Richmond and Sam W. Haynes (College Station: Texas A&M University Press, 2013). On the case of León Martínez, see also Alton Hughes, *Pecos: A History of the Pioneer West*, 2 vols. (Seagraves, TX: Pioneer Book Publishers, 1978), 1: 193–96.

26. Clifford B. Casey, *Alpine, Texas: Then and Now* (Seagraves, TX: Pioneer Book Publishers, 1981), 18.

27. Arnoldo De León and Kenneth L. Stewart, *Tejanos and the Numbers Game: A Socio-Historical Interpretation from the Federal Censuses, 1850–1900* (Albuquerque: University of New Mexico Press, 1989), 12; Arnoldo De León and Kenneth L. Stewart, "Tejano Demographic Patterns and Socio-Economic Development," *Borderlands Journal* 7, no. 1 (1983): 3, 6, table 1.

28. Patrick Dearen, *Crossing Rio Pecos* (Fort Worth: Texas Christian University Press, 1996), 66–67; Joe C. Primera, "Los Hermanos Torres: Early Settlers of Pecos County," *Permian Historical Annual* 20 (1980): 89, 91–94.

29. San Angelo *Standard*, September 21, 1889, 1; De León, *San Angeleños*, 16; Raht, *The Romance of the Davis Mountains and Big Bend Country*, 194–96; Daggett, *Pecos County History* 1: 158; Jacqueline M. Moore, *Cow Boys and Cattle Men: Class and Masculinities on the Texas Frontier, 1865–1900* (New York: New York University Press, 2010), 87.

30. El Paso *Times*, July 22, 1886, 3. Mexican Americans nonetheless remained engaged in local politics as of the mid-1880s. Juan Flores, part of San Angelo's first Hispanic families, ran for the position of constable, Precinct 1, in 1884. See San Angelo *Standard*, September 13, 1884, 4.

31. "Presidio, Texas," in Ron Tyler, ed., *New Handbook of Texas*, 6 vols. (Austin: Texas State Historical Association, 1996), 5: 330.

32. De León, *San Angeleños*, 21, 22.

33. María Eva Flores, CDP, "The Good Life the Hard Way: The Mexican American Community of Fort Stockton, Texas, 1930–1945" (PhD diss., Arizona State University, 2000), 23.

34. Steven W. Prewitt, "'We Didn't Ask to Come to This Party': Self-Determination Collides with the Federal Government in the Public Schools of Del Rio, Texas, 1890–1971" (PhD diss., University of Houston, 2000), 35, 41–42.

35. Casey, *Alpine*, 18. See further Paul Wright, "Life on both Sides of the Tracks in Early Alpine," *West Texas Historical Association Yearbook* 73 (1997): 98, and Paul Wright, "Residential Segregation in Two Early West Texas Towns," *Southwestern Historical Quarterly* 102 (January 1999): 297, 301.

36. Wooster, *Frontier Crossroads*, 41, 126; Wright, "Residential Segregation in Two Early West Texas Towns," 298–99, 302–5.

37. Robert Wooster provides one example in *Frontier Crossroads*, 126.

38. San Antonio *Herald*, May 25, 1868, 2; De León, *San Angeleños*, 15, 18; Letter of Mrs. W. S. Veck to J. Evetts Haley, September 12, 1931, W. S. Veck Vertical File, West Texas Collection; Raht, *The Romance of the Davis Mountains and Big Bend Country*, 163; Clayton W. Williams, *Texas' Last Frontier: Fort Stockton and the Trans-Pecos, 1861–1895*, ed. Ernest Wallace (College Station: Texas A&M University Press, 1982), pp. 135, 136, 309, 370; Wooster, *Frontier Crossroads*, 41; John Ernest Gregg, "The History of Presidio County" (master's thesis, University of Texas, Austin, 1933), 55.

39. Kenneth L. Stewart and Arnoldo De León, "Education, Literacy, and Occupational Structure in West Texas, 1860–1900," *West Texas Historical Association Yearbook* 60 (1984): 131.

40. San Angelo *Standard-Times*, June 2, 1888, 1; De León, *San Angeleños*, 15; San Antonio *Express*, June 28, 1889, 4; Williams, *Texas' Last Frontier*, 208.

41. San Angelo *Standard*, September 21, 1889, 1; Alexander Soto Cano, "The Mexican American Community of Knickerbocker," *West Texas Historical Association Yearbook* 79 (October 2003): 26, 29; Wright, "Population Patterns in Presidio County in 1880," 192. On the scarcity of steady (reliable) work opportunities that forced many Tejanos into the general labor pool, see Stewart and De León, "Education, Literacy, and Occupational Structure in West Texas, 1860–1900," 130.

42. De León, *San Angeleños*, 18; R. D. Holt, ed., *Schleicher County, or Eighty Years of Develop-*

ment in Southwest Texas (Eldorado, TX: Eldorado Success, 1930), 38; Galveston *News*, October 6, 1892, 11; San Angelo *Standard-Times*, October 19, 1889, 2; Paul H. Carlson, *Texas Woollybacks: The Range Sheep and Goat Industry* (College Station: Texas A&M University Press), 114, 161.

43. San Angelo *Standard-Times*, November 1, 1884, 3.

44. Austin *Statesman*, December 31, 1891, 1; San Angelo *Standard-Times*, January 9, 1892, 3; San Antonio *Express*, January 16, 1892, 2; January 17, 1892, 2.

45. De León, *San Angeleños*, 16, 23–25, 28.

46. San Antonio *Express*, February 16, 1886, 7; Galveston *Weekly News*, October 6, 1892, 11; De León, *San Angeleños*, 26; Daggett, *Pecos County History*, 1: 258–59; Thompson, *History of Marfa and Presidio County*, 1: 315, 328.

47. Prewitt, "We Didn't Ask to Come to This Party," 38.

48. Flores, "The Good Life the Hard Way," 45–46.

49. San Angelo *Standard-Times*, May 9, 1885, 3; September 10, 1887, p. 2; September 22, 1894, 3; September 21, 1895, 3; September 30, 1899, 1; De León, *San Angeleños*, 25, 29.

50. San Angelo *Standard-Times*, January 18, 1896, 2.

51. San Antonio *Express*, November 5, 1894, 2.

52. Mody C. Boatright, "The Devil's Grotto," in *Texas and Southwestern Lore*, ed. J. Frank Dobie, vol. 6 of Publications of the Texas Folklore Society (Austin: Texas Folklore Society, 1927), 102–6.

53. Raht, *Romance of the Davis Mountains and Big Bend Country*, 77–81. But see also "Santiago Peak," in Tyler, ed., *New Handbook of Texas*, 5: 891.

54. San Angelo *Standard*, September 28, 1889, 2; Mrs. Mattie Belle Anderson, "Reminiscences of Mrs. Mattie Belle Anderson, Teacher, Fort Davis, Texas," Eugene C. Barker Texas History Center, University of Texas Archives, Austin, Texas (1929), 1, 2, 3, 9, 12; Jennie Parks Ringgold, *Frontier Days in the Southwest* (San Antonio: Naylor, 1952), 11; Prewitt, "We Didn't Ask to Come to This Party," 40; Brenda B. Wharton, "The Davis-Herrera Ranch Site, 41PS622: Presidio County, Texas," *Journal of Big Bend Studies* 19 (2007): 242; Wright, "Population Patterns in Presidio County in 1880," 193; Wright, "Residential Segregation in Two Early West Texas Towns," 314; Daggett, *Pecos County History*, 1: 247; Jack Richard Chappell, "El Polvo" (A Paper Presented to Dr. Clifford B. Casey in Partial Fulfillment of the Requirements for the Course History 432, Sul Ross State College, 1964), 22; Earl H. Elam, "Acculturation on the Rio Grande Frontier: The Founding of San José del Polvo and the Family of Lucía Rede Madrid," *Journal of Big Bend Studies* 5 (January 1993): 89. For the educational standing of Tejanitos in West Texas, see Stewart and De León, "Education, Literacy, and Occupational Structure in West Texas," 134–35.

55. San Angelo *Standard-Times*, June 22, 1895, 3.

56. See San Angelo *Standard-Times*, October 20, 1894, 1; October 27, 1894, p. 1.

57. San Angelo *Standard*, September 28, 1889, 2; Taylor, *The Coming Empire or Two Thousand Miles in Texas on Horseback*, 333; Ringgold, *Frontier Days in the Southwest*, 8. An anthropological study on *jacales* (and by comparison, adobe homes) is Joe S. Graham, *The Jacal in the Big Bend: Its Origin and Evolution*, ed. Robert J. Mallouf (Alpine, TX: Chihuahuan Desert Research Institute, 1988).

58. Raht, *Romance of the Davis Mountains and Big Bend Country*, 130, 149, 217, 256; Anderson, "Reminiscences of Mrs. Mattie Belle Anderson," 1; Woolford, "The Burr G. Duval Diary," 497.

59. Daggett, *Pecos County History*, 1: 126, 135–36. Another method for culling out wheat is described in Gregg, "The History of Presidio County," 132.

60. Terry G. Jordan, *North American Cattle Ranching Frontiers: Origins, Diffusion, and Differentiation* (Albuquerque: University of New Mexico Press, 1993), 219.

61. Woolford, "The Burr G. Duval Diary," 493–94; San Angelo *Standard*, September 21, 1889, 1; Carlson, *Texas Woollybacks*, 161. Wages in West Texas did not increase much for Mexican ranch workers (both *vaqueros* and sheepshearers) in the early twentieth century. In Sutton County during the 1910s, vaqueros who lived in their own quarters made between one-half to two-thirds of what Anglo ranch hands did, which was about $75 to $100 a month. B. Youngblood and A. B. Cox,

An Economic Study of a Typical Ranching Area on the Edwards Plateau of Texas, Texas Agricultural Experiment Station Bulletin, No. 297 (College Station: Agricultural and Mechanical College of Texas, 1922), 308–9.

62. Alice Evans Downie, *Terrell County, Texas, Its Past, Its People: A Compilation, Pictures of and Writings by or about People, Places, and Events in Terrell County* (Sanderson: Terrell County Heritage Commission, 1978), 60–62.

63. Daggett, *Pecos County History*, 1: 222.

64. Thompson, *History of Marfa and Presidio County*, 1: 134; Chappell, "El Polvo," 11, 18–20.

65. Gregg, "The History of Presidio County," 128–31.

66. Quote is from San Antonio *Express*, May 25, 1877, 2. See further, Doug Braudaway, "Torres Founders of Langtry," online publication for Val Verde County Historical Commission, accessed November 28, 2013; Ringgold, *Frontier Days*, 8; Williams, *Texas' Last Frontier*, 120, 126, 205–7, 211–12; Dearen, *Crossing Rio Pecos*, 65; Daggett, *Pecos County History*, 1: 126, 134–35, 222.

67. Kenneth Baxter Ragsdale, *Quicksilver: Terlingua and the Chisos Mountains Mining Company* (College Station: Texas A&M University Press, 1976), 16–17, 40, 47–48.

68. Clifford B. Casey, *Soldiers, Ranchers, and Miners in the Big Bend* (Washington, DC: National Park Service Division of History, Office of Archeology and Historical Preservation, 1969), 26–27.

69. "Saragosa, Texas," in Tyler, ed., *New Handbook of Texas*, 5: 894–95.

70. "Brogado, Texas," in ibid., 1: 746. See also Hughes, *Pecos*, 1: 99–100, 245–46.

71. "Casa Piedra, Texas," in Tyler, ed., *New Handbook of Texas*, 1: 1008; Gregg, "The History of Presidio County," 56.

72. Casey, *Soldiers, Ranchers, and Miners in the Big Bend*, 28.

73. Albert Tucker, "The Lost Communities of San Vicente," *West Texas Historical Association Yearbook* 72 (1996): 105, 108; "San Vicente, Texas," in Tyler, ed., *New Handbook of Texas*, 5: 893.

Education, Literacy, and Occupational Structure in West Texas, 1860–1900

Kenneth L. Stewart and Arnoldo De León

Americans hold to the principle that education serves as a vehicle for upward mobility. While schooling did turn out beneficial for Anglo-Americans in nineteenth-century West Texas, it did not for Tejanos. At least two reasons explain this consequence. First, poverty, isolation in frontier areas, and the general belief that education was not for Mexicans deprived Tejanitos of adequate schooling. Second, educators designed schooling, where made available to Mexicans, with understandings that Tejanos would assume lower-level functions in the job market. Consequently, Mexican American youngsters faced disadvantages in making material progress.

Until about 1865, the region west of the 100th meridian and south of the 32nd parallel was mainly Indian Territory. Only a few permanent town sites dotted this vast and parched terrain. These were vestiges of seventeenth-century Spanish explorations and missionary expeditions, for the area had proved largely unyielding to the civilizing efforts of New Spain and Mexico, then of the Republic of Texas and the United States. Four of these tenacious settlements—El Paso, Socorro, San Elizario, and Ysleta—were situated in the El Paso Valley and became the first communities of the west to be annexed into the state when El Paso County was organized in 1850.[1] Presidio County, created in the same year, contained only 574 inhabitants at the time the first census of the region was taken in 1860.[2] On the eve of the Civil War, West Texas remained a wilderness but was on the verge of a fundamental transformation.

With the reoccupation of military forts at Mason, McKavett, Clark, Lancaster, Bliss, Davis, and Stockton after the war, and with the erection of

This chapter was originally published in the *West Texas Historical Association Yearbook* 60 (1984): 127–43.

new garrisons like Fort Concho in 1867, the section began its era of intense growth and modernization.[3] Around these installations sprouted new towns like San Angelo and others, and the forbidding task of Indian pacification was at long last finished. Civilians—Anglos and Mexicans in the main—streamed into the growing region. The railroad, probably the most potent single factor in the taming of West Texas, spurred further immigration in the early 1880s as it cut through the region on its way to El Paso and beyond to California.[4] As new towns appeared, many of them along the path of the rails, the one-time wilderness was transformed, first to a frontier and then to a thriving and distinctive cultural appendage of modern Texas society.

This chapter focuses on the transition of West Texas from wilderness to modernity. Its aim is to describe changes that took place in the region's occupational system and to ascertain attendant patterns of education and literacy. Well entrenched by this time was the idea that education serves in the scheme of modernization by acting as an escalator that lifts individuals to a social standing commensurate with their abilities.[5] By empirically exploring the nexus of relations between occupation, literacy, and educational patterns in West Texas, this study tests the validity of the American belief of mobility through education. In some ways the maxim holds true, in others it falters.

A general picture of the occupational changes that occurred in West Texas as the section moved from wilderness to modernity[6] may be gained from table 3.1. By 1860, the seeds of transition were already planted—the proportional size of the service occupational sector in that year makes that evident. Nearly 36 percent of the labor force was engaged in service work (professional, public, and personal tasks), and one of the largest components of this group was comprised of men who were literally "in the service." Military personnel made up 28 percent of the service sector and about 10 percent of the total labor force in West Texas. Their presence, of course, was reduced by the demands of the Civil War, but by 1870 soldiers returned to the West Texas frontier in such numbers that they comprised a full one-third of the entire regional labor force.[7] Service workers swelled in 1870 to 44 percent of the employment pool, and military men formed about 76 percent of those providing services that year. Such a military buildup purged the frontier of Indian resistance as well as a real or perceived threat of Mexican insurgence. Furthermore, it made for an orderly and tamed environment and encouraged the political-economic development of the region. Nonetheless, the military presence did not fade as an element in the region's occupational structure until the closing years of the century.

Table 3.1. Occupational classification of workers in West Texas, 1860–1900[1]

Occupational classification[2]	*1860*	*1870*	*1880*	*1900*
Agriculture	18.5%	5.0%	23.5%	19.8%
Services[3]	35.9%	44.0%	31.7%	18.9%
Trade & Transport	13.5%	5.2%	7.2%	21.4%
Manufacture & Mechanical	9.5%	9.1%	4.9%	12.2%
General (Unspecified) Labor	22.6%	36.8%	32.8%	27.7%
Sample N	654	505	1328	3094

[1]Data for 1890 are not included here or elsewhere in the chapter because the original census returns were destroyed by fire. As time passed, of course, new counties were formed in the West Texas region, and these data reflect the multiplication of political units. The 1860 and 1870 samples include El Paso and Presidio Counties only. For 1880 Crockett, Pecos, and Tom Green Counties were added to the sampling frame. The data for 1900 were drawn from a total of eight counties including Crane, Crockett, El Paso, Pecos, Presidio, Sutton, Tom Green, and Val Verde.

[2]The occupational classes used here were employed by the Census Bureau for reporting purposes beginning in 1870.

[3]The "services" category includes professionals, public servants, and personal service workers.

By 1900 the service sector had waned to 18.9 percent of the labor force, and military people had shrunk to just 9 percent of the service providers and less than 2 percent of all workers.

The unspecified general labor pool in the 1860 occupational structure also signaled the transitory nature of things in West Texas. Consisting of low-skill workers, mostly Mexicans, who hired out on a seasonal or daily basis to farmers, ranchers, and regional entrepreneurs, this group comprised a sizable unattached and mobile labor force compelled by the necessities of survival to perform the marginal jobs that accompany the dynamic process of commercial economic development everywhere. In 1860 this sector approximated 23 percent of workers. In the 1870s and 1880s, the proportion of general laborers in the region climbed to over 30 percent, and then declined in the closing years of the era, reaching a level of about 28 percent in 1900.[8] During the years of transition from wilderness to modernity, it seems, West Texas entrepreneurs took advantage of the presence of a conspicuously exploitable labor group that performed the most menial tasks of development.

Though temporary enlargement of the service sector with military personnel and the availability of a vulnerable general labor class were necessary accoutrements to the modernization process in West Texas, the agricultural, trade, transport, manufacturing, and mechanical components of the labor force manifested the more definitive effects of the transformation of the region's occupational structure. As table 3.1 shows, there were no dramatic changes in the proportion of the workforce engaged in these more specialized phases of economic activity, though slight increases in the percentages for each category did take place between 1860 and 1900. Beyond these mild increases, however, important changes occurred in the qualities of the jobs performed in these labor segments.

In the agricultural sector, for instance, the essential change in the nature of work was not so much along the lines of more highly specialized labor tasks and roles. Instead, there was a pattern toward the enlargement of large landholdings. In each of the censuses in West Texas between 1860 and 1900, the most frequently used descriptions of pastoral workers were "farmer," "stockraiser," "herdsman," and "cowboy" or "*vaquero*," and persons working in these capacities consistently comprised 70 percent or more of the agricultural labor force. Over the years, however, the proportionate sizes of these particular segments of the workforce changed dramatically. In 1860, those identified as *farmers* and *stockraisers*—designations implying a degree of land ownership or control—composed more than 80 percent of the agricultural workers. At the same time, workers described as hired hands, such as *herdsmen* and *cowboys*, amounted to just 18 percent. By 1900, this picture of the agricultural labor market had changed significantly and had nearly inversed, as the farmers and stockraisers accounted for just 40 percent of the workers in agriculture and hired hands comprised about 50 percent.[9] What occurred with the onset of modernization and development, then, was a "proletarianization" of agricultural labor. The landowning class became proportionally smaller while an expanding number of workers turned to the "market" to sell their talents and energies.

The trade, transportation, manufacturing, and mechanical sectors of the labor force also evidenced distinct patterns of occupational change. Shifts in these areas of economic activity generally inclined toward specialization and displacement of labor. In trade and transport, for example, approximately thirteen specific job designations were recorded by census takers in 1860, and the most frequently held occupations were those of teamster, traveler, merchant, wagoner, and clerk. These five jobs absorbed nearly 78 percent of the region's trade and transportation workers. By 1900, the composition of the trade and transport sector had changed substantially. Census takers recorded about forty-nine different occupations that year, nearly four times the number of specific designations recorded forty years earlier. Additionally, many of the occupational types that appeared in the 1860 census were either not designated in the 1900 records or denoted with far less frequency. Teamsters accounted for some 22 percent of the region's trade and transport workers in 1860, for instance, but by 1900, this had declined to just 6.2 percent. At the same time, the later records show numerous occupational designations that did not appear in the first census of 1860. Most significant among the new job titles were various types connected to the iron horse, such as railroad hands and section foremen. Altogether, railroad laborers comprised approximately 37 percent of the trade and transport workers by 1900.[10] In the manufacturing and mechanical labor force, a similar proliferation of more specialized work tasks and displacement of old job types with new ones was evident.[11]

With economic modernization and the corresponding evolution of the occupational structure in West Texas came an interest in educational development that eventually stimulated the rise of a public school system. Economic change, of course, was not the sole factor behind all this. As elsewhere in the state and nation, West Texans saw in public schooling a mechanism for inculcating proper values of citizenship and a means to teach higher moral virtues to defend against crime and poverty.[12] The economic advance provided both resources and incentives for establishing formal schooling to carry out these aims.[13]

From the 1860s through the 1880s, education in West Texas was in a crude state, and development was slow. As late as the 1880s, most schools were of the one-room variety and accommodated pupils through just the elementary levels of learning. Ordinarily, one school was to be found in the more populated towns, and in the sparsely settled areas, one in the entire county. Learning conditions left much to be desired. Equipment was scarce and teachers frequently did not have the best preparation for the task at hand.[14] Slowly, however, the system of education improved and by the turn of the century formal instruction was ongoing at most locations throughout the region.

Both the achievements and the failures of the vigorous development of education in West Texas during the late nineteenth century are reflected in the rates of school attendance among children of the so-called scholastic ages.[15] As table 3.2 shows, the general pattern of the region's educational progress included a virtual abandonment of formal instruction at the end of the Civil War. Under Spain and Mexico, education had been both a missionary concern designed to pacify and "civilize" the indigenous Indian population and a frontier attempt to maintain culture and social order. As a result of such a tradition, some 30 percent of the enumerated scholastic

Table 3.2. School attendance rates among children ages 8–17 in West Texas, 1860–1900[1]

Year	*All children*	*Anglos*	*Tejanos*	*Ages 8–10*	*Ages 11–14*	*Ages 14–17*
1860	30.3%	25.0%	27.7%	34.7%	40.5%	8.9%
1870	6.6%	13.3%	5.5%	12.2%	5.6%	1.3%
1880	20.2%	30.7%	17.3%	23.0%	25.0%	9.2%
1900	49.5%	67.2%	33.3%	47.9%	60.9%	33.3%

[1]The Census Bureau routinely defined the "school-aged population" as ages 5–20 during this period, and school attendance within one year of the taking of the census was regularly recorded for persons of that age group. However, the states differed from the Census Bureau in their definitions of the "scholastic population," and the official state-level definitions also varied over time. The 8–17 year-old age group is used here because that cohort was established as the official scholastic population in the state of Texas in the 1890s.

population was involved in some formal instruction in 1860, primarily in El Paso County.[16] Subsequent events brought this system to its end, so that by 1870 the rate of school attendance among 8–17 year-olds in the sampled West Texas counties diminished to just 6.6 percent. After that, however, the schools that were to become the region's modern system of education began to evolve, and by 1900 nearly half of the scholastics received public schooling.

On the other hand, serious flaws marked the rapid expansion of education. The system quickly took on discriminatory features based on ethnicity and proved incapable of providing anything more than an intermittent and incomplete exposure to learning for the area's Mexican Americans.

The discriminatory character of the developing schools is reflected in a comparison of Anglo and Tejano rates of school attendance (table 3.2). In the earlier frontier years, when the remnants of the old Spanish/Mexican educational tradition were still intact, the attendance rate of Hispanic children actually outdistanced that of Anglos by a small margin, though it should be noted that whites were a very small proportion of the scholastic-aged population. With the reduction of educational efforts during the 1860s, however, what educational opportunities remained were more readily available to the Anglo children, so that by 1870 the rate of attendance for white scholastics stood at 13.2 percent compared to just 5.5 percent for Tejanos. Though these low rates in 1870 were not predictive of those to follow, the discriminatory nature of education was already taking root. Hence, by 1900 a full two-thirds of Anglo children were being schooled while just one-third of the Tejanos in the region received instruction.[17]

Another shortcoming in the development of education in West Texas was the region's inability to expand the instructional process beyond a truncated exposure to formal education. Though schools in the area reportedly taught a curriculum ranging from ordinary subjects to music, calisthenics, politeness, patriotism, and reverence for God,[18] the age-specific attendance rates in table 3.2 indicate that such instruction was not received continuously by children in the officially defined scholastic group. By 1900 less than half of those ages 8–10 attended school and only one-third of the 15–17 year-olds were enrolled in teaching institutions. The briefer age period of 11–14 years was the time in a child's life when formal schooling was most likely received. Nearly 61 percent of this age group reported attendance at the turn of the century. For the region's Mexican American children, furthermore, these educational patterns also mixed with discriminatory elements in the system to create additional schooling handicaps. Tejano children, if they got to school at all, were far more likely than Anglos to receive only a brief formal learning experience.

The vicissitudes of the late-nineteenth-century educational development in West Texas were reflected in the skills that people in the region brought to adult life, particularly ones in literacy (table 3.3). With the replacement of the Mexican schooling system in the post–Civil War years, rates of literacy among the region's adult population stagnated. In 1860, the

Table 3.3. Literacy rates among West Texans aged 21 and over[1]

Year	*Region*	*Anglos*	*Tejanos*
1860	41.6%	96.5%	23.4%
1870	34.0%	91.9%	15.7%
1880	42.5%	89.1%	20.0%
1900	68.2%	96.1%	36.2%

[1]In 1870 the Census Bureau began to distinguish between degrees of literacy, designating some persons as fully literate while others were classified as having only partial literacy skills. Both full and partial literates were included in the calculations shown here.

Table 3.4. Literacy rates by occupational classification for West Texans aged 21 years and over[1]

Occupational classification	*1860*	*1870*	*1880*	*1900*
Economically nonactive	27.9%	22.6%	37.3%	61.6%
Economically active	42.3%	39.9%	45.2%	72.5%
Agricultural workers	39.0%	50.0%	53.0%	69.3%
Professional and domestic services	88.3%	48.0%	40.5%	96.9%
Personal service workers	29.7%	36.4%	43.4%	77.1%
Trade and transport workers	68.3%	76.2%	87.1%	82.1%
Manufacture and mechanical workers	44.4%	71.1%	68.3%	86.9%
General (unspecified) laborers	25.5%	15.3%	27.4%	49.5%

[1]Partial literates are included in computation of the rates of literacy

rate for persons aged 21 and over stood at 41.6 percent. Ten years later, the literacy rate dipped to just 34 percent, but climbed back to approximately the 1860 level by 1880. Only in the last twenty years of the century did the regional rate increase dramatically, up to 68.2 percent in 1900. The separate rates for the region's two major ethnic groups showed a similar pattern, first of stagnation and then of significant increase, especially among Tejanos in the closing decades.[19]

In the occupational marketplace, the commonly accepted notion that modernization yielded certain advantages to literates does not seem to be entirely accurate in the case of West Texas. In reality, the competitive edge for literates already existed prior to the struggle toward development and was not created by that transformation. In comparison to 1900, reading and writing abilities were a stronger requirement in 1860 for participation in the region's economy (table 3.4). In the earlier era, forty-two out of every one hundred persons participating in job markets were literate compared to just twenty-eight out of every one hundred people not holding jobs. By 1900, the rate of literacy among the economically active approached 73 percent compared to 62 percent for the nonactive. An ironic effect of modernization, thus, was to make literacy a superfluous requirement for economic participation. As schools increased general literacy by the end of the century, such skills had less effect in determining the opportunity people would have in the economy of West Texas.

The reduced impact of literacy in the era of modernization is apparent also if one studies the particular kinds of jobs the gainfully employed people of West Texas were able to obtain. As table 3.4 shows, the professional and domestic service[20] sector of the labor force showed the highest degree of literacy in 1860 with a rate of 88.3 percent. Trade and transportation workers also were a skilled group with a rate of 68.3 percent, and all the other labor sectors had literacy levels well below 50 percent. Thus, in 1860 literate workers were privileged by virtue of having the greatest opportunity to move into professional positions and key roles within regional commerce and transportation.

By 1900, however, literacy rates in all specialized labor sectors (agriculture, the services, trade, transportation, and manufacturing) reached levels of 69 percent or more, so that reading and writing skills no longer were of central importance in determining which of these sectors workers would occupy. The remaining influence of literacy was more pronounced in separating those in general labor and specialized tasks. Illiterates, in other words, were more likely to be confined to the general labor pool while literates more frequently found jobs in one of the specialized occupational sectors. It appears, then, that education in West Texas was so effective in promoting the general literacy of the population that by the turn of the century, the acquisition of such skills had become a redundant requirement for participation in almost all phases of the economy.

Simultaneously, literacy remained a requirement for participation within the labor structure and those not having it found jobs in the specialized tasks hard to acquire. Among these were the Mexican Americans of West Texas whose access to schooling was less than that of whites. Furthermore, the educational system of the region was oriented toward creating a type of labor segmentation.

A brief discussion of two competing twentieth-century scholarly views of the nature of linkage between modern educational systems and occupational markets seems appropriate at this point. The first of these schools, which may be summarized for convenience as the "human capital" perspective, maintains that the development of schooling has been and remains an essential investment for both society and the individual. Society, it is claimed, gains from the skills taught by the formal schooling process, skills that add up to a more capable and productive workforce. The individual, on the other hand, gains opportunities that would not otherwise be open by investment in his or her education. Schooling, in this view, is a mutually beneficial undertaking; both society and the individual gain.

A major alternative perspective found in contemporary writing is the "sorting machine" concept.[21] According to this line of analysis, the modern educational enterprise serves as a mechanism for selecting and channeling potential workers into an array of job designations and reproducing inequities in the occupational structure. In this view, society enjoys the use of a system that manipulates workers to meet labor requirements. At the level of the individual, however, some gain opportunities and others lose as the development of personal potential and ability is subordinated to the social need for sorting and selecting.

Tragically, the second of these views seems confirmed in part by what happened in the development of education in West Texas. To be sure, formal schooling did prepare some of the region's people for occupational opportunities, and it probably added to the productivity of labor and economic processes. Yet for the Mexicans of West Texas, modern education as it emerged, faltered as a vehicle for upward mobility. As the school system evolved, it did not attract Tejanitos as it did Anglo children, and it exposed Mexican students to briefer periods of formal instructions. Moreover, as the Chicano historian Mario T. García has shown in his study of education in El Paso, instruction provided in the "Mexican schools" of that city was based upon the assumption that this special class of children needed to be prepared for participation in the lowest order occupations.[22] By 1900, a full 55 percent of the Tejano workers were concentrated in just two marginal low-grade sectors of the West Texas labor structure, the personal servant segment and the general labor groups.

Education in the western counties of the state, then, developed in a way that nourished social inequities. For Anglos it functioned as an investment in human capital as it provided them with literacy and other skills essential for effective job competition. For the Mexican Americans of the region, however, the system of formal education became a dynamic of exclusion rather than a facilitator of opportunity.

Notes

1. Walter Prescott Webb, ed., *The Handbook of Texas*, 2 vols. (Austin: Texas State Historical Association, 1952), 1: 562–63. For purposes of this chapter, West Texas is geographically defined as the region stretching from the western edge of the Texas Hill Country into the El Paso Valley. It is bordered on the south by the upper waters of "Big Bend" section of the Rio Grande, and on the north by the line of Texas counties running along the 32nd parallel or southern border of New Mexico. The Panhandle section of the state is excluded from the analysis.

2. *Population of the United States in 1860*. Ser. No. 1860.0 (Washington, DC: Government Printing Office, 1864), 475, table 1.

3. See William Curry Holden, *Alkali Trails; or, Social and Economic Movements of the Texas Frontier, 1846–1900* (Dallas: Southwest Press, 1930) for a panoramic history of the development of the West Texas frontier.

4. Calculations based on sample data taken from the original census reports of eight West Texas counties (including Crane, Crockett, El Paso, Presidio, Pecos, Tom Green, Sutton, and Val Verde) for the decennial censuses of 1860 through 1900 show that the region's total population multiplied by about ninefold between 1860 and 1900. Most of this growth occurred during the last twenty years of the century when the population increased by nearly 280 percent. The Mexican American segment of the region's people grew by nearly 200 percent between 1880 and 1900, while the number of Anglos increased by more than 500 percent. At the turn of the century, there were approximately equal numbers of Mexicans and Anglos in the population as a whole, though the two groups were relatively segregated into different geographical sections. See Arnoldo De León and Kenneth L. Stewart, "Tejano Demographic Patterns and Socio-Economic Development: A Research Note," *Borderlands Journal* 7, no. 1 (1983).

5. Among the more prominent twentieth-century critics of the idea that education in fact does serve as an avenue to mobility are Samuel Bowles and Herbert Gintes, *Schooling in Capitalist America: Educational Reform and the Contradictions of Economic Life* (New York: Basic Books, 1976). Others who question the historical accuracy of the concept include Michael B. Katz, *Class, Bureaucracy, and Schools: The Illusion of Educational Change in America* (New York: Praeger, 1971), and Colin Grear, *The Great School Legend* (New York: Basic Books, 1972). Diane Ravitch has written a fine review and critique of the so-called radical attack on American education in *The Revisionists Revised: A Critique of the Radical Attack on the Schools* (New York: Basic Books, 1977).

6. Unless otherwise indicated, the data in this chapter came from an ongoing study of the original census schedules from twenty counties selected to represent demographic and social trends in South, Central, and West Texas from 1850 through 1900. The entire database includes information on more than 100,000 individuals who lived in the South, Central, and Western regions of Texas. Eight counties located in West Texas were included in the ongoing study, and information on 14,353 residents of the section between 1860 and 1900 was gathered. Individuals were selected for the study by a random procedure, and it is estimated that about 21 percent of all residents at Crane, Crockett, El Paso, Pecos, Presidio, Sutton, Tom Green, and Val Verde Counties over the last forty years of the century were included.

7. Although military personnel made up large percentages of the West Texas labor force in the 1860s, 1870s, and 1880s, it should be pointed out that the area was scantly populated in those days. Thus, in raw numbers, the buildup of military personnel is in hundreds, rather than thousands of men. It is estimated, in fact, that the total number of military men in the entire frontier fort system running from Red River to the Rio Grande Valley never exceeded 1,500. Nonetheless, it is undeniable that the opening of West Texas for development involved military conquest. Lest the frontier era be romanticized, let it be repeated that at the end of the gun barrel laid the tragedy of Indian internment and suppression of Mexican Americans. For an excellent description of United States military operations in Texas during the era, see Robert M. Utley, *Frontier Regulars: The United States Army and the Indian, 1866–1891*, Wars of the United States (Bloomington: Indiana University Press, 1973), chaps. 1, 2, 11, 12, 13, and 18.

8. As might be expected, this general labor pool was not evenly distributed across the region. Instead, the general laboring population was clustered into the region's emerging commercial centers. In 1860, for example, about 25 percent of the labor force in El Paso County consisted of unspecified general laborers compared to just 9 percent in the more isolated setting of Presidio County. In 1900, concentrations ranging from 23 percent to almost 50 percent of the workers existed in El Paso, Pecos, Presidio, Tom Green, and Val Verde Counties while the then most remote farm and ranch areas such as Crane and Crockett Counties had general laboring populations of less than 4 percent of the workforce.

9. Census descriptions of the work done in agriculture also reflect changes in land usage. In 1860, the label "farmer" was most frequently used to describe the labor of those who had achieved some measure of land ownership. The title of "stockraiser" was more frequently used by 1900 in contrast.

10. Other examples of entirely new occupational designations appearing in the 1900 census records are "telegrapher" and "telephone operator." In addition, the 1900 records contain many specific designations hinting at the evolution of earlier more general work roles into more particularized forms. For example, labels such as "druggist" or "jeweler" appeared in the 1900 census to describe specialized mercantile operators, where in the 1860 records the general label of "merchant" was more frequently applied.

11. Technological development, of course, had much to do with the pattern of specialization and displacement in these labor sectors. The appearance of rail, telephone, and telegraph workers in trade and transport occupations by 1900 is indicative, as is the emergence of "wheel rights" and "machinists" as specialized workers in the manufacture and mechanical labor segment.

12. The statewide public debate in nineteenth-century Texas between those interested in the economic, civic, and moral potentials of schooling is an important theme of Frederick Eby's *The Development of Education in Texas* (New York: Macmillan, 1925). Eby argues that the schooling system that eventually emerged in Texas represented, in part, a compromise between these ideological interests.

13. Economic modernization and formal schooling movements, of course, have been associated with one another throughout the course of modern history. The correlation between the two, however, has come to be understood in contemporary literatures as a matter of extreme complexity. For an excellent recent analysis, see Lascelles Anderson and Douglas M. Windham, eds., *Education and Development: Issues in the Analysis and Planning of Postcolonial Societies* (Lexington, MA: D. C. Heath, 1982).

14. Descriptions of such conditions in various areas throughout the West Texas region are available in local histories, including Grace Bitner, "The History of Tom Green County, Texas" (master's thesis, University of Texas, 1931); R. D. Holt, ed., *Schleicher County: Or Eighty Years of Development in Southwest Texas* (Eldorado, TX: Eldorado Success, 1930); Alton Hughes, *Pecos: A History of the Pioneer West*, 2 vols. (Seagraves, TX: Pioneer Books Publishers, 1978); C. L. Sonnichsen, *Pass of the North: Four Centuries on the Rio Grande* (El Paso: Texas Western Press, 1968); Barry Scobee, *Old Fort Davis* (San Antonio: Naylor Company, 1947); and Clifford B. Casey, *Alpine, Texas: Then and Now* (Seagraves, TX: Pioneer Books Publisher, 1981).

15. The state's official definition of the scholastic population varied over time. In the 1870s, for example, the scholastic ages included 8–14 year-olds, but by 1900 the definition had been expanded to include children of ages 8–17. For purposes of standardizing the calculations presented here, the latter definition was adopted for the entire period.

16. This proportion is almost certainly inflated by a considerable degree since the census takers could hardly have been expected to enumerate the Indian population not Hispanicized by earlier missionization efforts. Nevertheless, the Indian children who were counted in the census had a higher attendance rate than either the Anglo or Mexican American children of the region.

17. These calculations can be feasibly explained on grounds other than discrimination. For example, one school of thought suggests that tradition-bound and indolent Mexicans never placed the value on education, as did the white community. A more thorough analysis discounting this hypothesis is in Kenneth L. Stewart and Arnoldo De León. "Education Is the Gateway: Comparative Patterns of School Attendance and Literacy between Anglos and Tejanos in Three Texas Regions, 1850–1900," *Aztlán: International Journal of Chicano Studies Research* 16 (1985).

18. Sonnichsen, *Pass of the North*, 234.

19. Of course, immigration was an important source of population increase in the late nineteenth century, and so the fluctuation in general literacy rates cannot be attributed solely to the region's educational system. Nevertheless, the correspondence between rates of literacy and the evolution of schools is both striking and noteworthy.

20. "Domestic service" as used here refers to public service occupations including military service.

21. This label is borrowed from the innovative title of Joel Spring's book, *The Sorting Machine: National Educational Policy since 1945* (New York: David McKay, 1976). Perhaps the most widely

acknowledged advocates of the sorting and selecting perspective are Bowles and Gintis, *Schooling in Capitalist America.* A prominent selection expressing the human capital view is Gary S. Becker, *Human Capital* (New York: National Bureau of Economic Research, 1964). A useful and insightful overview of the scholarly exchange and debate that has gone on between these two camps is in Jerome Karable and A. H. Halsey, eds., *Power and Ideology in Education* (New York: Oxford University Press, 1977), 307–65.

22. See Mario T. García, *Desert Immigrants: The Mexicans of El Paso, 1880–1900* (New Haven, CT: Yale University Press, 1981), chap. 6.

4

Tejanos in West Texas

As did other Texans, Mexican-origin people looked upon West Texas and Northwest Texas as lands of new beginnings. Once arriving in the region, Mexican laborers followed roads that took them to many settings, both rural and urban. They employed numerous strategies in their struggle for survival, overcame difficulties, and succeeded in efforts at community building. Over time, they contributed politically, economically, and culturally to their new homeland. By the twenty-first century, many Hispanics/Latinos had integrated themselves into the mainstream of society and imposed a Hispanic ambient on their surroundings.

During the mid-nineteenth century, people of Hispanic, usually Spanish-Mexican, descent constituted some 70 percent of the total white population living in West Texas. Until the last decades of that century, people of Hispanic origin outnumbered Anglos (non-Hispanic white settlers and residents) in what today are referred to as the Edwards Plateau and Trans-Pecos areas of the region. In modern-day Oldham and Hartley Counties in the Texas Panhandle, *pastores* (sheepherders) from New Mexico similarly held a demographic advantage over Anglos as late as 1880.[1]

Some prominent Hispanic names of the present day can be identified with West Texas before 1900: Casimero Romero, Pablo Alderette, and Paula Losoya Taylor. Romero led sheep ranchers from New Mexico into the Panhandle around 1876 and established the town that came to be known as Tascosa. Alderette arrived in the San Angelo area with his family around

This chapter was originally published in Paul H. Carlson and Bruce A. Glasrud, eds., *West Texas: A History of the Giant Side of the State* (Norman: University of Oklahoma Press, 2014), 107–18.

1869 or 1870 and served as a Tom Green County commissioner in 1875. History credits Losoya Taylor with cofounding Del Rio.[2]

For the most part, however, ordinary Tejanos, of Mexican origin or descent, worked as ranch and farm hands, as day laborers, as freighters, and as unskilled workers in an assortment of occupations in the predominantly agrarian society of West Texas.[3] Though post–Civil War Anglo immigration to the region began to dwarf the Mexican American presence there, people of Mexican descent remained a visible element in 1900. As present-day statistics show, in recent years they have again come to outnumber Anglos in many counties stretching from the Rio Grande to the Texas Panhandle.[4]

Tejanos, the name used today for Texans of Mexican descent, originally applied to people who inhabited the geographic area of Texas. In colonial times, when Texas was a northern territory of Mexico and most residents other than Indians spoke Spanish, *Tejanos* simply meant "Texans," people who lived in Texas. During the years of Texas independence the same geographical sense prevailed, and residents of the new republic were sometimes referred to as Tejanos. The shift in meaning, such that "Tejano" also denoted Hispanic language and culture as distinct from "Anglo" counterparts, seems to have gradually occurred over the mid- to late nineteenth century as the Anglo population rose and English became a more prevalent language.

Even so, West Texas was, and remains today, a land of geographic diversity, and Tejanos and Mexican immigrants, along with other ethnic incomers to the area in the early twentieth century, gravitated toward areas offering hospitable prospects for cattle, sheep, and goat raising. This pattern of settlement took them to Trans-Pecos ranch counties like Terrell, Pecos, and Reeves, but also Edwards Plateau livestock counties like Sutton and Val Verde. Others sought work in developing enterprises, such as the quicksilver (mercury) operations in the Big Bend. The Chisos Mining Company in Terlingua, for example, attracted workers from both sides of the border, so many that one contemporary in the early 1900s remarked that 1,000 to 1,500 Mexicans lived in tents and stone huts near the mine.[5]

During the period after World War I all of West Texas experienced new improvements in range management, in farming practices, and in oil drilling. The number of towns multiplied. Mexican American communities that had risen before 1900 kept pace with the times despite dire conditions: poverty, racial discrimination, condescending attitudes toward Mexican culture and intelligence, and even violence. In towns like Marfa, Presidio, San Angelo, Fort Stockton, and Ozona, *barrios* (labeled "Little Mexicos" by Anglos) sprouted around railroad depots or livestock yards, sites where unskilled jobs might be readily accessible to Mexican workers. These barrios afforded opportunities for community building, and Tejanos organized mutual aid societies to help members in need or to sponsor cultural activities; they founded churches of every denomination, celebrated *fiestas patrias* (patriotic Mexican holidays) under the tutelage of local *comités patrióticos*, and they enjoyed sports events—almost every community had its own *equipo*, or baseball team.[6]

New arrivals from Mexico or other parts of the state (many came from South Texas) augmented the existing Hispanic population in the region. But not all of them pursued their destiny in ranch settlements, as so many earlier Mexican workers had done. Instead, they sought new beginnings in counties such as Schleicher, Runnels, Concho, and McCullough, which were turning more and more to farm cultivation.[7]

They also further pursued possibilities for livelihood in sections of West Texas then undergoing oil exploration and discovery: Reagan and Ector Counties in the Edwards Plateau, and Pecos County in the Trans-Pecos region; in the Panhandle; and in such Rolling Plains counties as Scurry, Fisher, Jones, Howard, and Taylor. This new thrust drew Tejanos into the fledgling oil towns of Big Lake and Snyder and into embryonic barrios growing in Odessa, Midland, Abilene, Lubbock, and Amarillo.[8]

By 1930 people of Mexican origin or descent represented a rather insignificant proportion of the inhabitants settled throughout the wide expanse that is West Texas. According to calculations derived from population figures provided by the federal census of 1930, Americans of Mexican descent made up 7.6 percent of a total West Texas population of 843,922.[9]

The Great Depression and World War II led a greater number of Mexican workers northward from their homes in South Texas and in Mexico, as well as from southern West Texas counties, where many already resided. Although the Depression extended its reach into West Texas, it hardly caused the devastation there that it did in other parts of the country, and the region survived, due to the quick rebound of ranching, government help to farmers, and a surge in the oil industry.[10]

But the 1930s and 1940s did not bring better days to the Tejanos of West Texas or to the Hispanic workers and families moving into the region. Whether in ranching, farming, oil fields, or towns, most faced trying times. Traditionally ranchers had paid Mexican and Tejano cowboys less than they paid Anglo cowhands for doing the same work.[11] Anglo sheep and goat men negotiated through *capitanes*, or crew chiefs (themselves forced to survive on meager payments) for getting their sheep sheared, a system encouraging wage unfairness that hit the common *tasinque* (sheepshearer) hardest. In the San Angelo area in 1934, Mexican American sheepshearers went on strike protesting employment practices and low pay. The strike ended in failure.[12]

Migrant farm workers dealt with their own tribulation. By the early 1930s Mexican workers were responding to calls for cotton pickers throughout the region, and the demand came strongest from farm counties in Northwest Texas. Setting out from South Texas, the migrant laborers followed a trail that kept them on the road from about March to December. They crossed through the Coastal Bend counties on their way to Central Texas farms, then through Tom Green, Runnels, McCullough, and Concho County cotton fields, and up to Lubbock, Hale, Lamb, and Bailey Counties.[13]

On this Big Swing, as people called this cycle, Mexican American migrants encountered difficult conditions. They traveled at their own expense, either in an old car or on the bed of a large truck—they paid a *troquero*, or a truck driver, to transport them over the hundreds of miles along their route. Circumstances forced them to find shelter on their own, to determine what stores sold goods to Mexicans (some towns discouraged Mexicans from even stopping within their city limits), and to trust that work would await them once reaching their destination. Once arrived, they were plagued by a range of further problems, among these lack of proper sanitary facilities, lack of adequate protection from the weather (winters are cold in Northwest Texas), *troqueros* who might cheat them of their earning, ill treatment by farm owners, and of course, low wages for backbreaking labor.[14]

The recovery of the oil industry during the 1930s augured well for Permian Basin counties, Panhandle counties, and some southeastern counties in Northwest Texas, and many Tejano workers sought jobs in and around the oil fields. For the most part, racial and ethnic attitudes of the era precluded their taking the more desirable positions and better-paying tasks. They faced relegation to the dirtiest chores, including grubbing the land, cleaning oil-field debris, and helping transport oil-field supplies and heavy equipment. In small oil towns close to the oil fields, they survived by taking any type of employment: pick and shovel work, housecleaning, construction, dishwashing, or perhaps seasonal jobs in neighboring farms and ranches.[15]

Town life offered these workers no advantage over rural living. Housing in urban areas reflected the ambient poverty level in which most lived; dwellings were built with whatever earnings they could muster, generally on affordable property at the outskirts of a municipality. In any case, most Anglos in West Texas followed segregationist policies and prohibited

"Mexicans" (meaning anyone Hispanic) from setting up homesteads in the white areas of settlements and municipalities. Public facilities such as restrooms or parks were often off-limits to "Mexicans," as were schools. Educators seldom made provisions for schooling Tejano adolescents, and in any case, there existed unwritten rules that Mexican children could not attend school past elementary grades.[16]

Still, the clearest expression of Hispanic culture throughout West Texas was discernible in the towns—at least that is where present-day scholarship, albeit thin, has so far focused. Within the boundaries of the barrios, as in remote ranch and farm homes, life marched on as normally as people could possibly make it. Entrepreneurs set up business establishments, among them *tienditas* (small "mom and pop" general stores), restaurants offering Mexican-style food, Spanish-language theaters, and dance halls. Spanish-speaking priests and ministers tended to the spiritual needs of believers. Within the Hispanic community, people carried on old folkloric traditions, families observed conventional courtesies when interacting with one another and friends, and the young abided by established rules of courtship. Leisure included the observation of important religious or secular anniversaries, both Mexican and American (Fourth of July), or participation in recreative clubs that sponsored cultural activities, picnic outings, and dances. *Lo mexicano*, "the Mexican way," thus persisted during the Depression years throughout West Texas: in the Big Bend, in border towns such as Del Rio, in urban centers like San Angelo, and in Trans-Pecos towns such as Fort Stockton and faraway Van Horn.[17]

Despite these persistent socioeconomic problems, collectively and individually, Hispanics made efforts at community improvement. Mexican American leaders took it upon themselves to address local issues, as in the case of the League of United Latin American Citizens (LULAC), active in towns like San Angelo and Fort Stockton by the 1930s. By the war years, at least a few students had broken past societal barriers in West Texas to graduate from high school. Many young Hispanic men met the qualifications for military service and either enlisted or responded to draft calls, fighting gallantly both in Europe and in the Pacific.[18]

The Mexican and Mexican American influx into West Texas intensified after World War II, at least as indicated by population figures. In 1950, about 95,000 people of Mexican origin or descent lived in West Texas (8.6 percent of the total population), and this amount increased to more than 306,000 (20.0 percent of the total population) by 1980.[19]

Although between 1950 and 1980 the oil industry experienced fluctuation and farmers and ranchers faced their own woes, West Texans of Mexican descent still found options for material advancement in many sections of the region. Ranch counties attracted some workers, and cattle feeding enterprises and meatpacking plants established in Northwest Texas during the 1960s drew hundreds directly from Mexico and from poverty-stricken areas throughout the state. But the greatest lures to West Texas were the counties that continued to offer work in farming and oil production. Farms, now irrigated by electrically powered pumps, had a greater need for field hands, and oil counties along the northern rim of the Edwards Plateau and Trans-Pecos now offered job possibilities to Hispanic workers, who until past midcentury had not been permitted direct employment in oil drilling operations. And by the 1960s Tejanos and other Hispanic workers also saw better opportunities in the cities of West Texas, some that emerged as centers of finance, hubs for the ranching and farming industries, focal points for conducting financial transactions, or simply as oil towns. Thus by the 1960s and 1970s a general demographic trend was movement from the rural areas into large cities such as San Angelo, Midland, Odessa, Del Rio, Lubbock, and Amarillo and also into several county seats of less populous counties.[20]

Individually or as a group, Mexican Americans in West Texas attempted to find solutions to festering problems. Throughout the region, they still felt a need to tread lightly when entering public places; the route from Marfa, through Fort Stockton and then to Junction during the late 1940s (and presumably later) had a notorious reputation for "not serving Mexicans" at restaurants. During World War II even Mexican Americans in uniform themselves experienced rejection at eateries, barbershops, and gas stations.[21] Barrio leaders during the 1950s and 1960s bravely addressed matters of ethnic prejudice, police harassment, and de facto segregation in West Texas schools, among them the systems in Pecos, Midland, Ozona, Sonora, Alpine, and Snyder.[22] In these endeavors they found encouragement and support from LULAC and the American GI Forum (AGIF), the two leading groups at that time that looked into Mexican American concerns in Texas. In the hostile environment of that era, representatives from LULAC and AGIF went before city councils to request that attention be given to Mexican American neighborhoods needing city lighting, paved roads, and garbage collection. In rural areas, these advocates inquired into cases of Anglo abuse of Hispanic farm and ranch hands. To help uplift Hispanic communities, LULAC councils and AGIF chapters set up citizenship classes, encouraged people to pay their poll taxes and to vote, held dances to raise funds for school scholarships, sponsored athletic activities, and encouraged Mexican Americans to contribute to worthy causes, among them Red Cross drives. When Henry B. González of San Antonio launched his drive for governor in 1958, he counted on LULAC and the AGIF to help in his West Texas campaign. (He was defeated but went on to a long career in the US House of Representatives, 1961–99.)[23]

A more intense political drive intended to remove long-standing obstacles to Mexican American advancement occurred during the 1960s through the 1970s. This was the Chicano movement, a sometimes militant campaign led by young people coming of age during the tumultuous Vietnam era and by middle-class members of the World War II generation who had become increasingly dissatisfied with circumstances that stifled Mexican American ambitions. Chicanos joined such militant groups as the Mexican American Youth Organization (MAYO) and Raza Unida Party (RUP), or they joined older, mainstream organizations such as LULAC, AGIF, and the Mexican American Legal Defense and Education Fund (MALDEF). Assisted by liberal allies, they launched frontal attacks on racism and ethnic prejudice, on the political structure, on the capitalist system, and on social injustices generally.[24]

While area universities such as Texas Tech, Angelo State, and Sul Ross often received a lot of attention as a result of Chicano students' militant activism, many West Texas communities became politicized and active at the microlevel. In 1972 and 1974, when RUP put up candidates for statewide offices, many Mexican Americans in West Texas supported the party's platform, which called for a better funding system for schools, for single-member election districts, for the elimination of the Texas Ranger force, and for women's equality. Here and there RUP won some offices, among them in Marathon in Brewster County.[25] The momentum of the 1970s allowed for the election of Froy Salinas of Lubbock as state representative in 1978.

Chicano activists also dealt with the plight of the migrant farm laborer. In the late 1970s and continuing into the 1980s, the Texas Farm Workers Union (TFWU) arrived in Northwest Texas counties of Bailey, Castro, Deaf Smith, Hale, and Lamb to challenge the dire conditions—long hours, very low pay, and little social support—that had long afflicted Mexican Americans in the vegetable and cotton fields. TFWU organizers held marches, union rallies, and boycotts in efforts to win concessions from growers. Texas Rural Legal Aid (TRLA), TFWU's main ally, filed suits of various sorts, and court victories gradually prepared towns (such as Hereford) where migrants increasingly yearned for the day when Tejanos would gain office in municipal, county, and school district governance.[26]

During the latter decades of the twentieth century and into the first years of the twenty-first, Mexican Americans solidified their presence in West Texas. Having comprised about 20.0 percent of the total population in 1980, by the year 2000 Tejanos accounted for fully 30.8 percent of the total population in the region.[27] This occurred as West Texans wrestled with uncertainty. The oil industry, while still a mainstay in many counties, contended with the usual ebbs and flows, and farmers and ranchers annually struggled with bad weather and with a dwindling supply of the great reserves of water essential for irrigated lands. These and other factors led to a marked decline in the Anglo-American population and a rapid rise in the number of Tejanos who chose West Texas as their permanent home.[28]

Continuing population increases was not the only demographic development to occur among Tejanos. Americans of Mexican descent also continued their earlier movement away from the more remote ranch counties toward the oil counties of the Edwards Plateau and Trans-Pecos and the oil and farm counties of northwestern Texas. Though they remained a discernible presence everywhere in West Texas, the trend that had begun at midcentury, in the postwar years was toward the urban areas, such that Lubbock, Amarillo, and Big Spring in northwestern Texas became magnet cities for many. On the Edwards Plateau, the cities of Del Rio, Midland, Odessa, and San Angelo together housed about 50.0 percent of the entire Hispanic population living from the Hill Country in the region's east to Hudspeth County in Far West Texas.[29]

In sum, Mexican Americans stayed in or migrated into West Texas for a variety of reasons. As other West Texans did, Tejanos found that the region offers a pleasant environment for raising families and enjoying life in general. As opposed to big city problems such as pollution, congestion, highway traffic, crime, and drug dealing, rural areas for many residents offered generous space and a greater sense of safety and security. Also, Tejanos were following a general trend in American society whereby minority groups found rural areas more to their liking.[30]

Economic and social inducements also explain the Tejano preference for life in West Texas. Recent arrivals from Mexico, as well as native-born Tejanos, have taken jobs in the region's numerous farms and ranches, and in its oil fields, in the feedlots of Northwest Texas, in restaurants, hotels, and construction sites in cities, and in every business seeking unskilled manual labor.[31] Enterprising Mexican Americans, even in disadvantaged circumstances, have often established business enterprises catering to Hispanic tastes or meeting Hispanic needs for professional services. Attorneys' offices displaying signs reading "Se habla español" proliferated, for instance, in towns and cities where Tejanos came to live and work. In the wake of the social reforms won in the 1960s and 1970s, Hispanic professionals—previously an almost nonexistent class—have found openings in the educational field as teachers and college professors, in hospitals as doctors and nurses, and in local and federal government service. Others who once worked the fields have prospered sufficiently to buy farm land.

Hispanics also found politics, once closed to them, attractive. The work of groups such as LULAC and the AGIF, the impact of the Chicano movement, the initiatives taken in West Texas by the San Antonio–based Southwest Voter and Education Project (SWVEP), and TRLA's court victories in the early 1980s forced cities, counties, and school districts to hold single-member district elections.[32] This opportunity, coupled with the increase in the Hispanic population (and thus voting numbers), allowed Tejanos to win political appointments or elections to government posts. By the end of the twentieth century they had become increasingly visible in West Texas county commissioners' courts, on school boards, in the constabulary (including sheriffs), and on judges' benches.[33]

Over the years since the founding of the first Hispanic settlement, Tejanos have sunk deep roots in just about every county in West Texas, gaining a demographic majority in 2014 in Sutton, Reagan, Presidio, Pecos, Deaf Smith, and Castro Counties.[34] Demographers have predicted further population gains in other counties and have reasoned that even counties far removed from the Rio Grande border could well follow trends now well established in South Texas, with its prominent Spanish-language advertisements, bilingual transactions, commemorations of the holidays such as Cinco de Mayo, and much more that marks the incontestable presence of a Hispanic West Texas. Easy to overlook in the landscape of West Texas until recent decades, Tejanos have gained a secure foothold in the mainstream of the region's affairs and have seen their culture come to be celebrated as another component of the American way of life.

Notes

1. Arnoldo De León and Kenneth L. Stewart, "Tejano Demographic Patterns and Socio-Economic Development," *Borderlands Journal* 7 (Fall 1983): 3, 6; Anna J. Taylor, "Hispanic Settlement of the Texas Panhandle-Plains, 1876–1884," *Panhandle-Plains Historical Review* 70 (1997): 36.

2. Taylor, "Hispanic Settlement of the Texas Panhandle-Plains," 46, 52; Arnoldo De León, *San Angeleños: Mexican Americans in San Angelo, Texas* (San Angelo: Fort Concho Museum Press, 1985), 15–16; Whitehead Memorial Museum, *La Hacienda: An Official Bicentennial Publication* (Del Rio: The Museum, 1976), 3, 5, 369.

3. Kenneth L. Stewart and Arnoldo De León, "Education, Literacy, and Occupational Structure in West Texas, 1860–1900," *West Texas Historical Association Yearbook* 60 (1984): 131.

4. De León and Stewart, "Tejano Demographic Patterns and Socio-Economic Development," 3, 6; Arnoldo De León, "Mexican Americans in the Edwards Plateau and Trans-Pecos Region,

1900–2000," *Southwestern Historical Quarterly* 112 (October 2008): 167–69; Arnoldo De León, "Tejanos in Northwest Texas: Rural Folks or Urbanites?" *West Texas Historical Association Yearbook* 86 (2010): 15.

5. De León, "Mexican Americans in the Edwards Plateau and Trans-Pecos Region," 155–57, 160–61; Arthur Gómez, *A Most Singular Country: A History of Occupation in the Big Bend* (Santa Fe: National Park Service; Salt Lake City: Charles Redd Center for Western Studies, Brigham Young University, 1990), 123.

6. De León, *San Angeleños*, 25–28, 40–41; María Eva Flores, CDP, "The Good Life the Hard Way: The Mexican American Community of Fort Stockton, Texas, 1930–1945" (PhD diss., Arizona State University, 2000), chaps. 2 to 5. See further Paul Wright, "Life on Both Sides of the Tracks in Early Alpine," *West Texas Historical Association Yearbook* 73 (1997): 98; Paul Wright, "Residential Segregation in Two Early West Texas Towns," *Southwestern Historical Quarterly* 102 (January 1999): 297–99, 302–5; and Paul Wright, "A Tumultuous Decade: Changes in the Mexican-Origin Population of the Big Bend, 1910–1920," *Journal of Big Bend Studies* 10 (1998): 180, 182.

7. De León, "Mexican Americans in the Edwards Plateau and Trans-Pecos Region," 157, 160.

8. Ibid., 155–56, 161; De León, "Tejanos in Northwest Texas: Rural Folks or Urbanites?," 10–12.

9. De León, "Mexican Americans in the Edwards Plateau and Trans-Pecos Region," 158–59, tables 3 and 4; De León, "Tejanos in Northwest Texas: Rural Folks or Urbanites?," 19–24, tables 1 and 2. To determine percentages for 1930, I divided the Mexican population by the total population to get 7.6 percent.

10. De León, "Mexican Americans in the Edwards Plateau and Trans-Pecos Region," 161; De León, "Tejanos in Northwest Texas: Rural Folks or Urbanites?," 10.

11. B. Youngblood and A. B. Cox, *An Economic Study of a Typical Ranching Area on the Edwards Plateau of Texas*, Texas Agricultural Experiment Station Bulletin, No. 297 (College Station: Agricultural and Mechanical College of Texas, 1922), 308–9.

12. Arnoldo De León, "*Los Tasinques* and the Sheep Shearers' Union of North America: A Strike in West Texas, 1934," *West Texas Historical Association Yearbook* 55 (1979): 3–16; Anita Torres Smith, "Shearing: *La Trasquila*, in the First Half of the Twentieth Century," *Journal of Big Bend Studies* 6 (1994): 99–117.

13. George O. Coalson, *The Development of the Migrant Farm Labor System in Texas, 1900–1954* (San Francisco: R&E Research Associates, 1977), 23, 25; Carey McWilliams, *Ill Fares the Land* (Boston: Little, Brown, 1942), 238–39; Zaragosa Vargas, *Labor Rights Are Civil Rights: Mexican American Workers in Twentieth-Century America* (Princeton, NJ: Princeton University Press, 2005), 18–21; Pauline R. Kibbe, *Latin Americans in Texas* (Albuquerque: University of New Mexico Press, 1946), 174–75; Yolanda G. Romero, "The Mexican American Frontier Experience in Twentieth Century Northwest Texas" (PhD diss., Texas Tech University, 1993), 31–37; Camilo Amado Martínez Jr., "*Vamos Pal West:* Let's Go West," *West Texas Historical Association Yearbook* 70 (1994): 40–56.

14. Kibbe, *Latin Americans in Texas*, 176–80; McWilliams, *Ill Fares the Land*, 238–39; Romero, "The Mexican American Frontier Experience in Twentieth Century Northwest Texas," chap. 3; Martínez, "*Vamos Pal West:* Let's Go West," 40–46.

15. Roger M. Olien and Diana Davids Olien, *Oil Booms: Social Change in Five Texas Towns* (Lincoln: University of Nebraska Press, 1982), 114, 117, 118, 119.

16. De León, *San Angeleños*, 50, 55; Olien and Olien, *Oil Booms*, 117, 119; Manuel Peña, *Where the Ox Does Not Plow: A Mexican American Ballad* (Albuquerque: University of New Mexico Press, 2008), 44–46.

17. Steven W. Prewitt, "'We Didn't Ask to Come to This Party': Self-Determination Collides with the Federal Government in the Public Schools of Del Rio, Texas, 1890–1971" (PhD diss., University of Houston, 2000), chaps. 2 and 3; De León, *San Angeleños*, chap. 4; Flores, "The Good Life the Hard Way," chaps. 2 to 5; Romero, "The Mexican American Frontier Experience in Twentieth Century Northwest Texas," 38–41, 88–93.

18. De León, *San Angeleños*, 54–56, 58; Salvador Guerrero, *Memorias: A West Texas Life* (Lubbock: Texas Tech University Press, 1991), chaps. 10–14; Flores, "The Good Life the Hard Way," chaps. 4 and 6.

19. De León, "Mexican Americans in the Edwards Plateau and Trans-Pecos Region," 158–59, tables 3 and 4; De León, "Tejanos in Northwest Texas: Rural Folks or Urbanites?," 19–24, tables 1 and 2. To determine percentages for 1950, I divided the Mexican population by the total population to get 8.6 percent. I performed the same calculation for 1980 to arrive at 20.0 percent.

20. De León, "Mexican Americans in the Edwards Plateau and Trans-Pecos Region," 161, 163–64; De León, "Tejanos in Northwest Texas: Rural Folks or Urbanites?," 11–13; Olien and Olien, *Oil Booms*, 114, 118.

21. Letter from Raymond Wheat to Mr. Everett Williams, identified as 180.23 in Dr. Héctor P. García Papers, Special Collections & Archives, Mary and Jeff Bell Library, Texas A&M University–Corpus Christi; Guerrero, *Memorias*, 101.

22. Jorge C. Rangel and Carlos M. Alcalá, "Project Report: De Jure Segregation of Chicanos in Texas Schools," *Harvard Civil Rights–Civil Liberties Law Review* 7 (March 1972): 367–68; "Alpine's School Situation," *Texas Observer*, August 15, 1969, 11.

23. De León, *San Angeleños*, 73–76; Flores, "The Good Life the Hard Way," 181–87; Romero, "The Mexican American Frontier Experience in Twentieth Century Northwest Texas," 137–41; Arnoldo De León, *Mexican Americans in Texas: A Brief History*, 3rd ed. (Wheeling, IL: Harlan Davidson, 2009), 113, 128, 137.

24. De León, *Mexican Americans in Texas*, chap. 9.

25. De León, *San Angeleños*, chap. 7; Romero, "The Mexican American Frontier Experience in Twentieth Century Northwest Texas," 151–52; Ignacio M. García, *United We Win: The Rise and Fall of the Raza Unida Party* (Tucson: Mexican American Studies and Research Center, University of Arizona Press, 1989), 168.

26. Romero, "The Mexican American Frontier Experience in Twentieth Century Northwest Texas," 153–66.

27. De León, "Mexican Americans in the Edwards Plateau and Trans-Pecos Region," 158–59, tables 3 and 4; De León, "Tejanos in Northwest Texas: Rural Folks or Urbanites?," 19–24, tables 1 and 2. To determine percentages for 2000, I divided the Mexican population by the total population to get 30.8 percent.

28. De León, "Mexican Americans in the Edwards Plateau and Trans-Pecos Region," 167–68; De León, "Tejanos in Northwest Texas: Rural Folks or Urbanites?," 13–14.

29. De León, "Mexican Americans in the Edwards Plateau and Trans-Pecos Region," 168; De León, "Tejanos in Northwest Texas: Rural Folks or Urbanites?," 13–15.

30. De León, "Mexican Americans in the Edwards Plateau and Trans-Pecos Region," 169–70; De León, "Tejanos in Northwest Texas: Rural Folks or Urbanites?," p. 16; William Kandel and John Cromartie, *New Patterns of Hispanic Settlement in Rural America*, Rural Development Research Report, no. 99 (Washington, DC: US Department of Agriculture, Economic Research Service, 2004).

31. De León, "Mexican Americans in the Edwards Plateau and Trans-Pecos Region," 170; De León, "Tejanos in Northwest Texas: Rural Folks or Urbanites?," 15.

32. De León, *Mexican Americans in Texas*, chap. 10.

33. Elizabeth Cruce Alvarez, ed., *Texas Almanac, 2008–2009* (Dallas: Dallas Morning News, 2008), 513–22.

34. *Texas Tribune*, Census 2010 Interactive Map: Texas Population by Race, Hispanic Origin, accessed January 17, 2012.

Mexican Americans in the Edwards Plateau and Trans-Pecos Region, 1900–2000

A Demographic Study

Native-born Tejanos and immigrants from Mexico during the twentieth century established themselves permanently in the vast range that stretches from the Texas Hill Country to Hudspeth County. They responded to job opportunities as ranching and farming prospered, as West Texas became a center of an oil boom, and as economic growth in the cities after World War II called for white-collar personnel and service-sector workers. By the end of the twentieth century, Tejanos had become a majority in several West Texas counties, although almost half of the Hispanic/Latino population in the Edwards Plateau and Trans-Pecos was concentrated in four cities: Del Rio, San Angelo, Midland, and Odessa.

As Texas Mexicans march almost inexorably toward becoming the majority population in the Lone Star State, historians hasten to learn more of what not long ago many regarded as an invisible minority. This endeavor has at the present yielded an impressive amount of scholarship in the form of monographs, articles, historiographic essays, bibliographies, edited collections of works, and much more. Still, scholars recognize that too much of Tejano history remains undiscovered, and their curiosity has led them to research long-neglected matters such as the military participation of Mexican Americans (especially in the two world wars); the lives of men and women who gave of their time to improve conditions around them; as well as subjects that some might consider peripheral, like religion and sports. Despite this juggernaut, little has been written on women, urban life, politics, entrepreneurship, and leisure activities, to highlight only a few topics yet to be fully explored.[1]

This chapter was originally published in the *Southwestern Historical Quarterly* 112, no. 2 (2008): 148–70.

Table 5.1. Statewide population for Texas

	1930	*1950*	*1980*	*2000*
Total Pop.	5,824,715[a]	7,711,194[b]	14,229,191[e]	20,851,820[f]
Anglo Pop.	4,283,491[a]	-------	9,350,297[e]	14,799,505[f]
Afr. Am. Pop.	854,964[a]	977,458[c]	1,692,542[e]	2,404,566[f]
Mex. Am. Pop.	683,681[a]	1,033,768[d]	2,752,487[e]	5,071,963[g]

[a]Fifteenth Census of the United States, 1930. *Population*, vol. 3, pt. 2, Montana to Wyoming (Washington, DC, 1932), Table 2: "Color, Nativity, and Sex, for the State, Urban and Rural: 1930, 1920, and 1910," p. 941.

[b]*United States Census of Population, 1950*, vol. 1, Number of Inhabitants, Sect. 10, Table 5: "Area and Population of Counties, Urban and Rural: 1930 to 1950," p. 43-13.

[c]*United States Census of Population, 1950*, vol. 4, pt. 3, Special Report, *Nativity and Parentage*, Sect. 6, Table 15: "Age of the Negro Population, by Sex, for Selected States, Urban and Rural, and for Selected Standard Metropolitan Areas, 1950-Con.," pp. 3B-58.

[d]*United States Census of Population: 1950*, vol. 4, pt. 3, Special Report, *Persons of Spanish Surname*, Sect. 9, Table 2: "Age of White Persons of Spanish Surname, for Selected Southwestern States: 1950," p. 3C-15.

[e]*1980 Census of Population*, vol. 1, *Characteristics of the Population*, Chap. B, General Population Characteristics, Part 45, Texas, PC80-1-B45 (Washington, DC: Dept. of Commerce, 1982), Table 16: "Total Persons and Spanish Origin Persons by Type of Spanish Origin and Race: 1980," p. 45-34.

[f]United States Census 2000, *Texas: Census of Population and Housing*, "Summary Population and Housing Characteristics," PHC-1-45 (Washington, DC: U.S. Dept. of Commerce, U.S. Bureau of the Census, 2000), Table 3: "Race and Hispanic or Latino: 2000," p. 126.

[g]Betsy Guzmán, *The Hispanic Population: Census 2000 Brief* (Washington, DC: U.S. Census Bureau, 2001), Table 2: "Hispanic Population by Type for Regions, States, and Puerto Rico: 1990 and 2000," p. 4.

Also insufficiently studied are Texas regions and the Mexican American presence therein. Much attention has been extended to South Texas, true enough, but this has been at the expense of the northern, eastern, and western sections of the state. As a partial effort to correct this imbalance, this study looks at the Mexican American population in thirty-nine counties in a section of the state that is among the least researched—namely, the Edwards Plateau and the Trans-Pecos. Specifically, this chapter seeks to determine the historical forces that have lured Mexican-origin folks into this region, discern the cycles of population growth there, trace the demographic patterns of Mexican American dispersal, and hopefully,

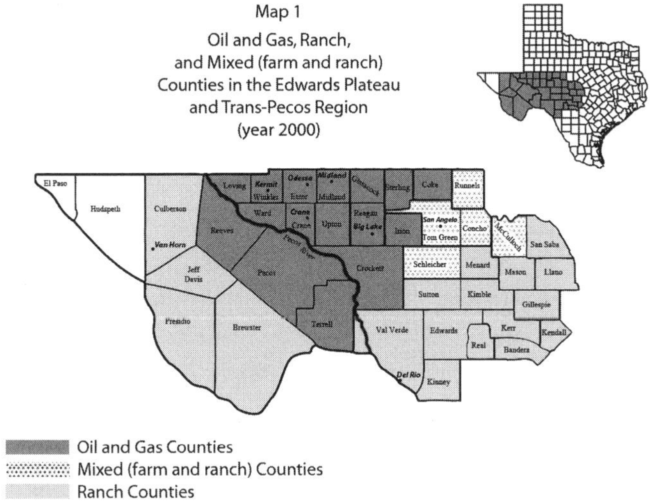

Map 1
Oil and Gas, Ranch,
and Mixed (farm and ranch)
Counties in the Edwards Plateau
and Trans-Pecos Region
(year 2000)

Map drawn for the author courtesy of Sharalyn Bell

prompt further scholarly study of Tejanos in that part of the state generally neglected in the literature (see map 1 and table 5.1).[2]

The area under study stretches along the 32nd parallel on the north and eastward toward the Hill Country counties of San Saba and Kendall, west from there toward the Rio Grande, and up the river toward Culberson County. This region of western Texas regularly experiences water problems; annually, precipitation there is perceptibly less than that which falls on the eastern third of the state. The terrain in this area of central and western Texas has been described as rough, rugged, and rocky, for such is the appearance given the landscape by the brush, range grasses, and thickets formed by live oak, cedar, juniper, and mesquite trees. Despite such drawbacks, much of the area lends itself aptly to livestock raising. Singular areas of the Edwards Plateau, moreover, do well under cultivation. In the "Concho Country"—a section within the Edwards Plateau embracing counties such as Runnels, Tom Green, Concho, McCulloch, and Schleicher—the soil runs deep, allowing farmers to raise cotton as well as grain sorghum and other crops that supplement the general ranching economy.[3]

As of the year 2000, the official United States federal census counted about 238,000 "Hispanic or Latino" people living in the counties constituting the Edwards Plateau and Trans-Pecos region. This figure represents only about 4.7 percent of the state's Texas-Mexican population—the 2000 census counted about 6,669,666 "Hispanics or Latinos (of any race)" in the Lone Star State, but of this number 5,071,963 were identified as Mexican origin Latino. Said differently, the aggregate population of Mexican Americans in the Edwards Plateau and Trans-Pecos is less than the entire Mexican (and other Latino) population in cities such as San Antonio, Houston, El Paso, and Dallas.[4]

In 2000, Mexican Americans made up only 35 percent of the total population (including African Americans, Asians, as well as Anglos—or Euro-Americans—and Mexicans) in the Edwards Plateau and the Trans-Pecos region. While almost negligible in some counties therein, Mexican Americans are prominent demographically in others. In ten of the counties, for instance, they comprise nearly 50 percent or more of the population, and in four of these, Mexican Americans constitute in excess of 70 percent of inhabitants (see table 5.2 and map 2).

At one point in the history of the Edwards Plateau and Trans-Pecos region, Tejanos actually were more numerous than Anglos in what was then an area of the state closely tied to the traditional livestock economy of the nineteenth century. Anglo Texans who had pushed westward into the eastern counties of the Edwards Plateau before the Civil War had discovered ranching to be the most convenient way of wresting a living from the land, and those who followed them into the center-west region after 1865 continued the pattern of livestock raising. Small-scale farming existed of course, but only as a secondary enterprise and in a supplementary capacity.[5]

In 1860, when census takers ventured into that frontier for the first time, Mexican-descent settlers made up almost three-fourths of all inhabitants, and though that standing declined through the rest of the nineteenth century, as of 1900 Tejanos still constituted half of all residents in the region. The causes behind this strong showing included natural reproduction and some in-migration from other parts of the state, but a major reason was immigration from Mexico. As of 1860, Mexicans of foreign birth represented 40 percent of the total Mexican population in the region; by 1880 foreign-born Mexicans constituted almost 60 percent of the total Mexican population, before dropping to about 50 percent as of 1900. Calls for labor from Anglo newcomers founding ranches and farms in the region as well as from pioneering Mexican landowners enticed poor folks across the international border.[6]

From the 1910s and continuing into the 1920s, the combined region of the Edwards Plateau and the Trans-Pecos began its remarkable ascent toward modernization. Several developments drove this change. Ranchers found improved ways to raise cattle under unfriendly environmental

Table 5.2. Population 2000

County	*Total Pop.*	*Mexican and Other Latino Pop.*	*% of Pop.*
Val Verde	44,856	33,849	75.5
Edwards	2,162	974	45.1
Kinney	3,379	1,707	51.0
Bandera	17,645	2,384	13.5
Kerr	43,653	8,353	19.1
Kendall	23,743	4,248	17.9
Gillespie	20,814	3,309	15.9
Sutton	4,077	2,106	51.7
Real	3,047	688	22.6
Menard	2,360	748	31.7
Kimble	4,468	926	20.7
Mason	3,738	783	20.9
Llano	17,044	875	5.0
San Saba	6,186	1,333	21.5
McCulloch	8,205	2,219	27.0
Schleicher	2,935	1,278	43.5
Concho	3,966	1,639	41.3
Tom Green	104,010	31,946	30.7
Runnels	11,495	3,372	29.3
Coke	3,864	653	16.9
Sterling	9,674	432	5.0
Irion	1,771	436	24.6
Reagan	3,326	1,646	49.5
Terrell	1,081	525	48.6
Pecos	16,809	10,262	61.1
Reeves	13,137	9,640	73.5
Crockett	4,099	2,242	54.7
Ward	10,909	4,580	42.0
Crane	3,966	1,753	44.2
Loving	67	7	10.0
Winkler	7,173	3,156	44.6
Ector	121,123	51,306	42.0
Midland	116,009	33,676	29.0
Glasscock	1,406	420	30.0

County	*Total Pop.*	*Mexican and Other Latino Pop.*	*% of Pop.*
Upton	3,404	1,449	42.6
Presidio	7,304	6,162	84.4
Brewster	8,866	3,867	43.6
Jeff Davis	2,207	783	35.5
Culberson	2,975	2,149	72.2
Total	666,953	237,881	35.0

United States Census 2000, *Texas: Census of Population and Housing,* "Summary Population and Housing Characteristics," PHC-1-45 (Washington, DC: U.S. Dept. of Commerce, U.S. Bureau of the Census, 2000), Table 3: "Race and Hispanic or Latino: 2000."

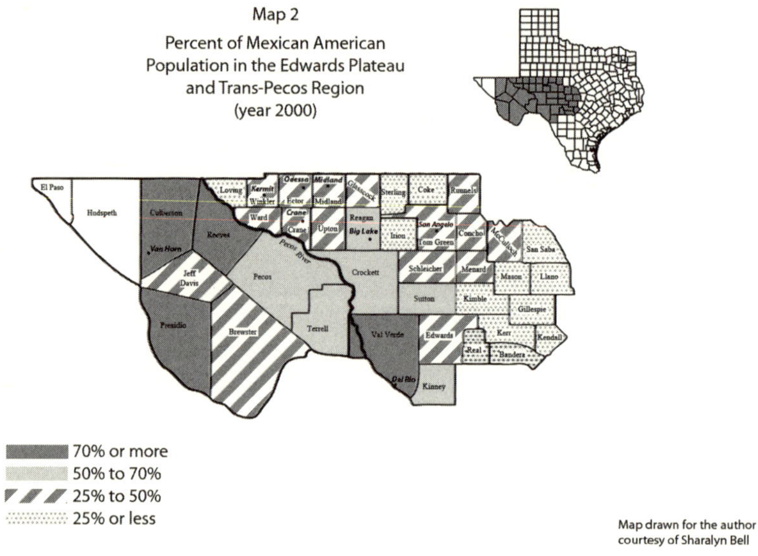

Map 2
Percent of Mexican American Population in the Edwards Plateau and Trans-Pecos Region (year 2000)

Map drawn for the author courtesy of Sharalyn Bell

circumstances. To water their herds of cattle, as well as sheep and goats, for instance, they made wider use of windmills, dug water wells, and constructed rock or concrete reservoirs. Farming technology also improved. Those placing their faith in cotton and then sorghum grains adopted practices of dry-land farming as a rational approach to cultivation. In May 1923, furthermore, wildcatters struck oil near Big Lake in Reagan County. The discovery augured well for the future of the Permian Basin within the Edwards Plateau and the Trans-Pecos region, and indeed, additional discoveries took place in the 1920s in neighboring counties, among them Tom Green, Upton, Crane, Glasscock, Winkler, Ector, Pecos, and Ward.[7]

These oil strikes (and advances in ranching and farming) proved to be of epic significance for the center-west region. After the late 1920s and certainly by the mid-1930s, the general economic framework in the region had been restructured: while some counties would still rely heavily on ranching, some would depend on a mix of ranching and farming, while others would turn predominantly to the oil (and gas) industry for survival. Such patterns persist today.

Growth within Tejano communities did not accompany the economic expansion that took place in the Edwards Plateau and the Trans-Pecos during the first three decades of the century. To the contrary, after 1900 Tejanos saw their numerical proportion decline precipitously so that by 1930 they constituted only about 19 percent of the total population of mainly Anglos and Mexicans in the region (see tables 5.3 and 5.4). This reversal resulted from a rapid influx of Anglo-Americans arriving in the region as part of the aforementioned economic development. During that period Anglos completed taking control of the political system, the social composition, and the economic structure (including rangelands, cotton fields, and mines) of counties constituting the Edwards Plateau and Trans-Pecos as they did in most areas of Texas where Tejanos once had dominated numerically.[8]

Mexican Americans and Mexican immigrants (either fleeing peonage and civil unrest in their home country or experiencing displacement from their lands by transnational businesses set on exploiting Mexico's natural resources), meanwhile, came to comprise much of the labor force that buttressed the flowering economy. They gravitated to areas needing cowhands, goat herders, and sheepshearers; to farms requiring cotton pickers; and to mining districts calling for common laborers willing to risk dangerous work.[9] For example, researchers from the Agricultural and Mechanical College of Texas in the early 1920s told of the work Mexican ranch hands performed (generally for a lower wage than Anglos got for doing the same work) in Sutton County in the Edwards Plateau and Trans-Pecos:

> The extra labor is also very largely Mexican. Most of the shearing is done by Mexican crews. Mexicans are secured to do most of the kidding and lambing. As a rule Mexicans come over from Mexico in the spring and do the shearing, lambing and kidding work on farms during the late spring and summer. When there is a very large crop of cotton in North Texas it is difficult to retain the laborers in Sutton County even though thousands of them come over from Mexico.[10]

Table 5.3. Total population

	1930	*1950*	*1980*	*2000*
Val Verde	14,924	16,635	35,910	44,856
Edwards	2,764	2,908	2,033	2,162
Kinney	3,980	2,668	2,279	3,379
Bandera	3,784	4,410	7,084	17,645
Kerr	10,151	14,022	28,780	43,653
Kendall	4,970	5,423	10,635	23,743
Gillespie	11,020	10,520	13,532	20,814
Sutton	2,807	3,746	5,130	4,077
Real	2,197	2,479	2,469	3,047
Menard	4,447	4,175	2,346	2,360
Kimble	4,119	4,619	4,063	4,468
Mason	5,511	4,945	3,683	3,738
Llano	5,538	5,377	10,144	17,044
San Saba	10,273	8,666	6,204	6,186
McCulloch	13,883	11,701	8,735	8,205
Schleicher	3,166	2,852	2,820	2,935
Concho	7,645	5,078	2,915	3,966
Tom Green	36,033	58,929	84,784	104,010
Runnels	21,821	16,771	11,872	11,495
Coke	5,253	4,045	3,196	3,864
Sterling	1,431	1,282	1,206	9,674
Irion	2,049	1,590	1,386	1,771
Reagan	3,028	3,127	4,135	3,326
Terrell	2,660	3,189	1,595	1,081
Pecos	7,812	9,939	14,618	16,809
Reeves	6,407	11,745	15,801	13,137
Crockett	2,590	3,981	4,608	4,099
Ward	4,599	13,346	13,976	10,909
Crane	2,221	3,945	4,600	3,966
Loving	195	227	91	67
Winkler	6,784	10,064	9,944	7,173
Ector	3,958	42,102	115,374	121,123
Midland	8,005	25,785	82,636	116,009
Glasscock	1,263	1,089	1,304	1,406
Upton	5,968	5,307	4,619	3,404
Presidio	10,154	7,354	5,188	7,304
Brewster	6,824	7,309	7,573	8,866
Jeff Davis	1,800	2,090	1,647	2,207
Culberson	1,228	1,825	3,315	2,975
Total	253,262	345,265	542,230	666,953

Sources for Tables 3 and 4:

For 1930: *Fifteenth Census of the United States: 1930,* Population, vol. 3, pt. 2 (Reports by States, Showing the Composition and Characteristics of the Population for Counties, Cities, and Townships . . .), Montana-Wyoming (Washington, DC: Government Printing Office, 1932), Table 17: "Indians, Chinese, and Japanese 1910 to 1930, and Mexicans, 1930, for Counties and For Cities of 25,000 or More," pp. 1014–15.

For 1950: *United States Census of Population, 1950.* Special Census Report P-E No. 3C: "Persons of Spanish Surname" (Washington, DC, 1953), Table 7: "Citizenship and Country of Birth of White Persons of Spanish Surname, for Counties and Urban Places of 10,000 or more in Selected Southwestern States: 1950," pp. 3C-44 to 3C-46.

For 1980: *1980 Census of Population,* Vol. 1, Characteristics of the Population, Chap. B, General Population Characteristics, pt. 45, Texas, PC80-1-B45 (Washington, DC: Dept. of Commerce, 1982), Table 16: "Total Persons and Spanish Origin Persons by Type of Spanish Origin and Race: 1980," pp. 45–43 to 45–46.

For 2000: *United States Census 2000, Texas: Census of Population and Housing,* "Summary Population and Housing Characteristics," PHC-1-45 (Washington, DC: U.S. Dept. of Commerce, U. S. Bureau of the Census, 2000), Table 3: "Race and Hispanic or Latino: 2000" pp. 126–97.

Table 5.4. Mexican American population

	1930	*1950*	*1980*	*2000*
Val Verde	9,542	10,488	22,001	33,849
Edwards	509	1,044	960	974
Kinney	1,606	1,432	1,221	1,707
Bandera	136	167	610	2,384
Kerr	1,165	1,400	3,560	8,353
Kendall	576	711	1,308	4,248
Gillespie	834	470	1,284	3,309
Sutton	1,051	1,577	2,037	2,106
Real	236	356	531	688
Menard	403	741	649	748
Kimble	319	599	701	926
Mason	400	357	582	783
Llano	89	137	249	875
San Saba	501	571	879	1,333
McCulloch	1,955	1,660	1,562	2,219
Schleicher	782	530	689	1,278
Concho	1,651	943	780	1,639
Tom Green	3,716	6,896	16,839	31,946
Runnels	1,376	1,372	2,215	3,372
Coke	194	260	363	653
Sterling	74	249	279	432
Irion	328	292	256	436
Reagan	101	148	1,271	1,646
Terrell	1,236	1,648	684	525

Table 5.4. (*cont.*)

	1930	*1950*	*1980*	*2000*
Pecos	2,439	3,576	6,901	10,262
Reeves	2,577	4,605	9,547	9,640
Crockett	713	1,404	2,301	2,242
Ward	1,379	2,524	3,626	4,580
Crane	18	34	1,099	1,753
Loving		45	16	7
Winkler	65	392	2,438	3,156
Ector	149	1,599	23,790	51,306
Midland	1,123	1,584	11,727	33,676
Glasscock	143	102	1,286	420
Upton	144	471	1,218	1,449
Presidio	6,774	5,133	3,905	6,162
Brewster	3,411	3,056	3,143	3,867
Jeff Davis	1,046	1,153	745	783
Culberson	583	719	2,056	2,149
Total	49,344	60,445	135,308	237,881
% of pop	19.0%	17.5%	25.0%	35.0%
Intercensal increase		22.0%	124.0%	76.0%

As table 5.4 indicates, Mexicans in 1930 were most heavily settled (1,500 persons or more) in the Big Bend; in predominantly ranch counties such as Val Verde, Kinney, Pecos, and Reeves; and in mixed counties (ranch and farm) like McCulloch, Concho, and Tom Green (see map 1). Not surprisingly, the Big Bend counties of Presidio and Brewster in 1930 had the largest concentration (except for Val Verde and Tom Green) of Mexican-descent inhabitants in the expanse that was the Edwards Plateau and Trans-Pecos.[11]

A second clustering of Mexican Americans during the early decades of the twentieth century was to be found in counties then mainly relying on cattle, sheep, and goat ranching. These included the aforementioned counties of Val Verde (a major sheep- and goat-raising center), Kinney, Pecos, and Reeves but also Kerr, Terrell, Sutton, Ward, and Midland; in each of these latter five counties, the Mexican population totaled between 1,000 and 1,500 (see table 5.4).

Mexicans and Mexican Americans also gravitated toward counties whose economies revolved around both ranching and farming, among them McCulloch, Runnels, Concho, and Tom Green. In those counties, Mexicans and Mexican Americans juggled seasonal employment on cotton fields during the spring and summer with miscellaneous work (e.g., sheepshearing, as indicated in the quote above) on ranches, although by the early decades of the twentieth century many had found San Angelo (Tom Green County) to be an attractive setting for permanent residence. Census figures for 1930 show relatively few (1,000 or fewer) Mexicans living in Hill Country counties such as Bandera, Kimble, Gillespie, Kendall, Mason, Llano, and San Saba (an exception was Kerr County).[12]

Hill Country counties were not the only ones Mexicans avoided. They also skirted Edwards, Real, Menard, Mason, Schleicher, Crockett, Coke, Culberson, Irion, Reagan, Sterling, Crane, Winkler, Glasscock, Upton, and Ector counties, all of which had fewer than 1,000 Tejano inhabitants. The geography there might in part explain the low representation: the Edwards Plateau and Trans-Pecos area feature stretches of land where the rainfall and topography test survival skills. Some of these counties (such as Ector) would later diversify economically and lure Mexican workers by the hundreds. However, at that early time they offered little occupational enticement. Ranching operations there were still fledgling enterprises.[13]

The economic upsurge that occurred in the agricultural and oil sectors of the Edwards Plateau and Trans-Pecos region during the early decades of the twentieth century sputtered, albeit briefly, during the early 1930s. Generally speaking, cotton prices held steady, there was a prompt recovery in wool and mohair production, and cattlemen experienced a small resurgence in livestock sales. The oil business faced reversals by the middle of 1931, but as with farming and ranching, it was not long before the industry rebounded (in fact, it did so by 1935). This resurgence between 1936 and 1939 revitalized the area, triggering both rural and urban growth, creating jobs, stimulating railroad traffic, and uplifting the optimism of inhabitants.[14]

By World War II and the years immediately following, ranching (cattle, sheep, and goats) and farming had regained their pre-Depression vitality. A parallel upswing took place in the oil fields. During the war the oil industry had entered a period of slump as it lost part of its international market, but once peace returned, pipeline construction began anew, facilitating the delivery of Permian Basin oil. As of 1952, Ector County ranked as the largest oil-producing county in the entire expanse of the Edwards Plateau and Trans-Pecos.[15]

Despite the midcentury boom, the Texas-Mexican population in counties within the Edwards Plateau and the Trans-Pecos region was only 60,445, an intercensal increase of about 22 percent for the score of years since 1930. In contrast, the increase for the rest of the population during that same time period was 39.7 percent. Overall, Mexican Americans and Mexicans remained a minority group in the region, for the Anglo (and small African American) population between 1930 and 1950 grew to the extent that the percent of Mexicans in center-west Texas declined: to 17.5 percent at midcentury as compared to 19.0 percent in 1930.[16]

What accounts for the disparity in growth? Mexican Americans (in Texas and throughout the United States for that matter) had faced deportation and repatriation pressures during the Depression years. Given the state of the economy and greater border vigilance by government officials, furthermore, the influx of workers from Mexico that had historically reinforced the existing Mexican element reached a state of temporary suspension. According to the 1950 federal census, approximately 84.3 percent of the Mexican population in the counties surveyed for this study was United States born, an indication that a downturn in immigration from Mexico in part contributed to the difference in Anglo and Mexican American population growth.[17]

The economic fluctuations of the age (a downturn during the early Depression years, followed by an upswing by the mid-1930s) did cause demographic realignments among Tejanos who moved to more prosperous counties in the region while abandoning those with less economic appeal. Out-migration was obvious from Kinney, McCulloch, Concho, Presidio, and Brewster Counties, most of which (the exception was Brewster County) experienced a drop not only in the Mexican population but also in total population. Among the most attractive settlement sites for Mexican-origin people was Tom Green County, where the Concho Valley had long been acknowledged as the "Sheep and Wool Capital" of the United States but had successfully diversified its economy with farming and industry.[18]

But the primary push among Tejanos during the twenty-year interval was into the several counties situated in the northern rim of the Edwards Plateau and into others straddling the Pecos River. The oil boom in this latter cluster of counties (referred to hereinafter as the "oil and gas counties") rejuvenated ranches and farms, stimulated railroad traffic, prompted urbanization (mainly the cities of Midland and Odessa, but also smaller-town growth as in Kermit and Crane), and created a new array of job opportunities. Indeed, these oil-producing counties between 1930 and 1950 saw an intercensal rise in the Mexican population of 77 percent; this compared to mixed (farm and ranch) counties wherein the increase was no more than 20 percent and where an imperceptible increase occurred in the mostly ranch counties (see table 5.5). For Tejano

Table 5.5. Intercensal increases* in the Mexican American population, 1930 to 2000

	1930	*1950*	*1980*	*2000*
Ranch Counties:				
Pop.	29,181	30,111	46,421	75,244
Intercensal Increase		3.20	54.2	62.1
Intercensal Increase, 1930 to 2000				157.9
Mixed Counties:				
Pop.	9,480	11,401	22,085	40,454
Intercensal Increase		20.0	94.0	83.2
Intercensal Increase, 1930 to 2000				326.7
Oil and Gas Counties:				
Pop.	10,683	18,933	66,802	122,183
Intercensal Increase		77.0	252.0	83.0
Intercensal Increase, 1930 to 2000				1043.7*

All calculations based on figures provided in table 5.4.*

workers and immigrants from Mexico wanting to join this era of modernization, this section of western Texas represented new possibilities. This occurred in spite of discrimination, which relegated many to construction occupations and "dirt work"—mainly site preparation and trucking—in the oil fields.[19]

To be sure, this demographic shift (1930–50) unfolded within a predominantly rural environment, for such is the milieu of western Texas. Thus, even if Mexicans after World War II gravitated toward the oil and gas counties, they hardly found themselves in metropolitan surroundings. Then (and in some cases now), an urban center in the Edwards Plateau and Trans-Pecos was a city (often the county seat) of 5,000 people or fewer having a symbiotic relationship with the agricultural sector: ranchers and farmers took hard-earned profits into town and the city provided them with needed goods and services. Only four cities in the Edwards Plateau and Trans-Pecos region at midcentury could claim a total population of 10,000 or more inhabitants; they were Del Rio (though little change occurred between 1930 and 1950 in Val Verde County), San Angelo, Midland, and Odessa. Still, the pattern foreshadowing today's concentration of Tejanos in these four largest cities of the region with the remainder of Mexican Americans dispersed throughout the ranches, farms, and the smaller towns was taking shape in the years immediately following World War II.[20]

Since the 1960s, economic trends in this center-west region have been in the direction of growth and concomitant diversification. Ranching in the area since then has benefited from twentieth-century modernization, including the provision of electric service to remote places, technological innovations, and progress in scientific methods applicable to range management. Farming has kept up with advances in methods of raising livestock. Electric irrigation pumps have transformed previously fallow ground into productive acreage. Immense and sophisticated sprinkler systems today dot areas of the Edwards Plateau and Trans-Pecos countryside where the local soil makes farming economically worthwhile.[21]

The expansion associated with ranching and farming over the last half-century pales compared to strides in oil production. Even as the industry has in recent decades experienced cycles ranging from slumps (during the late 1950s to the early 1970s and in the years after the early 1980s), to ones of quick recovery (early 1970s to the early 1980s, and then, with fluctuations during the 1990s, some resurgence by 2000), oil has brought material comfort to residents of many counties in center-west Texas, with the more fortunate beneficiaries being citizens of Ector and Midland Counties.[22]

From midcentury to about 1980 the Mexican population grew to a degree not evidenced earlier. By 1980, the number of people of Mexican descent in the counties that are part of the Edwards Plateau and Trans-Pecos region rose to 135,308. The intercensal increase for Texas Mexicans during this thirty-year period was an astounding 123.9 percent, so that as of 1980 they constituted one-fourth of the combined Anglo, Mexican, and African American population in the region (up from 17.5 percent in 1950). By contrast, the intercensal increase for the rest of the population had been only 42.9 percent. The Mexican-descent population in the Edwards Plateau and Trans-Pecos area had indeed surged sharply between 1950 and 1980, multiplying at a growth rate approximately triple that of the non-Mexican population. While this appears a healthy advance, the fact of the matter was that in real numbers, the Mexican American population during this time period had only risen by 74,863, whereas the non-Mexican population had increased by 122,102. Put another way, Tejanos toward the latter decades of the twentieth century still remained a minority population in most counties of the Edwards Plateau and Trans-Pecos, as had been the case since the early 1900s, except in the historically "Mexican" counties of Val Verde and Presidio. Only in Reeves County had the population growth between 1950 and 1980 transformed Mexicans into a majority group. Kinney and Culberson Counties may be added to this list of Mexican-dominant counties, but the total population there has always been small, less than 3,500 as of the year 2000.[23]

In reality, growth within both the Tejano and the total population between 1950 and 1980 was uneven throughout the Edwards Plateau and Trans-Pecos, and more so in some counties than in others, duplicating the trends manifest between 1930 and 1950. As had been the case throughout the decades, no appreciable increases occurred in the Hill Country counties of Bandera, Kimble, Gillespie, Kendall, Mason, Llano, and San Saba; only in Gillespie and Kendall Counties did the Mexican American population barely top 1,000 in 1980. Counties experiencing further declines (as they had between 1930 and 1950) among Mexican inhabitants between 1950 and 1980 were Kinney, Presidio, McCulloch, and Concho. Counties coping with Mexican American population losses for the first time included Edwards, Menard, Jeff Davis, Terrell, Irion, and Loving, although this latter set of counties was sparsely populated anyway; none of them hosted a total population of more than 2,350 in 1980. As noted, the geography in these several counties makes life more difficult than in other parts of the Edwards Plateau and Trans-Pecos, and the well-known drought conditions that afflicted center-west Texas during the 1950s may have highlighted for Mexicans the difficulty, if not futility, of staying there. After midcentury, moreover, Mexicans may have been seeking options other than working cattle, sheep, and goats. As shown in table 5.5, the intercensal increase in the "Ranch Counties" in 1980 was less than for the "Mixed Counties" and "Oil and Gas Counties."[24]

The move, expectedly, was into the Permian Basin and the expanse of lands immediately east and west of the Pecos River, the core of counties anchoring the West Texas oil boom. Still, dispersal into those counties was disparate, for as the oil boom in some of these counties fizzled after 1957 to 1974, the hunt for opportunity led people into Ector and Midland Counties, followed by Reeves and Pecos. The trek into Ector and Midland Counties seemed somewhat predictable, as their county seats, Odessa and Midland, respectively, had grown with the post–World War II oil boom and had since outgrown any other city in the oil and gas counties. Urban growth there (as well as in San Angelo) had heightened a demand for white-collar and service employment.[25]

As of the year 2000, the Mexican (and other Latino) population in the Edwards Plateau and Trans-Pecos stood at 237,881, with almost all of it due to in-migration and natural reproduction as the foreign-born population in the region averaged out to slightly more than 10 percent. In that twenty-year span between 1980 and 2000, the intercensal increase was 76.0 percent for Tejanos compared to a slight 5.4 percent for the non-Mexican (and other non-Latino) population. Because the rest of the population had increased by only 22,150 more than had the Mexican (and other Latino) population, Mexican Americans and immigrants from Mexico now made up 35 percent of the total population, up from 25 percent in 1980.[26]

What population shifts occurred during the twenty-year period? First, not much change took place in the Hill Country counties where Mexican Americans had always made up less than 20 percent of the total population. By the mid-1980s, with the oil bust in full swing, Mexican Americans continued to leave certain counties (and Mexican immigrants to avoid them) where oil production dropped off, among them Terrell, Crockett, and Glasscock, although apparently so did others (responding to the same economic contraction), as the total population in these counties also declined (in Glasscock County, the total population remained stagnant). On the other hand, Tejanos now emerged as a new majority in counties besides Val Verde and Presidio (where they had always made a majority), in Reeves where they gained majority status in 1980, and in sparsely inhabited Kinney and Culberson. Other counties where Mexicans and other Latinos as of 2000 constituted a majority of the total population included Pecos, Sutton, and Reagan, as well as Crockett and Terrell; in these counties the decline in the total population (as well as in the non-Mexican and other non-Latino population) that coincided with the waning of the wool and mohair industry now turned Tejanos into the majority. Natural increase accounted for this modification (for immigration, as noted earlier, did not appear to be a factor). But in-migration might also have accounted for it, as a national trend during recent decades has been the growth of the Mexican (and other Latino) group in rural areas of the country. Conversely (as in Terrell and Crockett Counties), there occurred an outflow in the non-Latino population.[27]

In reality, what happened in these rural counties does not exactly explain why by 2000 Mexicans (and other Latinos) constituted 35 percent of the total population in the Edwards Plateau and Trans-Pecos. The greatest population increases were centered in the urbanized areas, specifically the aforementioned cities of Del Rio, San Angelo, Midland, and Odessa. A total of 51.3 percent of the entire Tejano population that settled in the Edwards Plateau and Trans-Pecos as of 2000 now called these four cities home.[28]

What transpired in the latter years of the twentieth century, then, appeared to be a continuation of dispersal patterns traceable to the post–World War II era when the prosperity of the oil and gas counties began drawing people (of all races) out of the predominantly ranch and mixed counties. The greatest movement of Mexicans (and other Latinos) was indeed into Ector and Midland Counties, the heart of the oil-producing region (which by the 1990s was again seeing a recovery from the troubled times of the 1980s), with the remainder moving into the Concho Valley and into the border county of Val Verde. In Ector County the Texas Mexican population between 1980 and 2000 increased by 27,516, in Midland County by 21,949, in Tom Green County by 15,107, and in Val Verde County by 11,846. In the county seats of these four counties, the Mexican population during that score of years rose by 17,585 in Odessa, by 16,887 in Midland, by 13,487 in San Angelo, and by 6,888 in Del Rio.[29]

A set of factors explains the demographic patterns that unfolded in the Edwards Plateau and Trans-Pecos region over the course of one hundred years. There was, of course, historical agency. Mexican Americans, like other people in different settings, have taken initiatives in determining when the time has come to relocate and where best to settle. The lack or presence of opportunity also lay behind migration movements. For Mexican Americans, the time to move elsewhere came when there occurred, in certain counties, downturns in cattle, sheep, and goat ranching, as well as in the oil industry. On the other hand, Mexican Americans responded when new prospects beckoned them in those parts of the region experiencing boom periods or undergoing rapid economic development. The geography of the region further acted as a causal force behind population dispersals. On the one hand, the climate and topography in parts of central and western Texas coerced some to leave an area, yet the human instinct for coexisting with nature seduced others into staying there. Greater educational opportunities also explain demographic changes. When in recent decades improved access to education (and the growth of universities and community colleges) equipped Mexican Americans to compete professionally, many opted to move away from ranch and farm counties dependent on manual labor and head for the urban centers.[30]

What implications do the population advances made by Mexican Americans during recent decades have for the Edwards Plateau and Trans-Pecos region? Certainly, the Mexican and Latino population will continue increasing so that it will reflect patterns statewide. But will the region come to resemble South Texas, which some label a cultural "Tejano homeland"?[31] That is within the realm of possibility, and for several reasons. First, in-migration into the region is discernibly Mexican. Also, there exists white flight—a tendency brought on by a decline in the wool and mohair business and most apparent, by a lessening national reliance on domestic oil. As Anglo out-migration ensues, Mexican Americans and immigrants from Mexico take up vacated positions, both in the white and blue collar sectors. Such patterns have been quite manifest recently in the Permian Basin oil patch where Mexicans now constitute the bulk of the workforce. Although immigrants generally skirt the Edwards Plateau and Trans-Pecos region in favor of the larger cities in the state (most of them located along or east of I-35), they nonetheless search for work in center-west Texas as carpenters, roofers, gardeners, ranch hands, and field laborers, thus augmenting the overall Tejano population.

On the other hand, the same forces behind declines in the Anglo population play on Mexican American and immigrant groups. As Mexican-origin people in the Edwards Plateau and Trans-Pecos leave counties with less opportunity, they can (and do) depart for sections of the state with brighter prospects. Young Mexican Americans, especially those acquiring a college education, seek career opportunities in the big city (Dallas–Fort Worth, Austin, El Paso, San Antonio, or Houston). Second-generation immigrant children do likewise. Many either leave home to seek a university education or to find their destiny elsewhere once receiving their degree from one of the West Texas colleges.

Given the above forces at work, the Edwards Plateau and Trans-Pecos region seemingly will become a variant of the pattern of population settlement evident in South Texas. Unlike South Texas where almost every county is dominated by residents of Mexican descent, not all counties in the Edwards Plateau and the Trans-Pecos will become predominantly Mexican and Latino. The pattern instead will be (as it might in other regions of the state) an interspersion of Mexican and Anglo counties, with those in the Hill Country still mainly white and counties west from there, either mixed, or as in the case of the Trans-Pecos, predominantly Mexican. Some idea of this may be gained from the projections made regularly by the Texas State Data Center. Most assuredly, however, Mexican Americans will assert themselves more visibly in the political and social realm of this region where the Mexican American presence calls for further study.

Notes

1. No one term accurately identifies Texas Mexicans—that is, people of Mexican origin who live in Texas. Several terms are applicable—among them "Mexicans," "Mexican Americans," "Tejanos," and "Texas Mexicans"—and will be used interchangeably throughout the chapter. They should be understood to embrace the whole of the Texas-Mexican community, including both the native and foreign born. The words "Hispanic" and "Latino" have emerged as more popular labels during the last few years and will be used once the discussion reaches the post-1980 era. When singling out the foreign-born Mexican population, the word "immigrants" will be employed.

Studies reviewing the state of Tejano history may be found in Arnoldo De León, "Texas Mexicans: Twentieth Century Interpretations," in *Texas through Time: Evolving Interpretations*, ed. Walter L. Buenger and Robert A. Calvert (College Station: Texas A&M University, 1991), 20–49; and Arnoldo De León, "Whither Tejano History: Origins, Development, and Status," *Southwestern Historical Quarterly* 106 (January 2003): 349–64. See further the annual update (since 1995) on Tejano scholarship published in the *Quarterly* each October; Bruce A. Glasrud and Arnoldo De León, *Bibliophiling Tejano Scholarship: Secondary Sources on Hispanic Texans* (Alpine: Sul Ross State University Center for Big Bend Studies, 2003). The only available overview of Tejanos is Arnoldo De León, *Mexican Americans in Texas: A Brief History*, 2nd ed. (Wheeling, Il: Harlan Davidson, 1999).

Among major surveys on the Mexican American population in the United States are Rodolfo Acuña, *Occupied America: A History of Chicanos*, 6th ed. (Boston: Longman Publishing, 2006); Arnoldo De León and Richard Griswold del Castillo, *North to Aztlán: A History of Mexican Americans in the United States*, 2nd ed. (Wheeling, IL: Harlan Davidson, 2006); Manuel G. Gonzales, *Mexicanos: A History of Mexicans in the United States* (Bloomington: Indiana University Press, 1999); Oscar J. Martínez, *Mexican Origin People in the United States* (Tucson: University of Arizona Press, 2001); and Jorge Iber and Arnoldo De León, *Hispanics in the American West* (Santa Barbara, CA: ABC-CLIO, 2006).

2. Two counties in Far West Texas have been omitted from this study. Including El Paso County (and specifically the city of El Paso) would draw attention away from the coverage needed to be given to the Edwards Plateau and Trans-Pecos region. Also, the historical literature has not neglected El Paso as it has center-west Texas. See Bruce Glasrud and Arnoldo De León, "Tejanos in West Texas: A Selected Bibliography," *Journal of Big Bend Studies* 15 (2003). Hudspeth County was excluded because it is sparsely populated (its total population in 2000 was 3,344 and 75 percent Mexican and other Latino) and population changes there would not differ greatly from those of neighboring counties such as Culberson.

The scholarship published on the history of Mexican Americans in western Texas is reviewed in Glasrud and De León, "Tejanos in West Texas," and Arnoldo De León and Bruce Glasrud, "Bibliophiling Tejano Scholarship: A West Texas Collaboration," *West Texas Historical Association Yearbook* 80 (2004): 93–109. Many of the works are nonhistorical in nature, however, or cover the era before 1900. Further, only a few directly examine the Edwards Plateau and Trans-Pecos region. Because of the existing lacuna, this chapter relies on secondary sources (that demonstrate the influence that geographical and economic factors have on historical change) to construct the necessary backdrop that explains demographic movement in the Mexican American population.

Of importance to gaining a grasp of demographic patterns in both the region and the state is the work conducted by the Texas State Data Center and the Pew Hispanic Center. The former agency has as its mission distributing demographic data related to Texas while the latter engages in research on US Hispanic communities in an effort to determine how Hispanic population changes shape life in the United States. See www.txsdc.utsa.edu/ and www.pewhispanic.org. Also of significance to any study of demography in Texas are the works of Steve H. Murdock, specifically Steve H. Murdock et al., *The Texas Challenge: Population Change and the Future of Texas* (College Station: Texas A&M University Press, 1997), and Steve H. Murdock et al., *The New Texas*

Challenge: Population Change and the Future of Texas (College Station: Texas A&M University Press, 2003).

3. Ronnie C. Tyler, *The Big Bend: A History of the Last Texas Frontier* (Washington, DC: National Park Service, 1975), 5–10; Paul H. Carlson, *Texas Woollybacks: The Range Sheep and Goat Industry* (College Station: Texas A&M University Press, 1982), 101–2, 152–54; Rupert N. Richardson et al., *Texas: The Lone Star State*, 8th ed. (New York: Prentice-Hall, 2001), 5; Ron Tyler et al., eds., *The New Handbook of Texas*, 6 vols. (Austin: Texas State Historical Association, 1996): 2: 802–3; and 5: 548–49.

4. United States Census 2000, *Texas: Census of Population and Housing*, "Summary Population and Housing Characteristics," PHC-1–45 (Washington, DC: U.S. Dept. of Commerce, U.S. Bureau of the Census, 2000), Table 3, "Race and Hispanic or Latino: 2000," p. 126. Groups other than Mexican Americans, such as Puerto Ricans, Central Americans, and Cubans, have traditionally settled in the state's larger urban areas. It may be assumed, therefore, that the largest number of persons identified by the 2000 census as "Hispanic or Latino" living in center-west Texas are of Mexican descent and are not "other" Hispanic or Latino peoples.

Betsy Guzmán, *The Hispanic Population: Census 2000 Brief* (Washington, DC: U.S. Census Bureau, 2001), p. 4 (table 2: "Hispanic Population by Type for Regions, States, and Puerto Rico: 1990 and 2000") counts 5,071,963 Mexicans (of Hispanic type).

For a recent government study that examines the forces influencing the course of the border counties and forecasts their future, see John Sharp, comptroller, *Bordering the Future: Challenge and Opportunity in the Texas Border Region* (Austin: Texas Comptroller of Public Accounts, 1998). See further, Emily Skop, Brian Gratton, and Myron P. Gutman, "La Frontera and Beyond: Geography and Demography in Mexican American History," *Professional Geographer* 58 (February 2006): 78–98.

5. Arnoldo De León and Kenneth L. Stewart, *Tejanos and the Numbers Game: A Socio-Historical Interpretation from the Federal Censuses, 1850–1900* (Albuquerque: University of New Mexico Press, 1989), 17; Carlson, *Texas Woollybacks*, 40–47, 68–71, 84; Terry G. Jordan, *North American Cattle-Ranching Frontiers: Origins, Diffusion, and Differentiation* (Albuquerque: University of New Mexico Press, 1993), 219; Wilburn Oatman, *Llano, Gem of the Hill Country: A History of Llano County, Texas* (Hereford, TX: Pioneer Book Publishers, 1970), 45–58.

6. De León and Stewart, *Tejanos and the Numbers Game*, 17, 24–25, 28. For works on immigration to the United States and Texas during this time period, see Lawrence Cardoso, *Mexican Emigration to the United States, 1897–1931* (Tucson: University of Arizona Press, 1980), chap. 1; Arthur Corwin, ed., *Immigrants—and Immigrants: Perspectives on Mexican Labor Migration to the United States* (Westport, CT: Greenwood Press, 1978), chap. 2; Oscar J. Martínez, "On the Size of the Chicano Population: New Estimates, 1850–1900," *Aztlán* 6 (Spring 1975): 43–67; Arnoldo De León and Kenneth L. Stewart, "Lost Dreams and Found Fortunes: Mexican and Anglo Immigrants to South Texas, 1850–1900," *Western Historical Quarterly* 14 (July 1983): 291–310; Kenneth L. Stewart and Arnoldo De León, "Literacy among Immigrants in Texas," *Latin American Research Review* 20 (Fall 1985): 180–87; Mario T. García, *Desert Immigrants: The Mexicans of El Paso, 1880–1920* (New Haven, CT: Yale University Press, 1981), chap. 2; Paul Wright, "Population Patterns in Presidio County in 1880: Evidence from the Census," *Journal of Big Bend Studies* 7 (January 1995): 181–201; and Anna J. Taylor, "Hispanic Settlements of the Texas Panhandle-Plains, 1876–1884," *Panhandle-Plains Historical Review* 70 (1997): 36–58.

For Tejano pioneers in nineteenth-century West Texas, see Arthur R. Gómez, *A Most Singular Country: A History of Occupation in the Big Bend* (Santa Fe: National Park Service; Salt Lake City: Charles Redd Center for Western Studies, Brigham Young University, 1990), 156–57, 160; Clifford B. Casey, *Mirages, Mysteries, and Reality: Brewster County, Texas, The Big Bend of the Rio Grande* (Hereford, TX: Pioneer Book Publishers, 1972), 170–73; R. D. Holt, ed., *Schleicher County, or Eighty Years of Development in Southwest Texas* (Eldorado: Eldorado Success, 1930), 37; and Arnoldo De León, *The Tejano Community, 1836–1900* (Albuquerque: University of New Mexico Press, 1982), 77–86.

For Tejano early settlements elsewhere in the state, see Gilberto M. Hinojosa, *A Borderlands Town in Transition: Laredo, Texas, 1755–1870* (College Station: Texas A&M University Press, 1983); Armando Alonzo, *Tejano Legacy: Rancheros and Settlers in South Texas, 1734–1900* (Albuquerque: University of New Mexico Press, 1998); Joe Graham, *El Rancho in South Texas: Continuity and Change from 1750* (Denton: University of North Texas Press, 1994); Mary Margaret McAllen Amberson, James A. McAllen, and Margaret H. McAllen, *I Would Rather Sleep in Texas: A History of the Lower Rio Grande Valley and the People of the Santa Anita Land Grant* (Austin: Texas State Historical Association, 2003).

7. Gómez, *A Most Singular Country*, 103, 106, 109, 161–68; Crockett County Historical Society, *History of Crockett County* (San Angelo: Anchor Publishing, 1976), 58; Holt, *Schleicher County*, 40, 44, 43, 36–39; Carlson, *Woollybacks*, 191–92, 197–98, 202; Cecilia Thompson, *A History of Marfa and Presidio County, 1535–1946*, 2 vols. (Austin: Nortex Press, 1985), 2: 110, 280–81; Robert A. Ryan and Leonard G. Schifrin, *Midland: The Economic Future of a Texas Oil Center* (Austin: Bureau of Business Records, the University of Texas, 1959), 28–29; Casey, *Mirages, Mysteries, and Reality*, 167, 168, 169, 172; Midland County Historical Society, *The Pioneer History of Midland County, Texas, 1880–1926* (Dallas: Taylor Publishing, 1984), 35; A. E. Skinner, *The Rowena Country: A Short History* (Wichita Falls: Nortex Offset Publications, 1973), 71, 77; Marsha Lea Daggett, *Pecos County History* (Pecos County Historical Commission, 1973–83), 145–46; Richard R. Moore, *West Texas after the Discovery of Oil: A Modern Frontier* (Austin: Pemberton Press, 1971), 8–11, 14–15, 16; Robert L. Martin, *The City Moves West: Economic and Industrial Growth in Central West Texas* (Austin: University of Texas Press, 1969), 104–5, 107. For a fuller discussion of events surrounding oil discoveries during the 1920s, see Roger M. Olien and Diana Davids Hinton, *Wildcatters: Texas Independent Oilmen*, 2nd ed. (College Station: Texas A&M University Press, 2007), chap. 2.

8. Expediency explains the selection of the years 1930, 1950, 1980, and 2000 in the tables used herein. The federal census in those particular years provided specific information on Mexican Americans—under the categories of Mexican (1930), White Persons of Spanish-surname (1950), Spanish-Origin Persons (1980), and (for 2000) under Hispanic or Latino (of any race). Source at table 3 contains citation for 1930.

This process of Anglo domination in South Texas is discussed in David Montejano, *Anglos and Mexicans in the Making of Texas, 1836–1986* (Austin: University of Texas Press, 1987), chaps. 5 and 6; Benjamin H. Johnson, *Revolution in Texas: How a Forgotten Rebellion and Its Bloody Suppression Turned Mexicans into Americans* (New Haven, CT: Yale University Press, 2003), chap. 1; Evan Anders, *Boss Rule in South Texas: The Progressive Era* (Austin: University of Texas Press, 1982), chap. 8.

9. For studies of immigration during this time period, see Mae M. Ngai, *Impossible Subjects: Illegal Aliens and the Making of Modern America* (Princeton, NJ: Princeton University Press, 2004), intro. and part 1; Mark Reisler, *By the Sweat of Their Brow: Mexican Immigrant Labor in the United States, 1900–1940* (Westport, CT: Greenwood Press, 1976); Cardoso, *Mexican Emigration to the United States*; Corwin, *Immigrants—and Immigrants*, chap. 3; García, *Desert Immigrants*, chap. 3; Hubert J. Miller, "Mexican Migrations to the United States, 1900–1920: With a Focus on the Texas Lower Rio Grande Valley," *Borderlands Journal* 7 (Spring 1984): 165–205; Paul Wright, "A Tumultuous Decade: Changes in the Mexican-Origin Population of the Big Bend, 1910–1920," *Journal of Big Bend Studies* 10 (1998): 163–87; Manuel Bernardo Ramírez, "El Pasoans: Life and Society in Mexican El Paso, 1920–1945" (PhD diss., University of Mississippi, 2000), chap. 3.

For the impact that foreign-owned corporations had on the displacement of people in Mexico and who then trekked north to the United States, often to find work with the same corporations that had dislodged them, see Gilbert G. Gonzalez and Raul A. Fernandez, *A Century of Chicano History: Empire, Nations, and Migration* (New York: Routledge, 2003), 29–49. Regarding recruitment efforts undertaken by beet companies in the US Midwest, see Dennis Nodín Valdés, *Al Norte: Agricultural Workers in the Great Lakes Region, 1917–1970* (Austin: University of Texas Press, 1991), 10–15.

As to the work performed during this time in this center-west region, see De León and Stewart, *Tejanos and the Numbers Game*, 12; Gómez, *A Most Singular Country*, 156–57, 160–67, 107–9, 123, 125–29; B. (Bonney) Youngblood, "An Economic Study of a Typical Ranching Area on the Edwards Plateau of Texas," Bulletin no. 297 (College Station: Agricultural and Mechanical College of Texas, 1922), 307–15; Midland County Historical Society, *The Pioneer History of Midland County*, 35; Skinner, *The Rowena Country*, 73, 75, 76; Thompson, *A History of Marfa and Presidio County*, 3–4; Paul Wright, "Characteristics of Big Bend Mining Towns, 1885–1920," *Journal of Big Bend Studies* 9 (1997): 107–9; Paul Wright, "Work among Anglos and Hispanics in the Big Bend, 1910," *West Texas Historical Association Yearbook* 71 (1995): 24–26, 28.

10. Youngblood, "An Economic Study," 308–9, 311, 312 (quotation).

11. Economic categorizations in map 1 are based on information provided for each county in Tyler et al., eds., *The New Handbook of Texas*.

12. Arnoldo De León, *San Angeleños: Mexican Americans in San Angelo, Texas* (San Angelo: Fort Concho Museum Press, 1985), chap. 4; Skinner, *Rowena Country*, 73, 75–76, 111; Camilo Martínez, "Vamos Pal West: Let's Go West," *West Texas Historical Association Yearbook* 70 (1994): 40–56. On work done throughout other parts of the state, see George Coalson, *The Development of the Migrant Farm Labor System in Texas, 1900–1954* (San Francisco: R&E Research Associates, 1977); Neil Foley, *The White Scourge: Mexicans, Blacks, and Poor Whites in Texas Cotton Culture* (Berkeley: University of California Press, 1997); Victor B. Nelson Cisneros, "*La Clase Trabajadora en Tejas*, 1920–1940," *Aztlán* 6 (Summer 1975): 239–65; Montejano, *Anglos and Mexicans in the Making of Texas*, chap. 9; Emilio Zamora Jr., *The World of the Mexican Worker in Texas* (College Station: Texas A&M University Press, 1993), chap. 2.

13. Martin, *The City Moves West*, 88, 91.

14. Gómez, *A Most Singular Country*, 109; Skinner, *Rowena Country*, 109; Carlson, *Woollybacks*, 200–201; Sutton County Historical Society, *Sutton County, 1887–1977* (Sonora: Sutton County Historical Society, 1979), 281; Thompson, *History of Marfa and Presidio*, 2: 552; Moore, *West Texas after the Discovery of Oil*, 16–17, 79, 87; Martin, *The City Moves West*, 107, 108; Samuel D. Myers, *The Permian Basin: Petroleum Empire of the Southwest* (El Paso: Permian Press, 1977), 15–16, 18; and Roger M. Olien and Diana Davids Olien, *Oil Booms: Social Change in Five Texas Towns* (Lincoln: University of Nebraska Press, 1982), 169.

For the conditions that Mexican Americans faced during the decade of the Depression, see Julia Kirk Blackwelder, *Women of the Depression: Caste and Culture in San Antonio, 1929–1939* (College Station: Texas A&M University Press, 1984); Richard García, *Rise of the Mexican American Middle Class: San Antonio, 1929–1941* (College Station: Texas A&M University Press, 1991); Arnoldo De León, *Ethnicity in the Sunbelt: Mexican Americans in Houston* (Houston: Mexican American Studies Program, University of Houston, 1989); Irene Ledesma, "Unlikely Strikers: Mexican-American Women in Strike Activity in Texas, 1919–1974" (PhD diss., Ohio State University, 1992); Zaragosa Vargas, "Tejana Radical: Emma Tenayuca and the San Antonio Labor Movement during the Great Depression," *Pacific Historical Review* 66 (November 1997): 553–80; María Eva Flores, "The Good Life the Hard Way: The Mexican American Community of Fort Stockton, Texas, 1930–1945" (PhD diss., Arizona State University, 2000); Nora Ríos McMillan, "The Immigration Issue between 1929 and 1954 as Seen through *La Prensa*," *South Texas Studies* 6 (Victoria, TX: Victoria College Press, 1995), 20–52.

15. Carlson, *Woollybacks*, 205; Crockett County Historical Society, *History of Crockett County*, 58, 59, 60; Daggett, *Pecos County History*, 145–46; Myers, *The Permian Basin*, 20–21, 27–28, 29, 30, 340–41; Martin, *The City Moves West*, 113; Olien and Hinton, *Wildcatters*, 67, 82–84.

16. The 1950 census counted white persons of Spanish surname, and those figures were used to compile the 1950 column in table 4. Calculations were derived using figures in tables 3 and 4.

17. On this topic, see Gómez, *A Most Singular Country*, 167. See further Ngai, *Impossible Subjects*, chap. 2; Francisco E. Balderrama, *Decade of Betrayal: Mexican Repatriation in the 1930s* (Albuquerque: University of New Mexico Press, 1995); R. Reynolds McKay, "Texas Mexican Repatriation during the Great Depression" (PhD diss., University of Oklahoma at Norman, 1982);

Nora E. Ríos-McMillan, "The Repatriation of Mexicans during the Great Depression," *Journal of South Texas* 11 (1998): 44–72; Marilyn Rhinehart and Thomas H. Kreneck, "'In the Shadow of Uncertainty': Texas Mexicans and Repatriation in Houston during the Great Depression," *Houston Review* 10 (1988): 21–34; *United States Census of Population, 1950*. Special Census Report P-E No. 3C: "Persons of Spanish Surname" (Washington, DC, 1953), table 7, "Citizenship and Country of Birth of White Persons of Spanish Surname, for Counties and Urban Places of 10,000 or more in Selected Southwestern States: 1950," pp. 3C-44 to 3C-46.

18. Carlson, *Texas Woollybacks*, 213; De León, *San Angeleños*, chaps. 4 and 5.

19. Olien and Olien, *Oil Booms*, 114, 117, 118. Some generalizations went into the classification of counties under the broad economic categories of ranching, mixed (ranching and farming), and oil and gas counties. Some oil and gas counties, for instance, also have farming and ranching, among them Pecos, Reeves, Irion, Midland, and others. Conversely, Tom Green and Schleicher County, with much ranching and farming, also depend on an oil and gas economy.

On labor segmentation common during that era, see Ngai, *Impossible Subjects*, 129–38; Mario Barrera, *Race and Class in the Southwest: A Theory of Racial Inequality* (Notre Dame, IN: University of Notre Dame Press, 1979); Montejano, *Anglos and Mexicans in the Making of Texas*; Nelson Cisneros, "La Clase Trabajadora en Tejas," 239–65; García, *Rise of the Mexican American Middle Class*, chap. 2; Mario T. García, "Racial Dualism in the El Paso Labor Market, 1880–1920," *Aztlán* 6 (Summer 1975): 197–218.

20. *United States Census of Population, 1950*, Table 7, "Citizenship and Country of Birth of White Persons of Spanish Surname, for Counties and Urban Places of 10,000 or more in Selected Southwestern States: 1950," p. 3C-46, gave the following figures for Mexican-descent people living in these four cities: Del Rio, 9,293; San Angelo, 5,912; Midland, 1,420; and Odessa, 254.

21. Crockett County Historical Society, *History of Crockett County*, 58–60; Daggett, *Pecos County History*, 145–46.

22. Olien and Olien, *Oil Booms*, 167, 168, 169; Olien and Hinton, *Wildcatters*, 114–16, 138–39, 141–43, 161–69, xiii–xv, xx–xxii.

23. The 1980 census counted "Spanish-Origin Persons," and those figures were used to compile the 1980 column in table 4. See *1980 Census of Population*, Volume I, Characteristics of the Population, chap. B, General Population Characteristics, Part 45, Texas, PC80–1-B45 (Washington, DC: Dept. of Commerce, 1982), Table 16, "Total Persons and Spanish Origin Persons by Type of Spanish Origin and Race: 1980," pp. 45-43 to 45-46.

By comparison, the cultural geographer Daniel D. Arreola states: "In South Texas, where close to half of all Texas Mexicans resided, 71 percent of the region's population [in 1990] was Texas Mexican, giving the area the most extensive regional concentration of Mexican Americans in the United States." Daniel D. Arreola, *Tejano South Texas: A Mexican American Cultural Province* (Austin: University of Texas Press, 2002), 58. For Tejano population trends across the state since 1960, see Terry G. Jordan, "A Century and a Half of Ethnic Change in Texas, 1836–1986," *Southwestern Historical Quarterly* 89 (April 1986): 399–400.

24. Studies that look at Mexican Americans searching for work opportunities in Texas urban areas during this time period include De León, *Mexican Americans in Texas: A Brief History*, chap. 8; De León, *Ethnicity in the Sunbelt*, chap. 8; and Carlos E. Cuéllar, *Stories from the Barrio: A History of Mexican Fort Worth* (Fort Worth: Texas Christian University Press, 2003).

25. *1980 Census of Population*, Table 16, "Total Persons and Spanish Origin Persons by Type of Spanish Origin and Race: 1980," pp. 45-35 to 45-43, gives the following figures for Mexican Americans living in the four major cities of the Edwards Plateau and Trans-Pecos region: Odessa, 90,027 (total pop.), 20,086 (Mexican); Midland, 70,525 (total pop.), 10,656 (Mexican); Del Rio, 30,034 (total pop.), 20,558 (Mexican); and San Angelo, 73,249 (total pop.), 15,834 (Mexican).

26. The 2000 census counted "Hispanics or Latinos (of any race)" and those figures were used to compile the 2000 column in table 4. See United States Census 2000, *Texas: Census of Population and Housing*, "Summary Population and Housing Characteristics," PHC-1-45 (Washington,

DC: U.S. Dept. of Commerce, U.S. Bureau of the Census, 2000), Table 3, "Race and Hispanic or Latino: 2000" pp. 126–97.

The percentage of foreign born that the 2000 census gave for each county was for the total population, but it may be assumed that most of those were born in Mexico, with the remaining ones being European born. *Texas: 2000, Summary Social, Economic, and Housing Characteristics, 2000 Census of Population and Housing,* PHC-2-45, Part I (Washington, DC: U.S. Dept. of Commerce, 2003), Table 1, "Place of Birth, Residence in 1995, and Language: 2000," pp. 1–37.

For a breakdown of the several racial or ethnic groups in these counties, see information provided by the Texas State Data Center at www.txsdc.utsa.edu/txdata/redistrict/dre-popcnt.php ("Counties by Detailed Race/Ethnicity Population Counts").

27. Population losses occurring in western Texas and the Panhandle regions have become topics of discussion recently. See San Antonio *Express-News,* March 25, 2001, p. 1A, and August 27, 2006, p. 1B. For further information, see the reports issued by the Texas State Data Center at www.txsdc.utsa.edu/txdata/redistrict/dre-popcnt.php. Regarding Mexican American and immigrant movements into the US countryside and into small-town America, see William Kandel and John Cromartie, *New Patterns of Hispanic Settlement in Rural America,* Rural Development Research Report, no. 99 (Washington, DC: U.S. Dept. of Agriculture, Economic Research Service, 2004).

28. The 2000 census reported the following figures: Odessa, 90,943 (total pop.), 37,671 (Latino); Midland, 94,996 (total pop.), 27,543 (Latino); San Angelo, 88,439 (total pop.), 29,321 (Latino); and Del Rio, 33,867 (total pop.), 27,446 (Latino). United States Census 2000, *Texas: Census of Population and Housing,* "Summary Population and Housing Characteristics" (Washington, DC: U.S. Department of Commerce, U.S. Bureau of the Census, 2000), Table 4, "Race and Hispanic or Latino: 2000," pp. 214, 230, 232, 240. Figure of 51.3 percent derives from adding up the Mexican (and other Latino) population in those four cities (121,981) and dividing it by the total Mexican (and other Latino) population of 2000 in the thirty-nine counties.

29. See note 25 and note 28. For the oil recovery of the 1990s, see Olien and Hinton, *Wildcatters,* xx–xxii.

30. On the struggle for educational equality in Texas after World War II and on new opportunities available to Tejanos by the 1960s, see Benjamin Márquez, *LULAC: The Evolution of a Mexican American Political Organization* (Austin: University of Texas Press, 1993); Craig A. Kaplowitz, *LULAC, Mexican Americans, and National Policy* (College Station: Texas A&M University Press, 2005); Carl Allsup, *The American G.I. Forum: Origins and Evolution* (Austin: Center for Mexican American Studies, University of Texas Press, 1982); Guadalupe San Miguel Jr., *"Let All of Them Take Heed": Mexican Americans and the Campaign for Educational Equality in Texas, 1910–1981* (Austin: University of Texas Press, 1987); Carlos Kevin Blanton, *The Strange Career of Bilingual Education in Texas, 1836–1981* (College Station: Texas A&M University Press, 2004); Guadalupe San Miguel Jr. and Richard R. Valencia, "From the Treaty of Guadalupe Hidalgo to *Hopwood*: The Educational Plight and Struggle of Mexican Americans in the Southwest," *Harvard Educational Review* 68 (Fall 1998): 353–412.

31. Arreola, *Tejano South Texas,* 58.

6

Tejanos in Northwest Texas

Rural Folks or Urbanites?

With the exception of larger cities such as Lubbock, Amarillo, and Abilene, Northwest Texas throughout the twentieth century remained largely rural. Expectedly, Tejanos initially arrived in the region seeking a livelihood in its countless farmlands. Census data indicate that Tejanos and immigrants from Mexico have since the 1950s assumed positions in other than farm work, finding employment in the oil fields, in feedlots, in construction, and in various other blue-collar occupations. Toward the last decades of the twentieth century, Hispanos/Latinos in Northwest Texas became urbanites, having relocated to town sites (usually the county seat) where many had acquired a middle-class standing.

According to the extant scholarly literature on Mexican Americans in Northwest Texas,[1] Tejanos did not found viable communities there until the 1920s. To be fair, Northwest Texas still appeared somewhat of a hinterland at the beginning of the twentieth century. As table 6.1 indicates, at a time in the modern age when reform Democrats kept Texas aligned with national Progressive politics, when Texans considered a public education a valuable asset in life, and when cities like Galveston, Houston, San Antonio, and others witnessed phenomenal growth, the expanse of Northwest Texas lingered in a state of arrested development. Only a few counties in the region could boast of having more than 2,000 residents. Those most likely to host that many inhabitants appeared ones to have been extensions (Donley and Floyd Counties do not fit into that pattern) of counties situated in the western sections of the Rolling Plains that during the late nineteenth century had expanded with the coming of

This chapter was originally published in the *West Texas Historical Association Yearbook* 86 (2010): 8–32.

the railroad and ranching.[2] Table 6.1 indicates that farther west or north of this cluster of counties, people had yet to find Northwest Texas—that is, the Panhandle and South Plains—an attractive locale for sinking roots. It might be surmised that only a scant number of Tejanos lived in Northwest Texas as of 1900.

But the region did not remain sparsely settled for long, as it soon fell under cultivation. As landowners by the 1890s foresaw dismal prospects for ranching, they began selling acreage to men of the plow. Within the first three decades of the twentieth century, the transformation of Northwest Texas had thus reached fruition, as many lands came to be devoted to the harvesting of wheat, grain sorghum, and after World War I, of cotton, especially around Lubbock and surrounding counties. Certainly, ranching as a profit-making industry did not vanish with the commitment to agriculture, and indeed, today remains a significant enterprise in the Northwest Texas economy. But for the meantime, livestock raising partnered with dry land farming.[3]

Oil discoveries furthered a transformation in Northwest Texas during this time period. Initial exploration for oil began during the World War I years, and shortly the effort produced meaningful results. In the upper Panhandle area, wildcatters struck oil in Carson County in 1921, and by the mid-1920s oil drilling had proved successful in Moore, Hutchinson, Potter, Carson, Gray, and Wheeler Counties. Almost at the same time, oil prospecting had made its way into the southeastern counties of Northwest Texas so that the oil business by 1930 surged as a going concern in Scurry, Fisher, Jones, Howard, Mitchell, and Taylor Counties.[4]

Tejanos probably did not participate in these developments, for as of 1930, they had not made any significant population inroads in Northwest Texas. Comparatively, more Mexican Americans resided in South Texas towns such as San Antonio (82,373) and Laredo (23,482), and for that matter, the Far West Texas city of El Paso (58,291), than lived in the entire Northwest section. The Mexican quarter in Houston, which had formed only in the first decades of the twentieth century, contained almost as many Tejanos (about 14,149) as did all counties on the Texas Plains.[5]

Still, Northwest Texas was luring folks with Spanish surnames. As table 6.2 shows, almost every county north of the Edwards Plateau featured Mexican American inhabitants. Most of them probably worked in the region's many farms. A few might have earned their living as cowhands, but almost certainly not as oil field laborers. Work in the oil patches at the time remained exclusively for white people, a pattern of occupation not substantially altered until the 1950s.[6]

Table 6.1. Total population

County	*1900*	*1930*	*1950*	*1980*	*2000*
Dallam	146	7,830	7,640	6,531	6,222
Sherman	104	2,314	2,443	3,174	3,186
Hansford	167	3,548	4,202	6,209	5,369
Ochiltree	267	5,224	6,024	9,558	9,006
Lipscomb	790	4,512	3,658	3,766	3,057
Hartley	377	2,185	1,913	3,987	5,537
Moore	209	1,555	13,349	16,575	20,121
Hutchinson	808	14,848	31,580	26,304	23,857
Roberts	620	1,457	1,031	1,187	887
Hemphill	815	4,637	4,123	5,304	3,351
Oldham	349	1,404	1,672	2,283	2,185
Potter	1,820	46,080	73,366	98,637	113,546
Carson	400	7,745	6,852	6,672	6,516
Gray	480	22,090	24,728	26,386	22,744
Wheeler	636	15,555	10,317	7,137	5,284
Deaf Smith	843	5,979	9,111	21,165	18,561
Randall	963	7,071	13,774	75,062	104,312
Armstrong	1,205	3,329	2,215	1,994	2,148
Donley	2,756	10,262	6,216	4,075	3,828
Collingsworth	1,283	14,461	9,139	4,648	3,206
Parmer	34	5,869	5,787	11,038	10,016
Castro	400	4,720	5,417	10,556	8,285
Swisher	1,227	7,343	8,249	9,723	8,378
Briscoe	1,253	5,590	3,528	2,579	1,790
Hall	1,670	16,966	10,930	5,594	3,782
Childress	2,138	16,044	12,123	6,950	7,688
Bailey	4	5,186	7,592	8,168	6,594
Lamb	31	17,452	20,015	18,669	14,709
Hale	1,080	20,189	28,211	37,592	36,602
Floyd	2,020	12,409	10,535	9,834	7,771
Motley	1,257	6,812	3,963	1,950	1,426
Cottle	1,002	9,395	6,099	2,947	1,904
Cochran	25	1,963	5,928	4,825	3,730
Hockley	44	9,298	24,407	23,230	22,716
Lubbock	203	39,104	101,048	211,651	242,628
Crosby	788	11,023	9,582	8,859	7,072
Dickens	1,151	8,601	7,177	3,539	2,762
King	490	1,193	870	425	356

Table 6.1. (*cont.*)

County	*1900*	*1930*	*1950*	*1980*	*2000*
Yoakum	26	1,263	4,339	8,299	7,322
Terry	48	8,883	13,107	14,581	12,761
Lynn	17	12,372	11,030	8,605	6,550
Garza	185	5,586	6,281	5,336	4,872
Kent	899	3,851	2,249	1,145	859
Stonewall	2,188	5,667	3,679	2,406	1,693
Gaines	55	2,800	8,909	13,150	14,467
Dawson	37	13,573	19,113	16,184	14,985
Borden	776	1,505	1,106	859	729
Scurry	4,158	12,188	22,779	18,159	16,361
Fisher	3,708	13,563	11,023	5,891	4,344
Jones	7,053	24,233	22,147	17,268	20,785
Andrews	87	736	5,002	13,323	13,044
Martin	332	5,785	5,541	4,684	4,246
Howard	2,528	22,883	26,722	33,142	33,627
Mitchell	2,855	14,183	14,357	9,088	9,698
Nolan	2,611	19,323	19,808	17,359	15,802
Taylor	10,499	41,023	63,370	110,932	126,555
Total	67,917	590,660	765,376	1,009,194	1,059,832

Sources for this table:

Fifteenth Census of the United States: 1930, Population, volume 3, part 2 (Reports by States, Showing the Composition and Characteristics of the Population for Counties, Cities, and Townships or Other Minor Civil Divisions), Montana-Wyoming (Washington, DC: Government Printing Office, 1932), Table 13: "Composition of the Population, By Counties: 1930," 975–990.

A Report of the Seventeenth Decennial Census of the United States. *Census of Population: 1950*, vol. 2, *Characteristics of the Population, Part 43: Texas* (Washington, DC, 1952), Table 42: "General Characteristics of the Population, For Counties: 1950," 43-204 to 43-218.

1980 Census of Population, Volume 1, Characteristics of the Population, Chapter B, General Population Characteristics, Part 45, Texas, PC80-1-B45 (Washington, DC: Department of Commerce, 1982), Table 16: "Total Persons and Spanish Origin Persons by Type of Spanish Origin and Race: 1980," 45-43 to 45-46.

United States Census 2000, Texas: Census of Population and Housing, "Summary Population and Housing Characteristics," PHC-1-45 (Washington, DC: U.S. Department of Commerce, U.S. Bureau of the Census, 2000), Table 4: "Race and Hispanic or Latino: 2000," 198–202.

Two discernible concentrations of Tejanos, according to the 1930 United States census, existed in Northwest Texas. One was in the oil and farm counties in the southeastern sections of Northwest Texas—that area where oil discoveries had been made in the 1920s. Attraction from economic growth therein, or perhaps migration from neighboring farm counties to the south (Runnels, Tom Green, or Concho, for example), might explain this convergence. Tejanos had also gravitated as of 1930 toward Potter and Lubbock Counties, at that time among the most heavily populated of all counties (except for Taylor County) in the region, and which, coincidentally, contained the two largest urban centers in Northwest Texas: Amarillo and Lubbock, respectively. To be sure, agriculture predominated in Potter and Lubbock Counties, but ranchers and farmers depended on the city for numerous supportive services, including the retail, banking, and transportation sectors. Amarillo and Lubbock certainly offered urban opportunities of many types, including ones in the service and unskilled trades that might have attracted Mexicans from surrounding cotton lands.

In the period between 1930 and 1950, Mexican Americans continued earlier movements into the Northwest Texas region. Economic growth beckoned them, for despite the Depression of the 1930s and the weather calamities of that era, the two decades proved fortuitous for the Panhandle and South Plains. On the one hand, oil companies made new finding. During the 1930s, the "oil and farm" counties of Yoakum, Gaines, and Andrews in the South Plains joined the ranks of earlier counties with oil deposits, and after World War II, Scurry County again (as it had in the 1920s) became a hub for oil field activity, albeit briefly.[7] Then, farming survived the era's difficulties; in fact, it expanded. Farmers took advantage of federal subsidies and escalated their use of irrigation. The shift to machine technology (including the tractor and modern field implements) and increased confidence in scientific agriculture during the 1940s led to greater production of cotton, grain sorghum, and corn.[8] But other crops lured Mexicans seasonally to Northwest Texas, among them the vegetable harvest such as that which flourished in counties like Deaf Smith. That section of the Panhandle by the 1940s gained recognition for producing highly profitable yields of potatoes, onions, lettuce, carrots, and cabbage.[9]

Up to midcentury, most Mexican Americans in Northwest Texas made their living as farm hands, and were considered by the majority white population as a social and demographic oddity. At least two factors might explain this anomaly. First, as Pauline Kibbe (executive director of the Good Neighbor Commission) put it, whites assumed Mexicans to be:

Table 6.2. Mexican American population

County	*1930*	*1950*	*1980*	*2000*
Dallam	264	508	855	1,766
Sherman	24	26	267	874
Hansford	15	5	674	1,690
Ochiltree	10	8	790	2,863
Lipscomb	53	20	270	633
Hartley	103	27	160	758
Moore	85	199	2,991	9,558
Hutchinson	25	230	982	3,506
Roberts	12	18	26	28
Hemphill	140	69	510	522
Oldham	16	16	95	241
Potter	1,032	1,847	9,895	31,921
Carson	340	169	230	458
Gray	89	81	1,003	2,959
Wheeler			235	664
Deaf Smith	20	618	8,215	10,654
Randall	124	101	2,549	10,718
Armstrong	36	76	28	116
Donley	79	17	125	243
Collingsworth	25	131	521	655
Parmer	77	140	3,395	4,927
Castro	1	78	3,785	4,279
Swisher	54	73	2,545	2,951
Briscoe	58	12	409	407
Hall	11	136	760	1,040
Childress	67	83	624	1,574
Bailey	12	147	2,512	3,119
Lamb	388	1,097	5,377	6,393
Hale	113	1251	12,010	17,532
Floyd	27	175	3,164	3,569
Motley	81	135	142	173
Cottle	94	311	411	360
Cochran	13	355	1,404	1,646
Hockley	113	1,000	6,057	8,459
Lubbock	1,017	6,477	39,435	66,609
Crosby	79	571	3206	3,460
Dickens	128	463	562	660
King	14	21	41	34

County	*1930*	*1950*	*1980*	*2000*
Yoakum		78	222	3,363
Terry	29	1,084	4,744	5,626
Lynn	123	1,117	3,150	2,923
Garza	203	612	1,217	1,810
Kent	216	125	72	78
Stonewall	254	155	168	199
Gaines		232	3,843	5,175
Dawson	60	2,885	5,938	7,222
Borden	83	110	123	87
Scurry	591	565	3,235	4,544
Fisher	772	809	1,046	928
Jones	790	1,222	2,402	4,346
Andrews		26	2,737	5,202
Martin	440	1,011	1,598	1,925
Howard	2,236	3,137	6,667	12,597
Mitchell	1,675	1,503	2,201	3,009
Nolan	1,330	1,215	3,301	4,431
Taylor	981	2,026	12,028	23,328
Total	14,622	34,603	170,952	294,812
% of pop	2.5%	4.5%	16.9%	27.8%
Intercensal Change		137%	394.0%	72.5%

Sources for this table:

Fifteenth Census of the United States: 1930, Population, volume 3, Part 2 (Reports by States, Showing the Composition and Characteristics of the Population for Counties, Cities, and townships or Other Minor Civil Divisions), Montana-Wyoming (Washington, DC: Government Printing Office, 1932), Table 17: "Indians, Chinese, and Japanese 1910 to 1930, and Mexicans, 1930, for Counties and for Cities of 25,000 or More," 1014–15.

United States Census of Population, 1950. Special Census Report P-E No. 3C: "Persons of Spanish Surname." (Washington, DC, 1953), Table 7: "Citizenship and Country of Birth of White Persons of Spanish Surname, for Counties and Urban Places of 10,000 or more in Selected Southwestern States: 1950," 3C-44 to 3C-46.

1980 Census of Population, Vol. 1, Characteristics of the Population, Chapter B, General Population Characteristics, Part 45, Texas, PC80-1-B45 (Washington, DC: Department of Commerce, 1982), Table 16: "Total Persons and Spanish Origin Persons by Type of Spanish Origin and Race: 1980," 45-43 to 45-46.

United States Census 2000, Texas: Census of Population and Housing, "Summary Population and Housing Characteristics," PHC-1-45 (Washington, DC: U.S. Department of Commerce, U.S. Bureau of the Census, 2000), Table 4: "Race and Hispanic or Latino: 2000," 198–202.

> Not a human being at all, but a species of farm implement that comes mysteriously and spontaneously into being coincident with the maturing of the cotton, that requires no upkeep or special consideration during the period of its usefulness, needs no protection from the elements, and when the crop has been harvested, vanishes into the limbo of forgotten things—until the next harvest season rolls around.[10]

Second, the small number of farm Mexicans hardly formed an identifiable ethnic element. As table 6.2 shows, in 1950 Mexican Americans constituted no more than 4.5 percent of the total population in Northwest Texas. Still, almost 20,000 more Tejanos lived in the region in 1950 than had in 1930. Many had decided that the region offered them a better opportunity than did South Texas (or wherever their home base) and settled there once the harvest season ended. Some faced no option but to stay in the rural Plains, unable to afford the drive home.

Where were they most likely to be settled? Looking at the 1950 census, and focusing on those counties having more than 1,000 Mexican American residents, it is clear that the migrants who remained in Northwest Texas stayed in the "farm" counties where cotton reigned as "king." It is no surprise that these several counties hosted the towns—among them *Lobika* (Lubbock), *Litlfil* (Littlefield), *Levelan* (Levelland), *Bigesprin* (Big Spring), *Sweetwata* (Sweetwater), and Lamesa—most remembered by the migratory generation of the 1930s and post–World War II era (see table 6.3).

Table 6.3. Mexican American population distribution by economic region, 1950

farm and livestock counties[11]		*oil and farm counties*		*oil and livestock counties*	
Lamb	1,097	Hockley	1,000	Potter	1,847
Hale	1,251	Martin	1,011		
Lubbock	6,477	Howard	3,137		
Terry	1,084	Mitchell	1,503		
Lynn	1,117	Nolan	1,215		
Dawson	2,885	Taylor	2,026		
Jones	1,222				
Total	15,133	Total	9,892	Total	1,847

To be sure, almost the entire Northwest Texas region at mid-twentieth century remained largely rural. The figures in table 6.4 indicate this point clearly. Exempting a few counties (wherein Mexican Americans as of the year 2000 made up 32 percent of the entire population), the majority of inhabitants of all races lived in settlements outside the county seat.[12] Moreover, most county headquarters then—as many do now—retained an old-fashioned, rural flavor (exceptions to this generalization might have been cities such as Lubbock and Big Spring). Given the racial attitudes of the period that precluded Tejanos from easy access to city jobs, the conclusion may be reached that Mexican Americans in Northwest Texas up to 1950 also lived (along with the general population) in rural areas. But their work was primarily that of farm hands or day laborers.

The agricultural growth of the preceding decades escalated during the 1950s as irrigated farming opened new acreage for cotton and grain sorghum. Indeed, "the South Plains became the major center for cotton production in Texas after World War II," writes historian Garry L. Nall.[13] By the early 1960s, eight counties in Northwest Texas together produced 40 percent of the total cotton yield in the Lone Star State, though the cotton economy experienced a downturn during the 1970s due to declining prices for the fiber and a drop in the water table. Farmers responded by planting feed for livestock. Other farm products like the vegetable crop around Deaf Smith and surrounding counties boomed. Despite the emerging trend toward crop variation, cotton still held its own as a major staple in many Plains counties.[14]

A new business appeared in Northwest Texas during the 1960s—that of controlled cattle feeding. Huge feedlots surfaced throughout the Panhandle, most prominently counties like Potter and Deaf Smith, as well as in South Plains counties like Hale and Lubbock, as major corporations found quick profits available in readying butcher cows for the meat market. Meatpacking plants inevitably sprung up as a concomitant industry in Northwest Texas, as beef producers sought to meet what seemed insatiable consumer demand.[15]

Startling demographic changes paralleled this economic transformation. Agribusiness required increased numbers of seasonal unskilled laborers capable of traveling from South Texas and other points of origin (including every part of Texas, or Mexico, and New Mexico) and working for survival wages in Northwest Texas.[16] The greatest increase (since Mexican Americans first arrived in Northwest Texas) in the Mexican-origin population thus occurred during this time period. These numbers climbed by 136,349, whereas the non-Hispanic population rose by only 108,189. An

Table 6.4. Percent of the total county population living in the county seat, 1950 and 1980, in counties where Mexican Americans constituted 32% or more of the population in 2000

County	*County Seat*	*% Living in in County Seat 1950*	*% Living in County Seat 1980*
Moore	Dumas	45.89	73.57
Deaf Smith	Hereford	57.15	74.90
Parmer	Friona*	20.77	34.50
Castro	Dimmit	26.97	47.55
Swisher	Tulia	39.06	51.76
Bailey	Muleshoe	32.63	59.28
Lamb	Littlefield	32.67	39.69
Hale	Plainview	49.78	59.02
Floyd	Floydada	30.47	42.64
Cochran	Morton	38.36	55.42
Hockley	Levelland	33.86	59.44
Lubbock	Lubbock	71.00	82.20
Crosby	Crosbytown	19.60	25.84
Yoakum	Denver City*	42.75	56.68
Terry	Brownfield	47.00	71.24
Lynn	Tahoka	25.82	37.91
Garza	Post	50.00	74.23
Gaines	Seminole	39.05	46.24
Dawson	Lamesa	56.00	72.85
Andrews	Andrews	65.85	83.02
Martin	Stanton	28.77	49.40
Howard	Big Spring	64.69	74.84

*denotes town with largest population in the county and not the county seat

Sources for this table:

www.texasalmanac.com/population/population-counties-history.pdf
www.texasalmanac.com/population/population-city-history.pdf

intercensal increase of 394 percent as of 1980 reflected the Mexican American population boom. Despite these immense strides in demographic growth, Mexican Americans constituted only 17 percent of the total population in the region as of 1980.[17]

Simultaneous with this population surge, Northwest Texas experienced a shift between midcentury and 1980 as most citizens came to prefer urban living (table 6.4). Compared to 1950, the majority of people in most of the counties (where Mexican Americans in the year 2000 composed more than 32 percent of a county's population) now (in 1980) resided in the county seat as opposed to the countryside. Mexican Americans made the same shift, from a rural population to an urbanized one, comprising almost the same percentage in each county, as did non-Mexicans (table 6.5).

Still, in counties where the Mexican American population in 1980 amounted to more than 5,000, only Lubbock (Lubbock County) and Abilene (Taylor County) could claim modern accoutrements. Big Spring (Howard) and Plainview (Hale County) might be thus categorized, but not county seats such as Hereford (Deaf Smith County), Littlefield (Lamb County), Levelland (Hockley County), and Lamesa (Dawson County). Said differently, Mexican Americans as of 1980 still resided in the "farm and livestock" counties and "oil and farm" counties. Potter and Moore Counties might be considered exceptions but in the former county, Mexican Americans constituted less than 32 percent of the county population in 2000.

The rise in the total population that occurred throughout Northwest Texas between 1950 and 1980 took an incredible dive during the last two decades of the twentieth century. As table 6.1 shows, about three-fourths of all counties in Northwest Texas lost residents during that time period. Scholars attribute the stark change to sluggish oil prices, annual struggles with fickle weather, a decline in the groundwater table upon which farmers had earlier relied, and the inclination of the younger generation to look for more attractive opportunities in other parts of the state.[18]

In the case of Hispanics or Latinos—as the 2000 census listed those of Hispanic descent—the opposite occurred (table 6.2). Their numbers rose throughout the region: specifically, by 123,860 between 1980 and 2000. This growth represented an intercensal increase of 72.5 percent as a whole.

The causes for this pronounced augmentation among Mexican-descent people after midcentury varied. On the one hand, they included the demand by the agricultural sector and meatpacking businesses for cheap laborers, the need by the construction, restaurant, and hotel industries for

Table 6.5. Percent of the non-Hispanic and Hispanic county population living in the county seat, 1980

County	*% Non-Hispanics Living in the County Seat*	*% Hispanics Living in the County Seat*
Moore	75.40	65.30
Deaf Smith	72.72	78.30
Parmer	32.40*	39.30
Castro	46.29	50.00
Swisher	50.88	54.30
Bailey	56.58	65.40
Lamb	41.47	40.90
Hale	60.51	55.90
Floyd	42.11	43.70
Cochran	49.14	70.70
Hockley	59.56	59.10
Lubbock	82.97	78.80
Crosby	25.86	25.80
Yoakum	59.55*	59.80
Terry	71.22	71.30
Lynn	43.76	28.00
Garza	71.64	84.00
Gaines	47.08	44.20
Dawson	70.64	76.70
Andrews	80.50	89.10
Martin	45.66	56.70
Howard	72.45	84.30

*denotes county wherein town with largest population is not the county seat

Sources for this table:

www.texasalmanac.com/population/population-counties-history.pdf

www.texasalmanac.com/population/population-city-history.pdf

1980 Census of Population, vol. 1. Characteristics of the Population, Chapter B. General Population Characteristics, part 45 Texas. PC80-1-B45, Bureau of the Census, Table 16: "Total Persons and Spanish Origin Persons by Type of Spanish Origin and Race: 1980."

people willing to work for lower wages, and the recent trend of Latinos to push into rural areas across the country.[19] Certainly, the quiet, rural, small town ambient of the Plains made the region attractive.

By the year 2000, consequently, Mexican Americans made up 27.8 percent of the total population in Northwest Texas, and as map 3 and table 6.8

show, they had come to be demographically noticeable in several counties. In two particularly, they formed more than 50.0 percent of the population. Not surprisingly, Deaf Smith and Castro Counties, situated at the core of farm and livestock production, owned this distinction. There, migrant workers arriving to pick the vegetable and cotton crops sometimes stayed (perhaps due to a lack of funds to return to their home source), hoping to

Table 6.6. Population losses and gains among non-Hispanics and Hispanics between 1980 and 2000 in counties where Mexican Americans constituted 32% or more of the population in 2000*

County	*Non–Hispanic Pop.*	*Hispanic Pop.*
Moore	−3,021	+6,657
Deaf Smith	−5,063	+2,439
Parmer	−2,554	+1,532
Castro	−2,765	+494
Swisher	−1,751	−406
Bailey	−2,181	+607
Lamb	−4,976	+1,056
Hale	−6,512	+5,552
Floyd	−2,468	+405
Cochran	−1,337	+242
Hockley	−2,916	+2,402
Lubbock	+3,803	+27,174
Crosby	−2,014	+254
Yoakum	−2,118	+3,141
Terry	−2,702	+882
Lynn	−1,828	+227
Garza	−1,147	+593
Gaines	−15	+1,332
Dawson	−2,483	+1,284
Andrews	−2,744	+2,465
Martin	−765	+327
Howard	−5,445	+5,930

– signifies loss
+ signifies gain

***Sources for this table are tables 6.2 and 6.8**

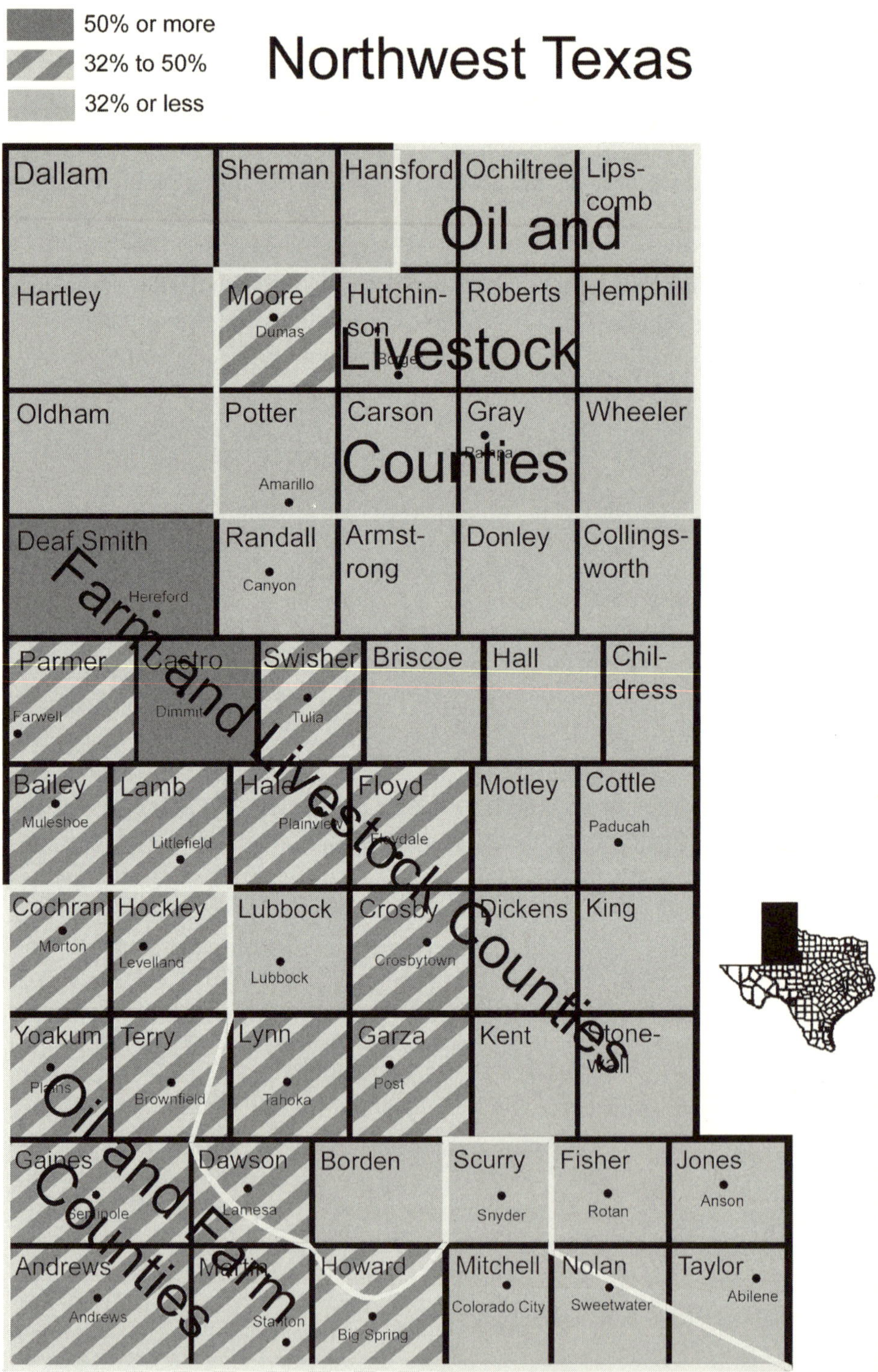

Map 3. Percent of Mexican American population in Northwest Texas.

Map drawn for the author courtesy of John Eusebio Klingemann

find employment locally. Indeed, work in the area's huge feedlots enticed many to remain, assuming they had the required tolerance for foul work and unpleasant smell.[20]

The remaining counties where Hispanics or Latinos (of any race) were demographically noticeable were those that counted on farming and rais-

Table 6.7. Percent of the Hispanic or Latino population living in the county seat, 2000

County	*Hispanic or Latino Pop.*	*County Seat*	*Hispanic or Latino Pop.*	*% Living in County Seat*
Moore	9,558	Dumas	5,876	58.30
Deaf Smith	10,654	Hereford	8,958	84.10
Parmer	4,927	Friona*	2,230	45.30
Castro	4,279	Dimmit	2,491	58.20
Swisher	2,951	Tulia	2,028	68.70
Bailey	3,119	Muleshoe	2,416	77.50
Lamb	6,393	Littlefield	2,982	46.60
Hale	17,532	Plainview	11,131	63.50
Floyd	3,569	Floydada	1,898	53.20
Cochran	1,646	Morton	1,210	73.50
Hockley	8,459	Levelland	5,045	59.60
Lubbock	66,609	Lubbock	54,786	82.30
Crosby	3,480	Crosbytown	893	25.80
Yoakum	3.363	Denver City*	1,879	55.90
Terry	5,626	Brownfield	4,360	77.50
Lynn	2,923	Tahoka	1,303	44.60
Garza	1,810	Post	1,581	87.30
Gaines	,179	Seminole	2,340	45.20
Dawson	7,222	Lamesa	5,271	73.00
Andrews	5,202	Andrews	4,049	77.80
Martin	1,925	Stanton	1,352	70.20
Howard	12,597	Big Spring	11,265	89.40

*denotes town with largest population in the county and not the county seat

Source for this table: *United States Census 2000, Texas: Census of Population and Housing,* "Summary Population and Housing Characteristics," PHC-1-45 (Washington, DC: U.S. Department of Commerce, U. S. Bureau of the Census, 2000), Table 4: "Race and Hispanic or Latino: 2000," 205–49.

Table 6.8. Percent of Mexican American population in northwest Texas counties, 2000

County	*Total Pop.*	*Mexican Am. and Other Latino Pop.*	*% Mexican American and other Latino Population*
Dallam	6,222	1,766	28.4
Sherman	3,186	874	27.4
Hansford	5,369	1,690	31.5
Ochiltree	9,006	2,863	31.8
Lipscomb	3,057	633	20.7
Hartley	5,537	758	13.7
Moore	20,121	9,558	48.0
Hutchinson	23,857	3,506	14.7
Roberts	887	28	3.2
Hemphill	3,351	522	15.6
Oldham	2,185	241	11.0
Potter	113,546	31,921	28.1
Carson	6,516	458	7.0
Gray	22,744	2,959	13.0
Wheeler	5284	664	12.6
Deaf Smith	18,561	10,654	57.4
Randall	104,312	10,718	10.3
Armstrong	2,148	116	5.4
Donley	3,828	243	6.3
Collingsworth	3,206	655	20.4
Parmer	10,016	4,927	49.2
Castro	8,285	4,279	51.6
Swisher	8,378	2,951	35.2
Briscoe	1,790	407	22.7
Hall	3,782	1,040	27.5
Childress	7,688	1,574	20.5
Bailey	6,594	3,119	47.3
Lamb	14,709	6,393	43.5
Hale	36,602	17,532	47.9
Floyd	7,771	3,569	45.9
Motley	1,426	173	12.1
Cottle	1,904	360	18.9
Cochran	3,730	1,646	44.1
Hockley	22,716	8,459	37.2
Lubbock	242,628	66,609	27.5

County	*Total Pop.*	*Mexican Am. and Other Latino Pop.*	*% Mexican American and other Latino Population*
Crosby	7,072	3,460	48.9
Dickens	2,762	660	23.9
King	356	34	9.6
Yoakum	7,322	3,363	45.9
Terry	12,761	5,626	44.1
Lynn	6,550	2,923	44.6
Garza	4,872	1,810	37.2
Kent	859	78	9.0
Stonewall	1,693	199	11.8
Gaines	14,467	5,175	35.8
Dawson	14,985	7,222	48.2
Borden	729	87	12.0
Scurry	16,361	4,544	27.8
Fisher	4,344	928	21.4
Jones	20,785	4,346	20.9
Andrews	13,044	5,202	39.9
Martin	4,246	1,925	45.3
Howard	33,627	12,597	37.5
Mitchell	9,698	3,009	31.0
Nolan	15,802	4,431	28.0
Taylor	126,555	23,328	8.4
Total	1,059,832	294,812	27.8

Source for this table:

United States Census 2000, Texas: Census of Population and Housing, "Summary Population and Housing Characteristics," PHC-1-45 (Washington, DC: U.S. Department of Commerce, U.S. Bureau of the Census, 2000), Table 4: "Race and Hispanic or Latino: 2000," 198–202.

---

ing livestock or were engaged in oil and farm production. As table 6.6 indicates, Anglos apparently no longer found many of these counties as attractive as earlier. Save for Lubbock County, Anglos sought flight from counties facing dismal economic prospects while Mexican Americans gravitated toward them.

Still, residence in predominantly "farm and livestock" counties and "oil and farm" counties do not make Hispanics or Latinos (of any race) a rural people. As table 6.7 indicates, in most cases, more than half of Tejanos in these counties lived in the county seat, and in some counties, as many as two-thirds of Hispanic or Latino residents preferred an urban setting. Even in Deaf Smith County, one of the two counties where Mexican Americans constituted more than half the population in 2000, 84.1 percent lived in Hereford!

This trend toward city residence obviously harked back to the mid-twentieth century, and as a comparison of tables 6.6 and 6.7 shows, the process accelerated after the 1980s. But does residence in the county seat make Tejanos urbanites? The matter is relative, of course. Because Northwest Texas still remains mainly rural, living in the county seat hardly parallels the experience associated with life in the state's larger metropolises or even in smaller cities, such as Corpus Christi, Waco, or Beaumont. In Northwest Texas, thus, Mexicans and Mexican Americans do not reside in what in the popular imagination symbolizes "the city" (freeways, crime, urban blight, and more). Yet, the smaller rural town (where town folks drive a few blocks out of the city limits into the countryside) appears an acceptable way of life on the Panhandle and South Plains. The county seat, particularly, permits Tejano urbanites to earn their livelihood in jobs (varying from the professional to the service sector) not readily available in the outlying communities. Commuters benefit from the amenities of city services even when they must routinely drive to work on local ranches, farms, or oil fields. Daily, also, Tejanos with homes in rural counties adjacent to Lubbock and Potter Counties go into Lubbock or Amarillo, respectively, to earn their weekly wage. Most face hardly any traffic in these daily commutes—a convenience that cannot be claimed by Tejanos living as true urbanites in more congested metroplexes.

Notes

1. The scholarship on Tejanos in Northwest Texas remains underdeveloped, at least in comparison to what has been written on Tejanos in South Texas and other parts of the state. Scholars generally associated with the history of Mexican Americans in the Northwest Texas are Yolanda Romero, Andrés A. Tijerina, and Jorge Iber. Romero's works include "The Mexican American Frontier Experience in Twentieth Century Northwest Texas" (PhD diss., Texas Tech University, 1993); "*Los Socios del Sementerio*: A Mexican American Burial Society in Early Lubbock, Texas," *West Texas Historical Association Yearbook* 63 (1987); "*Adelante Compañeros*: The Sanitation Workers' Struggle in Lubbock, Texas, 1968–1972," *West Texas Historical Association Yearbook* 69 (1993); "Trini Gámez, The Texas Farm Workers, and Mexican American Community Empowerment: Toil and Trouble on the Texas South Plains," in *Mexican Americans in Texas History*, ed. Emilio Zamora, Cynthia Orozco, and Rodolfo Rocha (Austin: Texas State Historical Association, 2000); and "Hispanics on the Texas South Plains," in *The Future of the Southern Plains*, ed. Sherry L. Smith (Norman: University of Oklahoma Press, 2003), hereafter ed. Smith. Tijerina's work, *The History of Mexican Americans in Lubbock County* (Lubbock: Texas Tech University Press, 1979),

has remained a standard for years. Most recently, Jorge Iber has also turned his attention to Tejanos in Northwest Texas. His works include "Bidal Agüero and *El Editor* Newspaper: The Varied Roles of a Spanish Surnamed Entrepreneur in a Lubbock, Texas Barrio, 1977–1999," *West Texas Historical Association Yearbook* 75 (1999); "A Vaquero in the Backfield: The Career of Bobby Cavazos, Texas Tech's First Hispanic All-American," *College Football Historical Society* 14 (August 2001); and "Becoming Raiders Rojos: Using Sport to Claim Hispanic 'Space' at Texas Tech University," *West Texas Historical Association Yearbook* 77 (2001). Certainly, others have written significant works on Tejanos in Northwest Texas, but these three authors are the ones generally associated with that history. See also Paul Carlson, *The Centennial History of Lubbock: Hub City of the Plains*, ed. Don Abbe and Monte Monroe (Virginia Beach, VA: Donning Company Publishers, 2008); and Scott Sosebee, "Dashed Hopes and Gained Opportunities: Mexican American Educational Experiences in Lubbock, Texas, from the 1920s through the 1960s," *West Texas Historical Association Yearbook* 83 (2007). The most comprehensive bibliography on the subject is Bruce A. Glasrud and Arnoldo De León's, "Tejanos in West Texas: A Selected Bibliography," *Journal of Big Bend Studies* 15 (2003). However, only about 10 percent of the numerous books and articles listed actually treat the history of Mexican Americans in Northwest Texas. Many focus, for instance, on El Paso or on communities located in the Edwards Plateau and Trans-Pecos. Further, many do not qualify as historical scholarship, fitting more appropriately into such fields as sociology, political science, and education. Some cover historical topics before 1900.

As might be gathered from the above summary, works on Tejanos in Northwest Texas tend to focus on cultural and social aspects of Mexican American communities. Many deal with Tejanos living in Lubbock County and other adjacent counties. Comparatively, this chapter offers a demographic portrait of Mexican Americans in Northwest Texas, and it examines population changes in the wider area that collectively constitutes the Panhandle and South Plains. In this chapter, several terms will be used to define the region under study. "Northwest Texas" embraces all counties north of the 32° parallel (see map 3). The "Panhandle" refers to that section of Texas consisting of the twenty-six counties north of the Bailey County to Cottle County boundary. The "South Plains" would include that area of Northwest Texas generally south from the Bailey County to the Cottle County line, excepting that section east of a divide running north–south from about Motley County to Mitchell County.

2. Ty Cashion, *A Texas Frontier: The Clear Fork Country and Fort Griffin, 1849–1887* (Norman: University of Oklahoma Press, 1996), 268–72, 275–77.

3. James Smallwood, "The Southern Plains and the Expansion of the Cotton Kingdom," *West Texas Historical Association Yearbook* 46 (1980): 37, 42, 44; John Miller Morris, "When Corporations Ruled the Llano Estacado," in *The Future of the Southern Plains*, ed. Smith, 51–52; Robert L. Martin, *The City Moves West: Economic and Industrial Growth in Central West Texas* (Austin: University of Texas Press, 1969), 15, 51–52, 55, 57, 59–63, 69, 70; Donald E. Green, *Land of the Underground Rain: Irrigation on the Texas High Plains, 1910–1970* (Austin: University of Texas Press, 1973), 102–3, 109–11.

4. Martin, *The City Moves West*, 101–3, 107–8; Richard R. Moore, *West Texas after the Discovery of Oil: A Modern Frontier* (Austin: Jenkins Publishing, 1971), 6–7.

5. Source for these figures is *Fifteenth Census of the United States: 1930*. Population. Volume 3, Part 2, Montana to Wyoming (Washington, DC, 1932). Composition and Characteristics: Table 17, "Indians, Chinese, and Japanese, 1910 to 1930, and Mexicans, 1930, for Counties and for Cities of 25,000 or More," 1015.

6. Roger M. Olien and Diana Davids Olien, *Oil Booms: Social Change in Five Texas Towns* (Lincoln: University of Nebraska Press, 1982), 119.

7. Moore, *West Texas after the Discovery of Oil*, 24, 46–52.

8. Garry L. Nall, "Just Where Are the Farmers in the West Texas Saga?" *West Texas Historical Association Yearbook* 78 (2002): 9–11; Smallwood, "The Southern Plains and the Expansion of the Cotton Kingdom," 45, 46.

9. *Deaf Smith County, Texas: The Land and Its People, 1876–1981* (Hereford, TX: Deaf Smith County Historical Society, 1982), 47; Bessie Patterson, *A History of Deaf Smith County, Featuring Pioneer Families* (Hereford, TX: Pioneer Publishers, 1964), 22.

10. Pauline R. Kibbe, *Latin Americans in Texas* (Albuquerque: University of New Mexico Press, 1946), 176.

11. Figures from table 6.2. For delineations of farm and livestock, oil and farm, and oil and livestock counties, see map 3.

12. The Texas State Data Center and Office of the State Demographer today divide the "Hispanic Percent of Total Population in Counties in the State of Texas, 2000" into four categories: 1.7 to 15.0 percent; 15.1 to 32.0 percent; 32.1 to 50.0 percent, and 50.1 to 97.5 percent. See http://txsdc.utsa.edu/maps/thematic/cnty.hipct.php, accessed August 16, 2009.

13. Nall, "Just Where Are the Farmers in the West Texas Saga?" 11–13.

14. Smallwood, "The Southern Plains and the Expansion of the Cotton Kingdom," 47–48; *Deaf Smith County, Texas, The Land and Its People*, 47; Patterson, *A History of Deaf Smith County*, 22.

15. Paul H. Carlson, *Amarillo: The Story of a Western Town* (Lubbock: Texas Tech University Press, 2006), 186–87.

16. Manuel Peña, *Where the Ox Does Not Plow: A Mexican American Ballad* (Albuquerque: University of New Mexico Press, 2008), 44–46.

17. This transformation is discussed briefly in Morris, "When Corporations Ruled the Llano Estacado," 87–88.

18. Elliott West, "Trails and Footprints: The Past of the Future Southern Plains," in *The Future of the Southern Plains*, ed. Smith, 18; Green, *Land of the Underground Rain*, 230, 237.

19. Morris, "When Corporations Ruled the Llano Estacado," 83–84, 88. William Kandel and John Cromartie, *New Patterns of Hispanic Settlement in Rural America*, Rural Development Research Report, no. 99 (Washington, DC: U.S. Dept. of Agriculture, Economic Research Service, 2004). See further, Jake Bernstein, "Demographic Destiny and Slowly but Surely, Hispanic Culture Will Define West Texas," *Texas Observer*, October 5, 2007, 24.

20. Morris, "When Corporations Ruled the Llano Estacado," 79.

7

Blowout 1910 Style

A Chicano School Boycott In West Texas

In 1968 in Los Angeles, California, Mexican American students dissatisfied with the city's school system walked out in what came to be called "blowouts." A like boycott took place in San Angelo, Texas, in 1910. Mexican American parents decided not to enroll their children in the segregated public schools, objecting to inferior facilities and inadequate educational programs. People in the community put up a gallant effort, sending their schoolchildren instead to the local Immaculate Conception Academy and the Mexican Presbyterian Mission School. Ultimately, boycott leaders determined that the school board would not accede to their demands. The blowout ended without success around 1915.

Race and class prevented Chicanos from securing the quality education Texas provided for white students in 1910. The pattern of segregation prospered statewide. In the majority of cities, school boards established so-called Mexican schools, staffed them with teachers ill prepared to instruct their charges, furnished them with inadequate physical materials including discarded textbooks, and in a number of other ways practiced policies that resulted in educational inequities for students of Mexican descent.[1]

Local governments and boards of education sanctioned the exclusion of Mexican children from public instruction in a variety of manners. Students attended overcrowded constructs in segregated areas of Pearsall, Devine, Kingsville, Del Rio, Asherton, Kyle, and Seguin. Desks and school equipment tended to be crude and outmoded. Chicanitos faced insults, abuses, and hazing from their white peers where integration was allowed. In places where the nearest school existed some distance from the Mexican *colonia*,

This chapter was originally published in the journal *Texana* 12, no. 2 (1974): 124–40.

the Chicano community endured promises for neighborhood instruction. Through conscious intent or subtle acts that alienated, humiliated, or antagonized Mexicanos, educational discrimination prevailed in Val Verde, Hays, Gonzales, Atascosa, Medina, Frio, La Salle, Dimmit, McMullen, Uvalde, Wilson, Williamson, Comal, Bastrop, Bee, Caldwell, and Blanco Counties. On such pretexts that separation was the better policy for the non-English speaking, that children were ill clad, that "greasers" were unclean and immoral, that proximity might lead to interracial contact, that Mexicanos were not white but Aztec- or Negro-descended, the separate policy developed in a pattern congruent with the ways whites felt about Mexicanos at that time.[2]

In San Angelo, a West Texas city of 10,000 people, a parallel arrangement existed. Similar racial notions about the few hundred Mexicans in the city[3] dictated the need for educational distance. The Mexican laboring elements, whites told a Chattanooga, Tennessee, correspondent in 1889, consisted of a "race of mongrels, chiefly Aztec, with a sprinkle of Spanish and negro." Native Indians of subtropical Mexico predominated, but the Mexicans' mixed-blood status made them "dark to the point of blackness." Whites described a people resigned to a halcyon life of gambling and drinking, a race unconcerned about its means of livelihood, inhabiting forlorn-looking huts on the edges of town and subsisting on two meals a day. Basically an immoral people, whites related, the Mexican elements had no particular morals concerning sexual relations, changing wives commonly and neither partner having much regard for proprieties when living together. They were incapable of education "even in the most moderate degree," and ignorance characterized them "except for their calling." A fondness for liquor and handouts, plus their inability to comprehend the significance of the ballot, made them susceptible to unscrupulous use by the political boss. Such virulent racism prevailed among San Angelo's white majority and had not abated by 1910.[4]

Not surprisingly, the town's decision to incorporate into a municipality in 1903 affected the white pupil only. Meant to improve an overcrowded situation and replace the inadequate "subscription" method with a system of city-controlled education, the move resulted, by school time in September of that year, in the addition of three new ward schools and added efficiency.[5] But the innovations ignored the pernicious Jim Crow pattern that continued—separate and unequal.

An average of fifty Mexican students composed the scholastic population of the designated school during that epoch. Low attendance marked the initial months of every school term, but following the cotton-picking season toward the end of the year, the number present generally improved, doubling for the most part by May.[6] The presence of the Mexican student concerned the white mind only peripherally. While regarding them as an imposition on society, San Angeloans still seemed to recognize a responsibility for the welfare of the Mexican,[7] and it was precisely that that resulted in the prevailing educational order. The staff, generally white but sometimes Mexican,[8] were ill prepared professionally. The inferior physical facilities and the poor quality of instruction the Mexican children received remained equally removed from the whites' educational philosophy, from the plans for curriculum reform or expansion of facilities, and from the laws amended to ensure "the continuance of civil liberty or the capacity of self-government."[9] In the Anglo mind, the 200 Mexican pupils of school age in 1910[10] existed as "the foreign class," as the "sons of Montezuma," and as "the natives from the Southern republic."[11] In an era when whites lavished praises upon themselves for their educational progressivism, conditions for Mexicans remained static and unimproved.

San Angeleños, then, had reason for resentment. When in early 1910, the Board of Trustees moved to provide Chicanitos with an old frame building abandoned by white students transferring to a recently finished schoolhouse, the Mexican element remonstrated.[12] Mexicanos protested quietly in April by withholding the names of school-aged children from the census enumerator on the claim that they did not receive the full benefit of the state fund's pro rata apportionment based at that time on the city's scholastic population.[13] But in June, represented by a committee of four and the legal firm of Anderson and Dumas of the city, Mexicans confronted the board demanding either the admission of the Mexican children to the white schools or the location of white and Mexican buildings on the same grounds. Basing their demands on the past provisions of inferior school facilities, the Mexicans argued that the furnishings were not commensurate with the amount of money designated for them, that the Mexican children were not learning anything under the existing system, and that certain changes must be made including the employment of competent male teachers. Startled by the Mexican move, the board conceded that the conditions of the Mexican school left much to be desired, assured the committee that they would be improved to a level equal to the white schools, said that it would do everything to acquire the male instructors, but absolutely refused to consider a policy of integration of whites and Mexicanos.[14] A few days later the board designated two male teachers to instruct at the Mexican school for the upcoming term.[15] They further issued orders for an immediate retaking of the census in the Mexican portion of the city.[16]

The committee found the proposals unsatisfactory. A few days following the exchange, a large percentage of the Mexican population—some 200 to 300 men, women, and children—congregated at a local meeting hall, resolving themselves to accomplishing their goals at any cost. Florentino Muñoz, a local barkeeper harboring Masonic interests, led the many heated speeches that expressed confidence in the law and optimism that they would secure their rights. Muñoz elaborated to the local press:

> Under the system which now prevails, the Mexican children are learning nothing—they have never learned anything, and we are simply seeking our just rights. We have the right to put our children in the white schools and we are going to do it, if we have to go to the highest authorities in the state.
>
> No, we will not accept the proposition of the school board, which is to give us a school north of the railroad and south of the river. This is not satisfactory to us. We want to send them from the school districts in which they live to the schools of that district. We repudiate the school board's offer and demand our rights.

The Reverend Alfred R. Penn; Francisco Aguilera, a tailor; José Luna, a barber; Carlos Rodríguez, another saloonkeeper; Dionicio Ramírez, a water hauler; José Flores, a furniture store employee; F. Arizpe; and B. R. Pérez, composing the remainder of the committee, shared the convictions of the leader.[17]

Upon hearing of the meeting, Sam Crowther, an English immigrant who had gained prominence in several capacities and now served as president of the school board, reiterated the trustees' stand that Chicanitos would be refused enrollment in the white schools and that their entrance "would be demoralizing to our school system." He continued:

> We have offered the Mexicans just as good school facilities as the white children. We are willing to give them everything they are entitled to. But the proposition of intermingling the whites and Mexicans would be a terrific blow to our school system and create a world of discord.
>
> The school board holds a meeting Tuesday night and we will endeavor to make terms that will satisfy the Mexicans but we do not intend to yield them this point.[18]

The white sector backed him. Mayor Joe D. Hassell, arguing that integration "would be absolutely a lightning stroke to our school system as it stands and demoralize it altogether," aligned himself strongly with the board.[19] The Central Labor Union, comprised of members from local trades, similarly promulgated a message of approval supporting the board, as it believed "that the Mexican children would be imposed upon the larger children and that would make unfriendly feelings, and we want harmony all the way round."[20] Citizens talked of endorsing the trustees' action through a public statement and of employing "stringent methods" should Mexicanos persist.[21]

The school board establishment sought compromise. They talked of a peaceable solution to the problem confronting them without retreating from their stand to prevent the Mexican children from entering the white school. Crowther, speaking for the board, stated:

> We are prepared to give the Mexicans a square deal but we will not think for one moment of admitting them into the white schools and thus demoralize our entire school system. It won't do and it shall not be done.

But the Mexicans in turn refused to retreat, threatening a legal fight. Notifying the board through their attorneys that the separate but equal policy was unacceptable, they resolved to carry the case to the highest state courts.[22] Still, in a unanimous decision, the board voted, in late June, to disregard the demands of the Chicano community and decided upon further plans for establishing the separate school for the "foreign class" with all possible educational advantages incorporated. It still proposed to have the Mexicans attend one or more of the old ward school buildings.[23]

But the issue remained. The Mexicans insisted that even better facilities would not provide the advantages of integration into the white schools. They continued agitating for what they declared to be their rights under the laws of the state. In response, whites pressured Crowther to call for a mass meeting and solve the dilemma once and for all.[24] "If you are interested in the welfare of San Angelo and its peerless educational facilities," editorialized the local paper, "you are urged to come out to the meeting Friday night and lend your aid in solving the difficult problem."[25] This mass meeting, by which whites hoped to arrive at a permanent solution, was postponed and never held.[26]

As school opening approached, whites maintained their position and went about their business of preparing the separate facilities for the Mexican children. On September 9, the board delineated the boundaries. Chicanitos were to attend two "Mexican schools" provided for them. Those living south of Beauregard Avenue were to attend a building in Fort Concho addition located near the Orient depot, and those living north of the line were to attend a frame structure in North Angelo located at the corner of Ninth and Randolph Streets, only a couple of blocks from the "Negro school."[27] Two male instructors were assigned to the task of teaching them.[28]

But the Mexican community stood its ground when the doors opened on September 19, 1910. Only two pupils appeared at the separate schools while seven Chicanitos appeared at the North Ward white school only to face expulsion. At this point the school board issued orders to the school system to block the entry of Mexican children, repeating its opinion that "to admit the Mexicans into white schools would be to demoralize the entire system and they will not under any pressure consider such a thing." In the meantime, the Mexicans conferred with Crowther hoping to change the board's mind.[29]

Faced with a stalemate, the Mexican community now sought the advice and assistance of the Mexican government. Muñoz, still the leader, announced confidently that

> we think we are in the right and are going to stand up for entrance into the white schools. We hope to have some encouraging information from the consul right away and we are going to do nothing until he is heard from. The consul is a man of influence and what we need is influence to carry our point.

Muñoz once more expressed his people's determination that if they could not send their children to the white schools, they wanted no school at all.

> We don't intend to do anything contrary to law and order. We don't intend to create a disturbance. Mr. Crowther and the school board have said "No." Maybe we can carry it over their "No." However, unless there is an unexpected weakening somewhere, we will not send our children to the separate schools. It doesn't benefit them any.

The whites also kept their stand.[30]

The confrontation at this point developed into speculation as to the role of the Mexican consul in the affairs of the city's Mexican community. Whites argued that they could not profit from an appeal to the consul, as, by Muñoz's own admission, all the committee members were legalized Texas voters and bona fide American citizens, circumstances that eliminated the interference of the Mexican government on their behalf. Whatever action to be taken under those conditions, they argued, would have to be done through the normal legal American channels such as appealing to the higher board of education in the state. Anglos argued further that according to legal opinions received, Mexicans had no right to complain so long as they were given equal school facilities with the whites, and in order to gain entrance into the white schools the Mexicans would have to prove that they were deprived of equal treatment.

On the other hand, the stand taken by the Mexican consul, Enrique Ornelas, in an interview with the San Antonio *Express*, greatly encouraged the Mexicans. The consul reported that he had taken the question up with Governor Thomas Campbell, with the Mexican government, and had communicated with President Taft. He further elaborated that so far as he was concerned, the San Angelo school board was in the wrong. Mexicans were committed to an equal burden of taxation along with whites, yet were deprived of equal facilities accruing to white children. The consul further elaborated as far as he knew, the Mexican community was law abiding, taxpaying, and respectable citizens who wanted nothing more than the equality they deserved. Once shown by law, precedent, and custom that they were in the wrong, Ornelas ended optimistically, the whites would recede from their position. Muñoz, in the meantime, admitted that he had erred in stating that all of the committee members were American citizens, that further investigation had revealed that at least some were Mexican nationals. He remained confident that the consul would be of help.[31]

The local press at this time commenced editorializing that internal dissension existed among the boycotters. It depicted a struggle between the rank and file and committee members, especially with the chairman, Muñoz. Citing an "authoritative source," the paper reported some 50 to 75 percent of the Mexican population ready to accede to the proffers of the school board and to the separate schools. The only obstacle to a solution, it elaborated, was the committee's ban, still declaring "White Schools or Nothing."[32]

The *Standard* also printed rumors of several prominent Mexican citizens equipping their children to attend the separate schools. It reported "one of the most influential Mexicans of the city" ready to buy books for some of the students and aid in breaking up the round of dissension. The paper quoted the source as saying:

> It is my opinion that the separate schools are best for the Mexicans and best for the whites. I think that if the children were allowed to intermingle

> there would be a constant strife and little good could accrue to either. You can't place the children of two nations in school together and keep down the trouble.
>
> The committee does not represent the Mexicans of San Angelo and only thinks it represents them. I want to see this trouble over with and so do some of the best and most influential Mexican citizens of San Angelo, and to that end I am going to gather up a squad of the youngsters, purchase books for them, and take them to schools set aside for them.
>
> I think Mr. Crowther and the school board have acted for the best. The Mexicans admire them for the firm stand they have taken to this matter and I think they will have little more trouble with the school situation.
>
> I am a Mexican by blood, but by birth I am an American, and I want to see things peaceful in San Angelo.[33]

The paper reported, however, that the committee still maintained that it and not others voiced the will of the Mexican population and that its opinion was unalterable.[34]

Notwithstanding the views of the press (and that "prominent citizen"), the committee had its way. Through persuasion, cajolement, or intimidation, the paper conjectured, Muñoz's committee had dominated and prevented the more moderate Mexicans from their plans to send the children to the separate schools. In the meantime, whites in the community denounced the committee as trying to override the will of their fellow countrymen, resolving to block the issue of integration "body and soul."[35] A week-and-a-half after the opening date of enrollment, the trustees decided to assign the teachers of the Mexican schools work in the white classrooms as no Mexican children had entered the separate facilities.[36] Aid from the consul never arrived.[37]

The boycott lasted throughout the 1910 school year with no Mexican children attending the separate school.[38] Many parents sent their children to Immaculate Conception Academy, the local Catholic school, but no records exist indicating what percentage stayed out completely. While allowing their attendance gratis, the policy at the academy also kept Mexicans from equal status interaction with whites by isolating them in "Mexican rooms" with a separate teacher provided. The boycotters' request for integration was turned down. Seemingly, the white Catholic membership was influential enough to thwart any similar ambitions Mexicans might have contemplated about imposing integration on that learning institution.[39]

At the beginning of the 1911 school term, the same segregated system awaited the Mexican youths. Despite renewed appeals for integration from the Mexican community, the board directed them to go to the one "Mexican school" south of the river, where enrollment passed uneventfully. Whites failed to take note of the space in the local paper reporting the denunciation of educational discrimination at the proceedings of the Primer Congreso Mexicanista in Laredo. Seven children showed up at the separate school in September of that year.[40]

Discontent continued. Enrollment in the "Mexican school" seemed to have approximated the preboycott enlistment in the following two years.[41] But defiance surfaced in 1913 and 1914. Attendance declined conspicuously in the segregated school in those years with no students attending in 1914–15. The local press gave no indication as to reasons and the official minutes of the school board reveal no motives, but it was obvious that the decline was related to the alternative provided when the Mexican Presbyterian Mission School opened for classes late in 1912.[42]

The Presbyterian Church, USA, having initiated efforts to evangelize Mexicans in Texas in 1908, decided to supplement its program with educational work. In San Angelo it had seen the school issue creating the potential for success and by November 1912 had plunged into the task of providing educational and religious privileges for all Mexicans in the city. The Mexican Presbyterian Mission school accepted students from six to eighteen years and instructed them in reading and writing in English and Spanish, arithmetic, geography, and physiology. It was an immediate success, and more students were attending it by 1913–14 than had ever attended the public school in any previous year. Some seventy-five students enrolled that term, an equal number attending it for 1914–15, when no students went to the public school.[43] The school continued to thrive in subsequent years, even as enrollment in the segregated school "south of the river" began picking up after 1915.[44]

Within a matter of years, then, things returned to the pre-1910 status quo. Whites remained indifferent to the wishes of the Chicano community and little accrued to Mexicans from their act of boldness. Several things had obstructed success. First, the mobilization, which developed spontaneously around the school issue, lost its fervor once the protestors realized the perseverance required for altering a tradition deeply rooted in the mind of the white community. Second, as a minority in the state without political "power capability," Mexicanos simply did not have the necessary strength at their disposal to extract from whites the changes they demanded. Third, concerning the commitment to "White Schools or Nothing," at least some sentiment of division prevailed. Militant action failed to follow the militancy espoused by the committee and its staunch supporters; indeed, the boycotters decided to send their children to the Catholic school where segregation thrived in a different form. Fourth, other forces subsequently drew away the leaders from the interest of the Mexican community. Those who knew them in later years remember some of them as businessmen virtually dependent on white patrons for their livelihood, a reality that certainly caused moderation.[45] And last, the demands, however much in keeping they were with American laws, remained out of place in a time when racial attitudes dictated that people of color keep to their place.

Still, the historical setting provides the blowout with its magnificence. A community rallied to attack a tradition profoundly ingrained in West Texas psychology. Refusing to resign themselves to continued injustice, the boycotters came together to dramatize glaring discrimination and attempted to help themselves despite adversity. The collective dissatisfaction with the public schools accounted for the extended success of the Mexican Presbyterian Mission School, and the continued attendance there suggests a concern among heads of families for first-rate educational benefits for their children.

Also, the blowout was one of many expressions by Chicanos publicizing the educational inequities of that time. Laredo's *La Crónica*, which noticed the San Angelo movement in June 1910, printed a series of articles later in the year calling attention to the educational exclusion of Mexican children in the state. Its fervent agitation led directly to a look into the matter by the Mexican government, albeit an artificial and inadequate one.

Finally, the protest exemplified the audacity of the Mexicans in an era when the wrath of whites almost automatically neutralized any impudence among racial minorities. No help could be expected from the outside. The Mexican government could not help. There existed no government agency to enforce desegregation, to ensure quality education, or to guarantee the rights promised by the Treaty of Guadalupe Hidalgo. A powerless people, and surely cognizant of that, Mexicanos appealed to the sensibilities of whites. It had to be done despite the odds if the Chicano community was to maintain any semblance of cultural autonomy and survival.

Notes

1. George I. Sánchez, *Concerning Segregation of Spanish-Speaking Children in the Public Schools*, Inter-American Education Occasional Papers 9 (Austin: University of Texas, 1951), 16–22; E. E. Davis, *A Report on Illiteracy in Texas*, University of Texas Bulletin No. 2328 (Austin: University of Texas, 1923), 30–31; Herschel T. Manuel, *Spanish-Speaking Children of the Southwest* (Austin: University of Texas, 1965), 135–37; Manuel, *The Education of Mexican and Spanish-Speaking Children in Texas* (Austin: University of Texas, 1930), 58–59; Thomas P. Carter, *Mexican Americans in*

School: A History of Educational Neglect (New York: College Entrance Examination Board, 1970), 67–130; Paul S. Taylor, *An American-Mexican Frontier: Nueces County, Texas* (Chapel Hill: University of North Carolina Press, 1934), 191–214; Arthur Rubel, *Across the Tracks: Mexican Americans in a Texas City* (Austin: University of Texas Press, 1966), 43–44; Everett Ross Clinchy Jr., *Equality of Opportunity for Latin Americans in Texas* (New York: Arno Press, 1974), 115–39; and, Guadalupe Salinas, "Mexican Americans and the Desegregation of Schools in the Southwest," *El Grito* 4 (Summer 1971). See also the fine study of José Limón, "El Primer Congreso Mexicanista de 1911: A Precursor to Contemporary Chicanismo," *Aztlán: Chicano Journal of the Social Sciences and the Arts* 5 (Spring and Fall 1974): 85–117.

2. *La Crónica*, Laredo, Texas, December 17, 1910, 1 and 3; December 31, 1910, 1; January 12, 1911. See especially the important issue of February 9, 1911, 1, where Mexicans wrote letters to the editor documenting the extent of racial separation in their respective towns. See further, Manuel, *Spanish-Speaking Children of the Southwest*, 135; Carter, *Mexican Americans in School*, 67–69; Davis, *A Report on Illiteracy in Texas*, 33; Sánchez, *Concerning the Segregation of Spanish-Speaking Children in the Public Schools*, 23–39.

3. Mexican Americans composed approximately 10 percent of San Angelo's 10,321 population in 1910 according to compilations from the *Thirteenth Census of the United States Taken in the Year 1910*, 3 vols. (Washington, DC: Government Printing Office, 1913), 3: 793, 846; and, according to estimates in B. A. Hodges, *A History of the Mexican Mission Work Conducted by the Presbyterian Church in the United States of America in the Synod of Texas* (Waxahachie: Woman's Synodical of Texas, 1931), 5, as reprinted in Carlos Cortes et al., *Church Views of the Mexican American* (New York: Arno Press, 1974).

4. San Angelo *Standard*, September 21, 1889, 1; September 28, 1889, 2; October 12, 1889, 2; October 19, 1889, 2. Nicolás Flores, an eighty-year-old resident of San Angelo, recalls with lucidity the intensity of racial feelings in the 1910s. From an interview with Nicolás Flores, San Angelo, Texas, April 16, 1975 (hereinafter referred to as an interview with Nicolás Flores, April 16, 1975).

5. San Angelo *Standard*, January 17, 1903, 1; February 7, 1903, 6; February 28, 1903, 3; March 21, 1903, 8; May 9, 1903, 6; May 16, 1903, 7; June 6, 1903, p. 6; June 20, 1903, 2; July 4, 1903 6; September 5, 1903, 6, September 26, 1903, 6; *Official Minutes Records of City Commission Book, 1903–1907*, vol. 5 (Office of City Secretary, City Hall, San Angelo, Texas), 14–15; *Thirteenth Census of the United States*, III, 793. See further, Grace Bitner, "The History of Tom Green County, Texas" (master's thesis, University of Texas, 1931), 77–81; E. L. Nunnally, "The San Angelo School System," *Texas Outlook* (May 1929): 21; and the brief review of San Angelo school history by the superintendent of schools, Felix E. Smith, in San Angelo *Standard*, December 7, 1913, 10.

6. See the Public School Reports as announced monthly in the San Angelo *Standard*: September 9, 1905, 8; October 7, 1905, 10; November 4, 1905, 4 ; January 13, 1906, 9; February 10, 1906, 9; April 7, 1906, 4; May 5, 1906, 5; October 21, 1909, 1; November 18, 1909, 3; December 16, 1909, 8; January 20, 1910, 2; February 20, 1910, 12; March 18, 1910, 4; April 14, 1910, 1; June 17, 1910, 1. The *Standard* for the period May 27, 1906, to August 31, 1909, is not available.

7. See, for example, the paternalism revealed by the trade members of the Central Labor Union, who, during the heat of the blowout, resolved that despite the fact that Mexicans were an imposition on "us," they still did not "lose sight of their welfare." San Angelo *Standard*, July 27, 1910, 1; May 16, 1910, 2.

8. San Angelo *Standard*, May 9, 1903, 6; September 26, 1903, 6; and, *Worley's Directory of San Angelo, 1911* (compiled and published by John Worley Directory Co., Dallas, Texas, 1911), 25.

9. See obvious examples where Mexicanos did seem to be outside the interests of those associated with the schools in San Angelo *Standard*, December 21, 1910, 1.; December 23, 1910, 4; January 14, 1911, 1; January 19, 1911, 8; January 27, 1911, 8; March 22, 1911, 5; February 6, 1911, 6; December 7, 1913, 10; May 8, 1914, 2; March 24, 1914, 1. Superintendent Felix Smith's recommendation for school improvements, printed in the September 12, 1915, 2, edition of the *Standard*, followed a similar vein. While briefly addressing himself to the curriculum of the "Negro school," suggesting a change of emphasis from "the study of Latin, history, and math," to "work having a direct bear-

ing on the lives of the pupils of the community," he made no mention of the Mexican students who were boycotting the system that year. See for the same thing, the *Official Minutes of the School Board*, vol. 1, located at the school vault, in the San Angelo School Administration Building. Note as well *La Crónica*, January 12, 1911, 1; and more importantly, see the discussions and elucidations that took place during the 1910 Annual Meeting of the State Teachers Association, attended incidentally, by San Angelo personnel, reported in the Abilene *Daily Reporter*, December 28, 1910. Nicolás Flores concurred that such was the case. Interview with Nicolás Flores, April 16, 1975.

The failure to establish a system of education was one of the indictments against the Mexican government in the Declaration of Independence of March 2, 1836. Manuel, *The Education of Mexican and Spanish-Speaking Children in Texas*, 56.

10. The census, taken in March of every year, disclosed about 200 Mexican children of school age in 1910. Reported in San Angelo *Standard*, June 15, 1910, 1. See also Manuel, *Education of Spanish-Speaking Children in Texas*, 39.

11. San Angelo *Standard*, June 8, 1910, 1; June 15, 1910, 1; April 18, 1910, 4; September 15, 1910, 1; and September 16, 1910, 5.

12. Hodges, *A History of the Mexican Mission Work*, 5, reprinted in Cortes et al., *Church Views of the Mexican American*. Also, San Angelo *Standard*, April 23, 1910, 5; April 29, 1910, 2.

San Angelo had seven schools in 1910: one high school with an approximate enrollment of 390 students; four ward schools: the East Ward (San Jacinto) school with approximately 370 students; Fort Concho school with approximately 245 students; Harris Avenue school with approximately 340 students; the North Ward (Reagan) school with approximately 375 students; a Mexican school with 45 students; and, a Negro school with approximately 114 students. See *Worley, 1910*, 42–43, and the *Minutes of the School Board*, vol. 1. The estimated enrollment is taken from the June, 1910, Public School System Report.

The reports show an increase in attendance in each school over the nine-month period. See San Angelo *Standard*, October 21, 1909, 1; November 18, 1909, 3; December 16, 1909, 8; January 20, 1910, 2; February 20, 1910, 2; March 18, 1910, 4; April 14, 1910, 1; June 17, 1910, 1. The above figures, according to the June 1910, report, comprised 93 percent of the city's scholastic population.

The scholastic population computed in March of every year was about 2,058 for 1910, including about 200 Mexicans, and 119 Negroes of school age. San Angelo *Standard*, May 25, 1910, 1; June 3, 1910, 1; June 15, 1910, 1; May 5, 1911, 5. In 1909, the school census showed about 1,835 of school age; in 1911, the scholastic population was about 1,819; in 1912, about 1891; and in 1913, about 1,968. San Angelo *Standard*, May 25, 1910, 1; June 26, 1912, 1; August 14, 1913, 1.

13. San Angelo *Standard*, April 16, 1910, 1; April 18, 1910, 4; April 30, 1910, 3; May 7, 1910, 1; May 25, 1910, 1; June 3, 1910, 1; June 8, 1910, 1.

14. Ibid., June 8, 1910, 1; June 21, 1910, 1; interview with Nicolás Flores, April 16, 1975; and, Hodges, *A History of the Mexican Mission Work*, 5, reprinted in Cortes et al., *Church Views of the Mexican American*. The San Angelo Public School holds no record dealing with the boycott. The earliest school board records start with May 26, 1914. Further, no one associated with the schools has any knowledge of the event. The Tom Green County Library, the Texas State Archives, and the Research Department of the Texas Department of Education Agency, have no record of the incident. (Based on letters in the author's possession, from personal visits to the several record-holding agencies, and interviews with members of the San Angelo School Administration.)

15. San Angelo *Standard*, June 18, 1910, 1.

16. Ibid., June 15, 1910, 1. A recount was necessary, the Mexicans felt, because they were not receiving their share of the apportionment. Under the Texas Constitution of 1876, the available school fund provided by the state was to be distributed to the several counties according to the population of youths of school age between seven and seventeen. Apportionment was based not on the actual number that attended school, but on the number of children of school age. The funds accruing to the schools on this basis were then disbursed by the local board of trustees, who discriminately spent the money on the maintenance of the white schools. Manuel, *Educa-*

tion of Spanish-Speaking Children in Texas, 56–58; Davis, *Illiteracy in Texas*, 33–34; Taylor, *An American-Mexican Frontier*, 200. While Mexicanos would acknowledge that not all Chicanitos in the census attended school, they complained that they still did not get the full benefit coming to them, seemingly, not even a quantity proportionate to the number attending. Being taxpayers, they protested, and contributing to the state school fund, the board was responsible for providing education for their children commensurate with the census count, just as it did for white children. San Angelo *Standard*, September 23, 1910, 1; Nicolás Flores interview, April 16, 1975; and *La Crónica*, December 24, 1910, 1. Texas later shifted to the "average daily attendance" method as a basis of financial support.

17. San Angelo *Standard*, June 20, 1910, 1, and the communication sent by the San Angelo correspondent to *La Crónica* in June 25, 1910, and reported in *La Crónica*, December 31, 1910, 1. See further, *Worley, 1910*, 230, and San Angelo *Standard*, November 23, 1913, 6, for information on Muñoz; the other committee members have been identified from *Worley, 1911*, and the one for 1912. Additional information on José Luna is provided by the *Standard*, July 3, 1914, 3. Also helpful in identifying the committee members have been interviews with Mr. José Flores Jr., son of José Flores, April 10, 1975; Mrs. Emma Boisse, stepdaughter of Florentino Muñoz, February 4, 1975; Mr. and Mrs. Inez Samarrón, old San Angelo residents, April 10, 1975; and, Nicolás Flores interview, April 16, 1975.

18. San Angelo *Standard*, June 20, 1910, 1; October 12, 1910, 5.

19. Ibid., June 21, 1910, 1. Crowther and Hassell did not elaborate their reasons for opposing integration.

20. Ibid., July 27, 1910, 1; May 16, 1910, 2.

21. Ibid., June 21, 1910, 1.

22. Ibid., June 21, 1910, 1. Research in the County and District Court records of Tom Green County fail to reveal that the case ever went to court. Also, interview with Nicolás Flores, April 16, 1975.

23. San Angelo *Standard*, June 22, 1910, 1.

24. Ibid., July 26, 1910, 1.

25. Ibid., July 27, 1910, 1.

26. Ibid., July 26, 1910, 1; July 29, 1910, 1.

27. Ibid., September 12, 1910, 2; July 20, 1911, 21; July 30, 1911, 8.

28. Ibid., September 18, 1910, 7.

29. Ibid., September 20, 1910, 1; September 21, 1910, 1. Interview with Nicolás Flores, April 16, 1975.

30. San Angelo *Standard*, September 21, 1910, 1.

31. Ibid., September 23, 1910, 1; September 24, 1910, 1; September 26, 1910, 1. See also the San Antonio *Express*, September 22, 1910, 9. Research in the Campbell Papers at the Texas State Archives, Austin, Texas, the Taft Papers, and communications with Don Ramón Meade, the Mexican consul at San Antonio, and with the Secretaría de Relaciones Exteriores in Mexico City, have failed to produce Ornelas's communiqués.

32. San Angelo *Standard*, September 23, 1910, 1; September 24, 1910, 1.

33. Ibid., September 25, 1910, 1.

34. Ibid., September 26, 1910, 1.

35. Ibid.

36. Ibid., September 29, 1910, 1.

37. Ibid., September 22, 1910, 1; September 26, 1910, 1.

38. Ibid., July 20, 1911, 2; September 17, 1911, 1. See also the Public School System Reports for that year in ibid., November 11, 1910, 1; December 8, 1910, p. 1; January 20, 1911, 1; February 16, 1911, 1; March 16, 1911, 1; April 8, 1911, 1; May 6, 1911, 1. Also the number enumerated in the census declined to 163, perhaps because Mexicanos again held back the names of eligible children as a form of protest. Ibid., June 26, 1912, 1.

In Gonzales, where a similar case of exclusion and inefficiency prevailed, one family contemplated moving to neighboring Wilson County where reportedly Mexicanos could attend the white schools. Apparently, Chicanos there did not go the route of the boycott. *La Crónica*, January 12, 1911, 1.

39. San Angelo *Standard*, September 22, 1910, 1. According to school authorities, the records maintained on attendance at Sacred Heart Cathedral school (Immaculate Conception Academy in 1910), date back only to the mid-1920s. Nicolás Flores, who attended the school about that time, notes that Immaculate Conception Academy was the only school in the city that allowed Mexicans into the program, but practiced the abovementioned policy of room segregation. Interview with Nicolás Flores, April 16, 1975. Also, Hodges, *A History of the Mexican Mission Work*, 5, in Cortes et al., *Church Views of the Mexican American.*

40. San Angelo *Standard*, September 17, 1911, 1; September 17, 1911, 4; September 19, 1911, 1; September 19, 1911, 2. Limón, "El Primer Congreso Mexicanista."

41. See the Public School System Reports in San Angelo *Standard*, October 19, 1911, 4; November 16, 1911, 5; December 17, 1911, 8; January 19, 1912, 4; February 18, 1912, 4; October 22, 1912, 1; November 22, 1912, 1; December 20, 1912, 1; February 20, 1913, 1; March 20, 1913, 1. Also, the scholastic census seemed to have declined about 19 from 1911, as only 144 were enumerated. Again, Mexicans may have held back names as in 1910, when the census takers enumerated close to 200. Ibid., June 26, 1912, 1.

42. Ibid., September 23, 1913, 1; October 16, 1914, 4. See further the Public School System Reports in the *Standard*, September 16, 1913, 1; October 8, 1913, 1; December 3, 1913, 1; January 15, 1914, 2; May 11, 1914, 2; September 23, 1914, 6; October 11, 1914, 12; November 10, 1914, 6; December 2, 1914, p. 4; January 14, 1915, 2; February 12, 1915, 3; March 12, 1915, 3; May 11, 1915, 3. The scholastic population declined further when the census was taken in 1915. It may have been that Mexicans saw no need to claim themselves now that they attended the Presbyterian Mission School anyway. Ibid., April 12, 1916, 1. Also, Hodges, *A History of the Mexican Mission Work*, 5, in Cortes et al., *Church Views of the Mexican American.*

43. San Angelo *Standard*, October 16, 1914, 4; September 22, 1915, p. 1; December 8, 1915, 6; September 19, 1916, 1; December 27, 1916, 1; December 24, 1917, p. 1; September 12, 1918, 4. Mrs. Jennie Suter directed the school with help from the Reverend Narciso Lafuerza, who served as pastor of the Mexican Presbyterian Church founded in 1915. Hodges, *A History of the Mexican Mission Work*, 4–11, in Cortes et al., *Church Views of the Mexican American*; and *Worley, 1915–1916*, 35. For the religious implications of this, see the incisive conclusion of José Roberto Juárez, "La Iglesia Católica y el Chicano en Sud Texas, 1836–1911," *Aztlán: Chicano Journal of the Social Sciences and the Arts* 4 (Fall 1973): 217–55.

44. See the Public School Reports in the San Angelo *Standard*, September 20, 1915, 1; October 14, 1915, 4; November 9, 1915, 1; December 10, 1915, 8; January 20, 1916, 2; February 17, 1916, p. 3; March 16, 1916, 3; April 12, 1916, 1; September 28, 1916, 1; January 12, 1917, 2; April 12, 1917, 1; September 18, 1917, 1; November 22, 1917, p. 2; January 9, 1918, 1; March 8, 1918, 6; September 15, 1918, 10; November 15, 1918, 2. According to eighty-year-old Juan Nava, long associated with the Mexican Presbyterian Church, the school instructed many a Catholic Mexican American in San Angelo. Interview with Juan Nava, April 18, 1975.

45. The above conclusions borrow from the insights developed by Armando Navarro, "The Evolution of Chicano Politics"; Carlos Muñoz Jr., "The Politics of Protest and Chicano Liberation: A Case Study of Repression and Cooptation," both in *Aztlán: Chicano Journal of the Social Science and the Arts* 5 (Spring and Fall 1974); Miguel Tirado, "Mexican American Political Organizations: The Key to Chicano Political Power," *Aztlán* 1 (Spring 1970); and Mario Barrera, Carlos Muñoz, and Charles Ornelas, "The Barrio as an Internal Colony," in *People and Politics in Urban Society*, ed. Harlan Hahn (Beverly Hills, CA: Sage Publications, 1972).

8

Los Tasinques and the Sheep Shearers' Union of North America

A Strike in West Texas, 1934

Strikes in ranches throughout the US West during the first half of the twentieth century seldom broke out, except ones led by the Sheep Shearers' Union of North America. In 1934, dissatisfied tasinques *(sheepshearers) in the West Texas area that encompassed San Angelo, Sonora, Ozona, and Del Rio sought the help of the Sheep Shearers' Union in their protest against poor wages and an unfair shearing contractor system. Their subsequent strike, which lasted throughout the spring of 1934, did not bear fruit, as the Mexican American tasinques could not fend off combined opposition from ranchers, police authorities, and nonunion shearers (scabs).*

In the latter decades of the nineteenth century, Mexican nationals arrived in the Concho Valley searching for work on the emerging Anglo-American ranches and farms. When a Tennessee journalist passed through San Angelo in 1889, he observed that the main laboring element in the region consisted of Mexicans, a people whom he described as a "race of mongrels, chiefly Aztec, with a sprinkle of Spanish and Negro." Mexicans tended the herds of sheep, cattle, and horses of the ranchers of West Texas, he noted, "but it is as herders that they are mostly employed. One Mexican fitted out with a small sack of flour, a 'hunk' of bacon and a keg of water will tend 2,000 to 2,500 sheep on the plateau prairies, alone, throughout the year."[1] In that early period, Anglos of the Concho Valley had come to regard the Mexican population as a class meant to perform menial labor. In an area where the ranches and land belonged to Anglos, where well-established Mexican American families did not own land or maintain a sociopolitical tradition (as compared to the older border cities of Brownsville, Laredo, El Paso, and others), and where the incoming Mexicans displayed perceptible Indian and Negro characteristics, Anglos naturally perceived *Mexicanos* in a condescending and even paternalistic manner.

This chapter was originally published in the *West Texas Historical Association Yearbook* 55 (1979): 3–16.

Quite naturally, Mexicans came to do the sheep-shearing as the Concho Valley blossomed into wool country, and San Angelo itself earned the sobriquet of "Wool Capital of the World." Gradually through these decades, a labor tradition evolved: hired white managers supervised the shearers working at unskilled ranch jobs while owners, living in nearby towns and cities, concerned themselves with commercial and financial arrangements with banks, loan companies, wool buyers or brokers, and wool and mohair warehouse companies. At the appropriate shearing time, these absentee owners turned to their Mexican hands for assistance in harvesting the wool crop. Through time, a labor connection unfolded in which ranchers could count on a ready supply of cheap labor at the right time. Attitudes of race and class permeated such a pattern.[2]

As men involved in large-scale, highly centralized enterprises designed to render sizable profits, Anglo sheep men attempted, like entrepreneurs elsewhere, to reduce costs by paying the shearers low wages. In the Concho Valley and other parts of West Texas, ranchers, bankers, loan company officials, the executive committee of the Sheep and Goat Raisers' Association (an organization advertising itself as one designed to gather and disseminate ideas about the sheep and goat industry), and members of the Texas Wool and Mohair Warehouse Association could meet informally, or convene in case of an emergency, and set the price of the shearing and tagging of sheep and goats.[3] Such "wage fixing" worked because of the pervasiveness of a cheap labor force (wage rates for sheepshearers and working conditions in Texas compared unfavorably with those in Wyoming, California, and Montana); because of the relative stability of that pool (management did not worry about the movement of wage laborers to areas with higher wage scales); and because Anglos attributed a different living standard and lifestyle to *Mexicanos.* As one Anglo put it, 90 percent of the shearers gambled away their earnings each night around the camps anyway.[4] Furthermore, a sense of paternalism governed the wage scale. According to the ranchers, they had taken care of their Mexican hands during sickness and health, in good and bad times, and had educated the Mexican children.[5] But the low wages did not fail to impress upon the *tasinques* (sheepshearers) the idea that they were an oppressed proletariat. Soon the rumblings of dissatisfaction expressed themselves in grievances against an entrepreneurial class that shearers identified as responsible for determining their living conditions and standards.

Aside from low wages, the *tasinques* disliked the system of working under shearing contractors, or *capitanes* (captains). According to the prevailing relationship, ranchers entered into contracts with captains responsible for furnishing the shearing machinery and accessory equipment, and the captain in turn paid the *tasinques* half of what he received from the owner for each animal shorn. Also, captains provided the men with transportation, board, and lodging. But according to the shearers, at times they did not get half of their earned wages and the food seemed invariably poor. Further, the captains carried no insurance for the protection of their employees. All of this only exacerbated already oppressive conditions, for the *capitanes*, like the ranchers, sought to augment their own income by discriminating against their own people.[6] The captains, on the other hand, argued that they traditionally advanced $50 to $400 to a shearer at the beginning of every year, and that once work began, they risked the possibility that the shearer might not work. They also pointed out that they bore the responsibility of finding work for the shearers and provided them with the needed equipment for shearing.[7]

In view of their grievances, the *tasinques* in the Concho Valley opted for unionization in 1934. In part, they had been inspired by the labor provisions of the New Deal's National Recovery Administration (NRA), which they thought extended to agricultural labor. Further, wages that fell behind the general price level grieved them. By late 1933, the wool industry had experienced the sharpest recovery ever in history, yet shearing wages remained stagnant and ranchers continued unresponsive to their needs. Sergio Gonzales Jr., a utility employee of Del Rio, Texas, had written to Montana for information on how to form a union, and from information received, he sought to emulate the Sheep Shearers' Union of North America, a union originally charted in Wyoming in 1912 and one that wished to expand into West Texas in 1933.[8] The organizers found legal assistance from Chicano attorneys in San Antonio as well as statewide support from the League of United Latin American Citizens (LULAC), an emerging civic organization in the early 1930s.[9] Thus, when the Butte, Montana–based Sheep Shearers' Union arrived in the Concho Valley in late 1933 seeking to organize the *tasinques*, many joined its ranks. Demanding recognition, the union, then 750 strong, called for a wage of six cents a head per sheep sheared, four cents per goat, and two cents for tagging, prices they felt were reasonable based upon the 100 to 150 sheep that good shearers could turn out daily. It also called for reforms in the *capitán-tasinque* system.[10]

The ranchers, however, balked at the demands. At meetings at Sonora (Sutton County) on January 4, 1934, in response to the sheepshearers' demands, ranchmen owning property in twenty-five West Texas counties and officials for wool and mohair warehouses established a maximum of eight cents a head for shearing sheep, five cents for goats, and two cents for tagging. Fearing the prospects of having to pay twelve cents per sheep, eight cents per goats, and four cents for tagging in order to meet the shearers' demands, the ranchers refused to bow to the Mexicans by not recognizing the union. According to President T. A. Kincaid of the Sheep and Goat Raisers' Association, who chaired the meeting, "Mexicans are being urged along like a bunch of sheep led by a lead goat into a car." Organization, he said, was akin to disloyalty. Mexican children, after all, received a free education; Mexicans paid little, if any taxes, had equality of opportunity on public works, indeed, derived more from the New Deal's Civil Works Administration (CWA) than anybody else in the ranch country. Collusion between sheep raising and urban business and financial interests reflected itself in the motions and amendments of several rancher delegates who proposed allowing banks, loan companies, and warehouses to determine the shearing rates.[11]

In a prepared statement, José M. Rodríguez, representing the Shearers' Union in San Angelo, answered the ranchers. First, Rodríguez said, shearers had lost battles before, but this one they would win. Second, the differences between the shearers and ranchmen did not involve a race struggle, for the "union is an American organization with American ideals and principles. Most of its members are thorough Americans, even though they are of Mexican extraction." The ranchers had no basis for saying that the United States government had amply cared for the Mexicans, for those receiving educational and relief benefits were American citizens and therefore entitled to employment and help. "As Americans we were ready to answer the call of our country during the World War. We fought in defense of our flag, and as Americans we are ready to defend it against all enemies, at any time." Moreover, he emphasized, the union accepted, in fact invited, Anglos into its ranks. Third, the demand for six cents was justifiable. Sheep-shearing demanded skill, experience, care, and accuracy, and, now that wool commanded a better price in the market, needed wages for shearers that increased commensurately. "We don't ask for anything out of reason," he said. "We are just asking for a fair price in our trade. We are entitled to it and deserve it. Give us a chance to have better homes and become better citizens of our country." And, turning to the problem with the *capitanes*, he accused them of responsibility for breaking shearing prices. He reiterated the shearers' complaint that *tasinques* often failed to get their share of the price paid to the captain, that the food provided them hardly compensated for the low wages, and that, given the prevailing arrangement, the shearers seemingly sacrificed themselves to provide the captains with good homes, automobiles, and plenty of money. Further, as contractors, captains cared naught for workman's compensation principles.[12]

From Del Rio, where the movement shared similar vigor, Sergio Gonzales Jr., Texas president of the Shearers' Union, stressed the point that the captains, not the shearers, were calling for a price of twelve cents for sheep and eight cents for goats so as to divide the wages in half and continue the old practice. Actually, he said, the ranchers did not have to pay the high price in order to meet the shearers' demands of six cents per sheep and four cents for goats. Gonzales argued that the shearers only desired a fair share of what the captains made, that dividing wages in half discriminated against the *tasinques*.[13]

Meanwhile, encounters between the antagonists occurred. Talk of removing Mexican shearers who declined a fair wage from relief rolls commenced circulating. The ranchers spoke of buying their own shearing machines and operating the equipment themselves. During the second week of January, a rumor circulated that Ygnacio Andrade of Del Rio, an antiunion captain, had been shot (the reports proved false). The next week, a captain in Paint Rock reported threats that his shearing machine would be stopped forcibly by the union unless he employed union men. On January 24, Sonora held an examining trial for a score of Mexicans charged with unlawfully assembling to break up a crew of nonunion shearers tagging sheep at the Fred Simmons Ranch (nine miles northwest of town). They were remanded to jail until released on bond. At the same time, reports from Del Rio stated that shearers had threatened a captain to use union men only, and that his shearing machine would be followed, should he leave town.[14] On January 29, Dan Flores of San Angelo asked the sheriff for an escort to the Irion County line, fearing that the union would prevent his tagging crew from sojourning to ranches there.[15] But labor leaders in West Texas remained undaunted and continued holding mass meetings and urging *tasinques* to join the union.[16]

On January 25, Andrés Aguirre, a captain from Ozona who described himself as the largest machine operator in Texas, issued an invitation to the ranchers, to all the shearing captains, and to the shearers and their representatives to a meeting in Del Rio on February 1. Given the existence of the Sheep Shearers' Union, its difference both with the captains and the ranchers, he elaborated, it seemed the only way for all concerned to arrive at an ultimate agreement regarding the price to be paid the *tasinques*. However, the sheep men deigned not to attend the meeting held at San Felipe High School. Kincaid explained to the press that he had no authority to attend such a meeting unless requested to do so by at least ten members of the association he headed. But the sheepshearers had consummated an agreement with some forty-two captains from fifteen southwestern Texas counties to meet the shearers' demands for six cents for sheep and four cents for goats. The captains had settled for less than half the wages, as had been traditional, and had agreed to contract with the ranchers for ten cents for a sheep and six-and-a-half to seven cents for goats. Satisfied with the results, Sergio Gonzales Jr. of Del Rio affirmed: "Members of our organization will not hold poor workmanship or rough treatment of sheep or goats nor uphold members being discharged for rough treatment of the animals. This union does not approve of our members leaving work without due notice."[17] Crews reportedly set out to work around Del Rio soon thereafter for prices nearing those agreed upon at the February 1 meeting.[18]

Simultaneously, however, the union faced the power of ranchers who refused to countenance talk of bargaining. On February 9, Kincaid and ranchmen from San Angelo, Sonora, and other West Texas towns discussed the labor situation in Austin with the administrator of state relief, complaining that Mexican shearers threatened to quit their jobs and work for the CWA unless ranchers submitted to their demands. The ranchers also visited with Governor Miriam A. Ferguson and asked her aid in protecting nonunion shearers from assault in those sections. Kincaid called a meeting of his organization for February 14, at Sonora where members could talk over the matter with CWA supervisors from West Texas ranch counties.[19] Plainly, the ranchers were prepared to employ the power at their disposal to break the obstinacy they faced.

At the Sonora meeting, the executive committee of the Sheep and Goat Raisers' Association and the Texas Wool and Mohair Warehouse Association decided to send a delegation of forty-seven ranchers from forty-four West Texas counties to Austin on February 21, to appear before the Texas Relief Commission and seek its aid in the labor troubles. With reports coming from Del Rio that two shearing machines had been destroyed by fire, the ranchers' association also took measures to secure the services of Texas Rangers to patrol the sheep and goat country. The ranchmen had also provided several relief boards with the names of *tasinques* involved in work boycotts. The Sutton County relief board had already dropped some forty shearers from the relief rolls since February 1, including many who had not worked at shearing in several years. The pattern of turning in names and blacklisting those men from the relief programs spread into other areas. Expressing the views of the committee, Kincaid stated:

> We are a pretty poor bunch of white men if we are going to sit here and let a bunch of Mexicans tell us what to do. They have organized a bunch of foreigners that this country has taken care of. Nobody objects to a shearers' union. There are many things about their laws that are excellent, but there is not a single Mexican shearers' crew in the state which can or will qualify under the American Federation of Labor (A.F. of L.) rules for the shearers' union.[20]

On February 21, the ranchers met in Austin with members of the state legislature and with C. R. Braun, assistant administrator of State Relief. They told Braun that union shearers had been stopping and harassing nonunion crews while finding refuge on the relief rolls. Braun assured them that neither the state nor federal government had any intent to give relief to persons who could make a living, and that no relief would be extended to shearers or other seasonal laborers involved in the stay-aways. From Senator Walter C. Woodward of Coleman, Senator K. M. Regan of Pecos, and Representative Penrose B. Metcalfe of San Angelo, the ranchers received assurances that the congressmen would do all they could to aid the ranchers. The executive committee of the Sheep and Goat Raisers Association arranged to have two Rangers convey and escort nonunion shearing crews from Blanco, Lampasas, Burnet, and Bandera Counties into West Texas. The committee turned down an offer from the legislature to pay the Rangers' salaries, stating that association funds could be used for this purpose.[21]

Nevertheless, the cause of the union persisted. While the ranchers mobilized behind their interests, out-of-state organizers arrived in West Texas to assist the sheepshearers. On February 15, W. R. Williams, special organizer for the A.F. of L., and Nelson Wilber, vice president of the Sheep Shearers' Union of North America, spoke before some 400 shearers at Díaz Hall in Del Rio. The two men assured the *tasinques* that, as skilled workers, they had much to be proud of; that they should respect the law, not sabotage equipment or fight with sheep men; that the union intended to better their living conditions and would assist them in cases of mistreatment by ranchers or unjust entanglement with the law. Only through unionization, they emphasized, could conditions be improved. The union would negotiate with the ranchmen, and if an understanding proved elusive, the Federal Labor Board would dispatch someone to the area to settle the problem. The Sheep Shearers' Union, they added, was totally behind their cause.[22]

Two weeks later, 250 unioneers met in San Angelo, with José M. Rodríguez acting as chairman. Wilber, the guest speaker, repeated the message of the Del Rio gathering. While the Sheep and Goat Raisers Association had refused to answer the union telegrams asking for an opportunity to negotiate a settlement, he said, "If you will continue along the lines you have been and stay organized, you will be recognized by ranchmen of this state." As to the problem with the *capitanes*, the union sought to transplant to West Texas the system employed in the Rocky Mountain states where unions agreed with sheep men on wages, based upon the price of wool that season, and captains then agreed on what they wanted for the use of their machinery, grinding tools, and for tying and shearing goats and sheep at prices closely approximating those demanded by the union.[23]

Despite the shearers' confidence, the wool raisers had gotten the upper hand. Sheriffs in Western Texas now took it upon themselves to protect nonunion crews; ranchers employed extralegal vigilante methods against strikers; Anglo crews replaced Mexican ones; the Sheep and Goat Raisers Association readied to pay for the Texas Rangers should they be needed; and Kincaid emphasized that the shearing dispute had just been settled.[24] At a Sheep and Goat Raisers' meeting held in Sonora on March 8, Kincaid assured his organization that it had no authority to negotiate shearing contracts on behalf of the sheep men and goat men of Texas as the association represented only a small percentage of those in the industry. In response to the Sheep Shearers' Union letters speaking of labor's right to bargain collectively under the NRA, Kincaid countered that qualified authorities had advised him otherwise. Since agriculture did not fall under the provisions of the NRA and its codes, ranchmen need not deal with organized labor backed by the A.F. of L.[25] In parts of West Texas, some of the shearers had indeed given in and worked for wages more or less the same as those of the previous year.[26]

Pulling out his trump card, Wilber revealed to a newspaper reporter that the union had notified the National Labor Board and the A.F. of L. of the difficulties between the ranchers and shearers and asked them for assistance in securing the six cents a head wage scale advocated by the union. Now, he thought, both the NRA and the National Labor Board would send investigators to the area, and upon the basis of their reports, better wages would be paid. In the meantime, the union would keep up its campaign by picketing nonunion crews while respecting the rights of private property and attempting peacefully to persuade nonunion shearers to join their ranks. If the ranchmen did not grant the shearers' demands, he said, the stay-aways would escalate into a strike. In such event, the Sheep Shearers' Union of North America would provide some financial support and legal talent to represent the men.[27] Then, on March 13, six sheep-shearers walked off the Tom Henderson Ranch in Schleicher County in protest of the price agreed to by the captains. Newspapers reported it as the first strike of union shearers in Texas.[28]

As time passed, however, the struggle of the union and the Mexicans slowly withered. Sheriffs continued making arrests of picketers, the Sheep and Goat Raisers' Association refused to negotiate, ranchers imported crews from outside West Texas, and relief agencies clamped down on relief cases.[29] Yet while some shearers succumbed to the reality of having to work for a living, union organizers went on about the business of setting up district headquarters in San Angelo and holding weekly meetings, while some union members adamantly stayed away from work until they got their demands.[30] In early May, representatives of the union persuaded a crew working at a Tom Green County ranch not to work for the eight cents a head. Eldorado reported similar incidents. Picketing continued and threats of physical violence upon strikebreakers became commonplace.[31]

By May, it was evident that a strike would not succeed. More and more shearers returned to work at old wages, as government conciliators sent to settle the labor troubles gave the unioneers little encouragement.[32] When Joseph Myers of the US Conciliation Commission of the US Department of Agriculture conferred with the executive committee of the Sheep and Goat Raisers' Association and other ranchers at Ozona on May 11, Kincaid reiterated to him that the association had no right to make wage contracts of any sort for the ranchmen, and that its primary business was gathering and disseminating information. Myers conceded that the association, in his opinion, had no power to make such contracts. But W. R. Williams, national organizer for the A.F. of L., admonished the ranchmen present to form a unit affiliated with the Sheep and Goat Raisers' Association for the purpose of making contracts for shearing. "If something is not done, the fight you have today is to continue to exist," he warned, and only by making contracts for shearing could ranchmen expect to meet the situation peacefully. But the Sheep and Goat Raisers' Association took no action on that request.[33] The ranchers left the meeting relatively satisfied, feeling Myers would report to the National Emergency Council that the position of the ranchmen in refusing to bargain collectively with the Sheep Shearers' Union was justified.[34]

Meanwhile, the fledgling union did the best it could under the circumstances. José Rodríguez in San Angelo announced in mid-May that more than 200,000 residents of the Mexican border country had signed petitions asking President Franklin D. Roosevelt to be more stringent in enforcing the immigration laws and in ending the practice of permitting laborers to work in the United States and live in Mexico. He stated also that five delegates from the Shearers' Union had attended the recent convention of the Texas Federation of Labor in Dallas. And on the subject of sheepshearing wages, he stated that the office in San Angelo regularly sent out union crews getting six cents a head as demanded.[35] Despite the optimism, however, the great campaign of the *tasinques* for unionization had failed.[36]

Many factors explain the *tasinques'* failure. First, the abundance of a cheap labor supply at a time when general unemployment forced people to take available jobs, weakened the shearers, and strengthened the hand of the sheep men. Second, the shearers faced a powerful tradition that considered them as inferior—organized landowners and warehousemen were not about to bargain with impertinent "Mexicans." Third, the ranchmen could muster their forces and wield power in several ways: by calling upon the governor and the legislature for assistance; by using police power, in this case the threat of using Texas Rangers to preserve law and order; by depriving the strikers of certain constitutional guarantees such as the right to relief and the right to picket. Fourth, they could play off a certain segment of the shearers' population against another, in this case the *capitanes* against the *tasinques.* Fifth, the wool industrialists could publicize their cause through their well-established monthly, *The Sheep and Goat Raisers' Magazine.* And last, as they did, ranchers could always turn to scab labor from the outside.

But on the other hand, several factors undermined the strike's potential from within. The shearers tried to bargain at a time when economic conditions throughout the country hardly lent themselves to negotiations. Second, other than the Sheep Shearers' Union of North America, few outside institutions supported them—government officials, the police, and even relief heads sided with the ranchers—and even the union exerted no influence among these groups. Third, poor organization frustrated it from the start: the whole thing radiated an aura of haste, no union news organization publicized the cause of the shearers, many of the *tasinques* themselves refused to be proselytized, the majority of the *capitanes* felt they would be the losers in any bargaining between shearers and ranchers, and the union had no financial capacity to support members during a long strike.

Notwithstanding its failure, the strike stands out as an exemplary case of audacity amid the odds. For Mexican Americans haughty of their history, and for social scientists who argue that Chicanos are an ahistoric people, the *tasinque* strike of 1934 is among those many salient manifestations of the Chicano will to manipulate circumstances to assuage adversity.

Notes

1. San Angelo *Standard*, September 21, 1889; June 2, 26, 1888.

2. Stuart Jamieson, *Labor Unionism in American Agriculture* (Washington, DC: U.S. Department of Labor, Bulletin No. 836, 1945; reprinted by New York: Arno Press, 1976), 225–26. For some of the better studies on Chicano agricultural labor movements taking place in the 1920s and 1930s in Texas and in other parts of the country, see the special report issue of *Aztlán: International Journal of Chicano Studies Research* (Summer 1975); Rodolfo Acuña, *Occupied America: The Chicanos' Struggle toward Liberation* (San Francisco: Canfield Press, 1972), 153–86; David Montejano, *Race, Labor Repression, and Capitalist Agriculture: Notes from South Texas, 1920–1930* (Berkeley: Institute for the Study of Social Change, 1977); and especially, the suggestive article of Professor Juan Gómez-Quiñones, "The First Steps: Chicano Labor Conflict and Organizing, 1900–1920," *Aztlán: Chicano Journal of the Social Sciences and the Arts* 4 (Spring 1972): 13–50.

3. Jamieson, *Labor Unionism*, 266; San Angelo *Morning Times*, January 2, 5, 1934; Del Rio *Evening News*, January 1, 1934; *Sheep and Goat Raisers' Magazine*, 14 (January 1934): 101, 115; and *The Co-Operator* (San Angelo) 4 (May 15, 1934): 5. Unless otherwise stated, all copies of the *Sheep and Goat Raisers' Magazine* and *The Co-Operator* contacted are those housed at the Sheep and Goat Raisers' Magazine headquarters at 233 West Twohig, San Angelo, Texas.

4. San Angelo *Morning Times*, March 2, January 5, 1934; Jamieson, *Labor Unionism*, 225. For an incisive essay on the use of "labor repressive" practices in agricultural labor, see Montejano, *Race, Labor Repression, and Capitalist Agriculture.*

5. Del Rio *Evening News*, January 1, 1934.

6. Mexican shearers averaged \$2.50 to \$3.25 per day during the season and an average yearly income of \$400 to \$700. In the off-season months, they customarily received \$1.00 to \$0.50 per day or \$20 to \$25 a month for steady employment. *Sheep and Goat Raisers' Magazine* 14 (September 1933): 23; and (January 1934): 101.

7. San Angelo *Morning Times*, January 5, 10, 1934; *Devil's River News*, Sonora, Texas, January 5, 1934.

8. San Angelo *Morning Times*, January 5, 11, 1934; *Sheep and Goat Raisers' Magazine* 14 (September 1933): 23. For a history of the Sheep Shearers' Union of North America, see Jamieson, *Labor Unionism*, 222–24.

9. San Angelo *Morning Times*, January 5, 1934; Del Rio *Evening News*, January 8, 1934. Sergio Gonzales Jr., one of the main organizers and Texas president of the Sheep Shearers' Union, served as vice president of the Del Rio LULAC chapter.

10. San Angelo *Morning Times*, January 5, 10, 11, 1934; *Devil's River News*, January 5, 1934.

11. *Devil's River News*, January 5, 1934; San Angelo *Morning Times*, January 5, 1934; *Sheep and Goat Raisers' Magazine* 14 (January 1934): 101, 115; and (March 1934): 141; *The Co-Operator* 4 (January 15, 1934): 9; Del Rio *Evening News*, January 1, 1934.

12. San Angelo *Morning Times*, January 10, 1934; *Devil's River News*, January 12, 1934.

13. Del Rio *Evening News*, January 8, 1934; *Devil's River News*, January 19, 1934.

14. San Angelo *Morning Times*, January 6, 10, 11, 21, 25, 26, 1934; *Devil's River News*, January 26, 1934; May 18, 1934.

15. San Angelo *Morning Times*, January 30, 1934. On February 22, the home of Captain Ynocente Gonzales on Fourteenth Street in San Angelo was burned down. Mrs. Gonzales blamed it on labor agitators. Ibid., February 23, 1934.

16. Del Rio *Evening News*, January 26, 1934.

17. San Angelo *Morning Times*, January 25, and February 2, 8, 1934; Del Rio *Evening News*, February 1, 1934.

18. Del Rio *Evening News*, February 15, 1934.

19. San Angelo *Morning Times*, February 10, 11, 14, 15, 1934; *Sheep and Goat Raisers' Magazine* 14 (February 1934): 126.

20. San Angelo *Morning Times*, February 15, 1934; San Angelo *Evening Standard*, February 16, 1934; *Devil's River News*, February 16, 1934; Del Rio *Evening News*, February 12, 1934; *Sheep and Goat Raisers' Magazine* 14 (February 1934): 126; *The Co-Operator* 4 (February 1, 1934): 11; and (February 15, 1934): 12.

21. San Angelo *Morning Times*, February 22, 1934; San Antonio *Express*, February 22, 1934; *Devil's River News*, February 23, 1934; *Sheep and Goat Raisers' Magazine* 14 (February 1934): 126.

22. Del Rio *Evening News*, February 16, 1934, 1.

23. San Angelo *Morning Times*, March 2, 1934; Del Rio *Evening News*, February 27, 1934.

24. San Angelo *Morning Times*, February 24, March 14, 1934; Jamieson, *Labor Unionism*, 228.

25. San Angelo *Morning Times*, March 1, 9, 1934; *Devil's River News*, March 9, 1934; *Sheep and Goat Raisers' Magazine* 14 (March 1934): 141; and (May 1934), 184; *The Co-Operator* 4 (March 1, 1934): 141.

26. San Angelo *Morning Times*, February 15, 20, and March 1, 4, 1934; *Sheep and Goat Raisers' Magazine* 14 (March 1934): 141.

27. San Angelo *Morning Times*, March 11, 1934.

28. Ibid., March 14, 1934.

29. Ibid., March 14, May 9, and April 19, 1934.

30. Ibid., April 7, 19, 1934.

31. Ibid., May 9, 1934

32. Ibid., May 3, 9, 12, 1934.

33. Ibid., May 11, 12, 1934; Del Rio *Evening News*, May 14, 1934; *The Co-Operator* 4 (May 15, 1934): 5.

34. San Angelo *Morning Times*, May 13, 1934.

35. Ibid., May 17, 18, 1934.

36. *Sheep and Goat Raisers' Magazine* 14 (March 1934), 141; and (May 1934): 184.

9

Wartime USA

West Texas Tejanos in World War II and Korea

Mexican American communities in West Texas contributed their share to World War II and Korean War efforts as much as did other Hispanic communities throughout the state. Soldados *(soldiers) from West Texas willingly answered the call to defend democracy overseas, saw combat in all theaters of the war, and performed valiantly under fire. Returning to the same kind of injustices they had faced when they entered the service, many West Texas veterans after World War II and during the 1950s joined civil rights organizations. They sought to gain victories at home just as they had won freedoms for people overseas.*

On the tragic day of December 7, 1941, twenty-two-year-old Salvador Guerrero of San Angelo took in a movie with one of his pals at the Royal Theatre on North Chadbourne and emerged onto the streets to learn firsthand the news of the Japanese attack on Pearl Harbor. He found fellow pedestrians by then totally infused with war fever. The buzz fully engulfed the *colonia mexicana* in the city—that is, the various segregated barrios throughout San Angelo. Guerrero learned as much walking home upon encountering a buddy who blurted: "*Simón, yo me voy* (Hell yes, I'm going)," adding "I can't wait to have a machine gun pointed at a Jap plane—Ta, Ta, Ta, Ta, Ta, Ta."[1]

Mexican Americans from West Texas, as might be supposed from the reactions exhibited in Hispanic San Angelo, shouldered their responsibility in fighting wartime enemies. This chapter aims to bring attention to their participation in the two mid-twentieth-century wars, as generally the scholarship neglects their role in those conflicts. Coming from the barrios of small towns and the many farms and ranches throughout the vast space that is West Texas, Tejanos from the Edwards Plateau and Trans-Pecos region fought for reasons akin to those that motivated others: patriotism and a desire to fight for the ideals of justice and democracy (even when drafted). Taking the culture of their upbringing into the military, they faced the enemy in every theater, displaying the same heroism as did other servicemen and earning medals and citations matching those obtained by their fellow citizens from South Texas or from the larger cities in the Lone Star State.

Many Mexican Americans would respond to President Franklin D. Roosevelt's and their country's call to retaliate against Japan for its unjustified and inhumane attack (and by extension, Germany and Italy, which honored the Tripartite Treaty of 1940 obligating them to aid Japan). Eligible for military duty since September 1940 under the provisions of the Selective Service Act were young men between the ages of eighteen and forty-five who passed the required physical examination. Certainly, most Mexican Americans from West Texas registered for the draft upon turning eighteen. Local newspaper listings that regularly posted the names of draftees, of men called for physicals, and of those taken to military camps upon qualifying for induction indicate compliance. Mexican American boys came from Concho Country communities such as Miles, Veribest, Rowena, and Millersview.[2] Numbers of draftees tended to be high in those counties having large Tejano populations, as in the instance of Culberson County where one-half of the 228 men who registered for the draft in October 1940 had Spanish surnames.[3]

Fighting men, both draftees and volunteers, from West Texas included mainly unskilled hands from farms and ranches or city workers engaged in low-level labor.[4] To be sure, their background as a minority in West Texas was diverse: some seemed no more than country hicks coming from remote areas of the Edwards Plateau and Trans-Pecos region, while other recruits hailed from the *barrios* of the many West Texas towns. Salvador Guerrero himself lived in the "Bulto Prieto" barrio section of San Angelo, while others came from "San Felipe" in Del Rio, "Little Mexico" in Fort Stockton, "Sinaloa" in Sonora, or the "Chihuahuita" enclaves of Fort Davis, Alpine, and Midland. Some of these men considered themselves a bit more "hip" than their country counterparts. These town dwellers may have acquired a bit more education than their rural cousins and capably expressed themselves through a mix of English and Spanish words (Spanglish, or Texas-Mex). Still others came from "*el otro cachete*," that is, from Mexico. But two days after the Pearl Harbor attack, Mexico's president Manuel Avila Camacho had urged those residing *en el estranjero* (in the United States) to fully cooperate with the war mobilization, including fighting their adopted country's wars. From these varied West Texas backgrounds stemmed the selectees to be sent off to Europe and Asia to fight totalitarianism.[5]

As in the case of other Americans, West Texas Tejanos looked at their prospects for war duty ambivalently. Some—feeling like the overly eager San Angeleño mentioned above—volunteered resolutely, as did twenty-year-olds Manuel "Mel" Nuñez and Antonio S. "Tony" Benavides of Fort Stockton. They decided one day to "join up." The two thence hitched a ride to Big Spring, the closest recruiting station to Fort Stockton, and there underwent processing. Accepted as soldiers, the two reported to Fort Bliss in El Paso for training.[6] Others waited for their draft call uneasily. Around the San Angelo barrios (and presumably throughout most West Texas Mexican American communities) an everyday question became: "*Saves a quien le cayó la leva?*" ("Guess who got caught by the draft?"). Surely some worried about the newspaper notices that appeared frequently, but others like Salvador Guerrero looked forward to the draft, and when the notification arrived, accepted it with glee. In February 1943 he took off with fellow San Angeleños for Abilene to undergo the physical examination required of all prospective troops. Happy to have earned an army uniform, Guerrero returned to town and decided to organize his own send-off to war. He hastily put together a "juke-box party" at a local clubhouse where friends and relatives came to wish the draftees good luck. The next morning, he reported to the Tom Green County Courthouse grounds where family members gathered for a ceremony wishing San Angeloans well in war (other communities held similar farewells). Guerrero then boarded the charter bus taking him and other recruits to the reception center at Camp Wolters in Mineral Wells, Texas. From there, the army ordered him to Camp Robinson at Little Rock, Arkansas, for boot camp.[7]

What motivated people like Nuñez, Benavides, Guerrero, and hundreds more from West Texas to eagerly don a military uniform? Born or raised in the United States, they felt "American" and held to the belief that patriotism compelled them to war service. They rejected insinuations of being non-US born; instead, they proudly asserted their citizenship as Americans and boasted of their homeland: West Texas.[8] Thus, many (with perhaps a mixture of apprehension and blessing from their families) complied with draft summonses. As elsewhere throughout the entire country, several men from the same family at times left West Texas towns and rural areas to serve wherever the armed forces assigned them. Of the Mexican American men from Sonora who went into the military, nine sets were brothers; three of these sets included three brothers.[9]

Military life also offered an escape from pervasive discrimination. Despite their citizenship and long residency in the Edwards Plateau and Trans-Pecos region, Mexican Americans daily encountered treatment as less than worthy people. White society limited their job opportunities and forbade their entry to many public establishments; even public schools and churches practiced racial exclusion. Alternately, then, the war presented an opportunity to eradicate such wrongs and possibly improve conditions for *la raza*. Guerrero wondered: "Could this episode of world history mark the turning point for the inequities of social life for Mexican Americans?" An optimist, he believed as much.[10]

Still other reasons drove West Texas Tejanos to view military enlistment favorably. Adventure awaited them outside their region in West Texas, and certainly overseas. In the military, they would have a unique chance to associate with other people, those from across the United States but particularly folks in Europe, Asia, and Africa.[11] Then, too, for the foreign-born military service offered a ready vehicle to US citizenship. West Texas was home to recently arrived Mexicans, others who had been in the United States for a few years, and still others who had been shaped by the complete American experience, among them Salvador Guerrero (who had even attended college). Several in this classification yearned for citizenship, among them Guerrero who in May 1943, "attained the desire that had burned inside my heart since my days at Sam Houston Elementary School."[12]

No one knows how many Mexican Americans from the United States saw military duty in World War II. Crude approximations run from 250,000 to 500,000—the government at that period did not keep records cataloged by nationality.[13] Consequently, it would be difficult to separate the number from Texas who made up part of that estimate and even more problematic to distinguish ones coming from the Edwards Plateau and Trans-Pecos region. Unquestionably, however, men and women from West Texas contributed as dutifully and bravely as did those from other places. Most acknowledged being the product of two cultures, having been shaped by the influence of their parents and molded by their years growing up in Texas.

Mexican-descent soldiers thus took the culture of their upbringing into the military (obviously, other soldiers from across the country also could not sever similar ties). Americanization among Mexican American communities advanced noticeably after World War II, but as of the late 1930s and early 1940s—given the many constraints under which Tejanos lived—strong sentiments still connected Mexican Americans to the ways of their parents and grandparents who had immigrated to the United States during the early decades of the twentieth century, or earlier. The enlisted men ranks included, therefore, those who had been fairly well exposed to Anglo-American life, perhaps through education or association in the workplace, but who remained "Mexican" by their residence in segregated barrios. Many others claimed not much more than a limited education and only partial contact with white people—they spoke little English and retained an attachment to the ways of their immigrant parents or grandparents. Newcomers to the United States knew little of their adopted country. Whatever their backgrounds, all swore allegiance to the United States and vowed to defend it, but they did not renounce "*lo mexicano*" (the sentiment they held for the culture their forebears had brought from Mexico).[14] The Spanish language acted as a common bonding element among them, of course, but so did the *pachuco* argot (or street talk) of that period as well as the *barrio* ritual of giving fellow cronies playful nicknames (*sobrenombres*). For example, Ramón G. Gutiérrez of Del Rio and Enrique Cardona and Dagoberto Chávez of Sonora carried their nicknames with them into the war theater: "*el sancudo*," "*el coyote*," and "*la galleta*," respectively.[15]

In the service, soldiers sometimes found their ethnicity to be a nonissue while at other times an attraction to bigotry. Several West Texas enlisted men reported that military life afforded them equality such as they had never experienced in their home towns or in the ranches and farms where they had lived. Some white soldiers freely associated with Mexican Americans who had similar interests as they, for instance.[16] Carlos Granado of Fort Stockton viewed the tolerance of white girls in the midwestern United States with wonder, for they saw past his ethnicity. He befriended one such woman and dated her while stationed in Wisconsin—a deed unthinkable in West Texas where social codes strictly prohibited Mexicans from consorting with white girls. On the other hand, many encountered prejudice that paralleled that entrenched in West Texas. Fellow soldiers and superiors derided them for being of Mexican descent or hurled racial slurs at them. Some white troopers refused to accept the fact that Mexican Americans made competent soldiers. Officers questioned the Tejanos' ability to perform complicated tasks in warfare.[17]

But Mexican Americans disproved any stereotype and served admirably in numerous capacities. Primary sources remain relatively silent on the contributions West Texas Tejanos made to the military cause as civilians. The broader literature on wartime USA says much of minority people and women manning defense plants based in America's largest cities, but such factories hardly existed in the Edwards Plateau and Trans-Pecos region. Certainly, however, some Tejanas and Tejanos would have worked as auxiliary staff in training installations such as Goodfellow Field in San Angelo, the Midland Army Air Flying School, Pecos Army Air Field, Marfa Air Field, or Gibbs Field near Fort Stockton. The latter facility, for instance, hired a small number of Mexican American men and women apparently as helpers on jobs at the hangars or as manual laborers at other locations on the site—construction work and truck driving for men and kitchen duty for women.[18]

But there also existed white-collar positions in the civilian sector, and at least some Mexican Americans from West Texas filled them. Elvira Peña Alfaro, then teaching in the Shafter school system (Presidio County), made the long journey to Washington, DC, to work in the Department of Justice.[19] Eva Camúñez of San Angelo found employment in San Antonio, then in Brownsville, and lastly in Laredo, working conscientiously and earning promotions to supervisor as a mail censor (mostly examining mail written in Spanish).[20]

In addition, the civilian community at large contributed to the war campaign in ways that mirrored efforts undertaken across the United States. In Presidio and neighboring border communities, for instance, Mexican American women participated in national goals by also tending to "victory gardens" and watching for subversive activities that might undermine the country's security.[21]

Enlisted men and women not assigned to combat units functioned responsibly as cooks; builders of roads, bridges, and railroads; administrative personnel; drivers; or recruiters, all mitigating the stereotype of the inept Mexican. Mel Nuñez from Fort Stockton, for instance, never left US soil; he worked with recruits throughout the war and won promotion to sergeant for his achievements. Anita Pineda of Fort Stockton served as a nurse in the Women's Army Corps (WACs), practicing her specialty in US posts far beyond West Texas. By war's end, the army had advanced her to corporal, recognized her duty with certificates of distinction, and awarded her medals for commendable performance.[22]

Whether in noncombat or combat roles, West Texas Mexican Americans in various branches of the military served in far-off places. Orders carried some to Europe and to countries—among them England, France, Belgium, Italy, Czechoslovakia, and of course Germany—known to many perhaps only from elementary school texts. Men from West Texas, like Tony Benavides of Fort Stockton, and Joe Mendoza and Cleto Fernández of San Angelo, fought in North Africa. Some saw duty in India, among them Silvestre Solis of Brady. Assignments took others to Australia, New Zealand, the Philippines, New Guinea, the Solomon Islands, Guam, Indonesia, New

Caledonia, and many other settings in the Pacific where the people, culture, and surroundings differed extremely from the milieu of West Texas.[23]

Wherever Tejanos served, they performed according to or beyond military expectations—racial pride, patriotism, and camaraderie sparked ethnic Mexicans to do so. In basic training, for instance, fellow Mexicanos prodded comrades to outperform the white soldier. Guerrero commonly heard a platoon buddy roar (in the parlance of the barrio) during strenuous military exercises: "*Órale, batos, no hagan a la raza quedar mal!*" ("Guys, do not let our people down!"). "Soldado Razo," a song many Spanish-speaking soldiers knew from home (it had become popular soon after the war broke out), stressed racial pride and extolled Mexican courage. The lyrics spoke of those ideals—family (especially motherhood), country, the church—dear to the *soldado razo* (the common soldier). At the same time, the words celebrated the Mexicans' valor: the soldado razo was joining other "*valientes muchachos*" (brave boys); was willing to die anywhere ("*mi raza sabe morir donde quiera*"); and was daring to gamble his life ("*aquí va otro mexicano que va a jugarse la vida*") in service to his nation.[24] Mexicanos abundantly displayed such qualities in combat.

Books and articles paying tribute to soldiers performing beyond the call of duty do not neglect West Texas Mexican Americans. Several writers, for instance, have documented the heroism of Manuel S. Gonzales in Italy on September 9, 1943. Gonzales belonged to the 142nd Infantry Regiment of the Thirty-Sixth Infantry Division from Texas. This division included many Tejanos who had been training together for many months before being shipped to the front and was part of Operation Avalanche, an Allied mission intended to capture the city of Salerno, Italy; subsequently, Allied forces would overcome the entire country and force it out of the war. Born and raised in the predominantly Spanish-speaking community of Fort Davis, Gonzales had married there and supported his family doing cement work. He had first been exposed to English upon joining the Civilian Conservation Corps in the late 1930s but then improved his speaking ability after joining the military in 1941. As a display of patriotism, he sported a tattoo of an American flag on his left arm. A model soldier, by the time of Operation Avalanche he had won assignment as squad leader, achieved the rank of staff sergeant, and had been flippantly nicknamed "*El Feo*," the ugly one, by his fellow Mexican American GI's in the Thirty-Sixth. Almost immediately upon landing on the beach in predawn hours alongside comrades, Gonzales sighted a German 88 mm artillery weapon taking a heavy toll on the landing crafts ferrying troops to the beachhead and effectively pinning down his unit. Gonzales advanced toward enemy lines, zeroing in on the 88 mm machine gun nest. Despite machine gun fire and grenades hurled at him, Gonzales took out the gun and crew. After that, he crawled under barbed wire toward another position, killing the two Germans guarding it. There (according to his own account):

> the gunners were down low and I couldn't get a shot at them. It had to be grenades. I crawled closer, up to a spot within 15 yards of the nest; then I threw a grenade. It was right on the bull's eye. The gun was silent.
>
> That left two more machine-guns and the mortar. It was my luck that they were all so busy firing at our troops on the beach they didn't look for anyone to be crawling up on them. Two grenades apiece finished the machine-gun nests. It took three grenades for the mortar.

Wounded in the attack, he managed to return to his outfit without help. Upon recovering, Gonzales continued his exploits on the front lines of the Italian campaign, gaining a reputation as a regular "Commando Kelly." The army recognized his heroism with a promotion to tech sergeant and with several awards and medals, including the Distinguished Service Cross. His hometown received him as a hero when the war ended, and Fort Davis veterans named VFW Post #7876 the "Manuel Gonzales Post."[25]

The bravado of Ramón G. Gutiérrez at the same battle at Salerno gained notice from the military historian Robert L. Wagner. Gutiérrez was also part of the 141st Infantry Regiment of the Thirty-Sixth Infantry Division to which Gonzales of Fort Davis belonged. Wagner wrote:

> Private Raymond [Ramón] G. Guttierez [*sic*] of Sonora, Texas moved forward firing his BAR [Browning Automatic Rifle]. Two enemy bullets pierced his helmet but failed to touch him. The third caught him in the arm. He continued to advance, located the enemy machine gun, closed in on it, and knifed the German gunner to death.[26]

Gutiérrez would go on to win other laurels. Military records, tributes by family members and acquaintances, and other sources place him also at the disastrous Rio Rapido Crossing in Italy in January 1944. Taken prisoner by the Germans as his division advanced into Italy, Gutiérrez escaped the Nazis, only to be recaptured; on a second attempt he managed a getaway to American lines. The army flew him to Texas in July 1944, eventually decorating him with nine medals, among them the Silver Star, which recognized his gallantry at Salerno, and the Order of Patriotic War 2nd Degree, awarded to him by the Soviet Union. Two towns claim him today: Del Rio, his hometown, and Sonora, where he enlisted in January 1941. A memorial in Del Rio's San Felipe Exes building honors him as the city's "Most Decorated Serviceman."[27]

The Normandy invasion of June 1944 most assuredly had its own heroes from West Texas, although the primary source record on Tejano participation remains lean. But Salvador Guerrero was there and remembered how he mustered up his own courage to overcome his fright of the Germans' artillery. As his landing craft prepared to make Omaha Beach on June 6, his soldier pal Rafaél Ramos encouraged him in street language familiar to the San Angeleño: "*No tenga miedo, chingón, si ya nos toca pos ni modo!*" ("Don't be afraid, big boy, if it is our time, what can be done?"). Scared witless but nonetheless pressing past bodies lying on the beach, Guerrero took momentary refuge from the continued fire of German 88 mm guns behind an immobilized tank. But he immediately heard a warning from another fellow Chicano: "*Ese, le 'stán tirando al tanque, bato.*" ("Hey man, they're shooting at the tank.") Alongside others performing heroic deeds at Normandy, Guerrero crossed the German lines and returned to West Texas to a long and productive life.[28]

It could be reasonably assumed that alongside men from other regions of the Lone Star State, West Texas Tejanos participated in many of the major battles of World War II. Secondary sources referencing men from West Texas place them at the Battle of the Bulge, Bastogne, Salerno, Guadalcanal, Iwo Jima, Okinawa, Manila, and of course at Omaha Beach in Normandy.[29]

How many Mexican Americans from West Texas became casualties of war (either killed or wounded), turned up missing in action, or became prisoners of war researchers find hard to learn. But various sources, among them Texas newspapers such as *La Prensa* of San Antonio, which through its column titled "Boletín del departamento de guerra" regularly published reports updating the tolls of war,[30] military records available through several databases,[31] and local histories that have been compiled by dedicated county historians (and by some professional scholars) acknowledge the extreme sacrifice that West Texas Tejanos paid. These men came from small communities like Van Horn, Sanderson, Alpine, Balmorhea, and Fort Stockton; from Big Bend villages such as Candelaria, Valentine, Marfa, Shafter, Presidio, Terlingua, and Redford; from towns in the Edwards Plateau like Sonora, Menard, Brady, Melvin, Paint Rock, Ballinger, and Del Rio; as well as larger cities in the region such as San Angelo and Midland.[32]

According to statistics compiled by the US War Department in 1946, some 134 men from West Texas lost their lives during the war. This amounted to approximately 24 percent of the total count of deaths suffered by men from the Edwards Plateau and Trans-Pecos region. Counties with heavy populations of Tejanos recorded high percentages of all soldiers dying either overseas or stateside, as table 9.1 indicates: Hudspeth 71 percent; Val Verde 70 percent; Reeves 60 percent; Presidio 52 percent; Brewster 52 percent; and Pecos 43 percent. Conversely, in those counties where Mexican Americans constituted a minority, Tejanos had lower percentages of total deaths, as in Tom Green, Reagan, and Coke Counties. In the upper-tier counties where few Mexican Americans resided, such as Ector, Crane, Winkler, and Glasscock, they experienced no deaths. Whatever their residence, some of the *soldados razos* who perished in war zones went by traditional names (considered old-fashioned today!) such as Espiridión Méndez and Amador Jácquez of Culberson County; Hilario O. Córdova and Epifanio Briceño of Brewster County; Cecilio Aragón and Paulino Lomas of Val Verde County; José Rosario Jiménez and Salomé G. Alvarado of Presidio County; Eulogio Lara and Felipe Rentería of Jeff Davis County; Bernardino D. Mora and Santiago Sánchez from Pecos County; and Pascual B. Acosta and Frutoso R. Chávez from Reeves County.[33]

The list of those reported wounded in action from the broader West Texas region[34] bolsters the ascribed gallantry of Mexican Americans; West Texas Tejanos endured their own share of injuries and like many of their comrades either found themselves at the battlefront after being patched up or having to spend weeks in hospital wards recovering. Some idea of the place of origin of these victims may be drawn from *La Prensa*'s compilation, the "Boletín del departamento de guerra," of Tejanos "*heridos en campaña*" (wounded in action). Like those killed in action, the wounded called home small communities like Brackettville, Paint Rock, Melvin, Langtry, or Valentine. Disproportionately represented on the lists were soldiers from Del Rio; such numbers bolster the aforementioned observation that in areas where Mexican Americans constituted a majority of inhabitants they suffered a higher percentage of total casualties.[35]

It is unclear how many others experienced life as prisoners of war. Certainly, there must have been many from West Texas who spent time in German captivity or Japanese detention, such as Willie Garza and Antonio "Tony" Tafolla of San Angelo, taken prisoners in the Philippines. The two men had joined the army in early 1941 and had received orders to the Philippines; there they found themselves when the Japanese attacked Luzon, the largest island in the Philippine archipelago, a few days after Pearl Harbor. Both fought at Bataan and Corregidor, but the record becomes hazy at this point regarding the fate of the two San Angeleños. Apparently Tafolla was

Table 9.1. World War II Spanish-surnamed* dead and missing: Edwards Plateau and Trans-Pecos counties

County	*KIA*	*DOW*	*DOI*	*DNB*	*FOD*	*M*	*all races*
Edwards	1	0	0	1	0	0	10
Val Verde	18	3	0	6	3	0	43
Kinney	7	0	0	2	0	0	24
Sutton	4	0	0	0	0	0	13
Schleicher	0	0	0	0	0	0	3
Tom Green	8	1	1	2	0	0	151
Coke	1	0	0	0	0	0	15
Sterling	0	0	0	0	0	0	4
Irion	1	0	0	0	0	0	6
Reagan	1	0	0	0	0	0	8
Terrell	4	1	0	1	0	0	16
Pecos	9	0	0	1	0	0	23
Reeves	10	0	0	2	2	0	23
Crockett	4	2	0	1	0	0	12
Ward	2	0	0	0	0	0	22
Crane	0	0	0	0	0	0	7
Loving	0	0	0	0	0	0	4
Winkler	0	0	0	0	0	0	17
Ector	0	0	0	0	0	0	25
Midland	2	0	0	0	0	0	41
Glasscock	0	0	0	0	0	0	4
Upton	0	0	0	0	0	0	8
Presidio	14	0	0	1	0	0	29
Brewster	6	1	0	4	0	0	21
Jeff Davis	1	0	0	0	0	0	5
Culberson	1	0	0	0	0	0	7
Hudspeth	1	1	0	2	1	0	7
Total	95	9	1	23	6	0	548

KIA = Killed in Action
DOW = Died of Wounds
DOI = Died of Injuries
DNB = Died, Nonbattle
FOD = Finding of Death
M = Missing

*Presumably Tejano

Source: United States Adjutant-General's Office, *World War II Honor List of Dead and Missing Army and Army Air Forces Personnel from Texas* (Washington, DC: War Department Bureau of Public Relations, 1946), http://www.archives.gov/research/military/ww2/army-casualties/texas.html.

among the 36,000 men forced to surrender at Bataan, a peninsula in southwestern Luzon. He then endured the infamous "Bataan Death March," the horrifying twelve-day, eighty-five-mile trek to Camp O'Donnell where he suffered further cruelties. On May 6, 1942, the Japanese government transferred from Camp O'Donnell and other stockades American captives taken at Bataan and those captured later (among them apparently Willie Garza) at the island fortress of Corregidor, located south of the Bataan Peninsula. There the American POWs became a slave labor pool for factories, mines, and various labor fields in Japan or in Japanese-controlled countries such as China and Korea. Reports listed Garza and Tafolla as Japanese POWs throughout the war years, as they did Thomas Gaitán of Del Rio, Jesús López of Midland, and Everardo Ramos of Ozona. Surrender terms finally freed Willie Garza from the Osaka Camp (in Japan) in September 1945. Fellow San Angeleño Tony Tafolla survived working in Japanese coal mines until the war ended and returned to his hometown and raised a family. The fate of Gaitán, López, and Ramos remains obscure.[36]

Whether killed in action, wounded in action, or having returned home safe and sound, West Texas Tejanos won their own share of military medals, decorations, and commendations (some of them given posthumously). Medals earned included Manuel S. Gonzales's Distinguished Service Cross, as well as numerous Silver Stars (among them Ramón G. Gutiérrez's), Bronze Stars, Air Medals, American Defense Medals, Oak Leaf Clusters, Battle Stars, and of course, Purple Hearts.[37] Sergeant Alberto L. Rede of Redford (the progeny of an accomplished family from the Marfa-Redford communities) received the Distinguished Flying Cross. As a crewmember of a C-47 cargo aircraft, he flew supply, transportation, and paratroop assault missions to such places in the Pacific theater as New Guinea, Indonesia, and the Philippines.[38] The medals amassed by West Texas Hispanics adds a new dimension to the significance of West Texas Tejano history and links it to the broader saga of Mexican American valor in World War II.

No more than five years passed before Mexican American young men from West Texas again answered the call to their country's commitment to world peace and demonstrated their courage under fire—this time in the Korean War (1950–53). As in the case of World War II (or earlier wars for that matter), no one has verified the number of Mexican Americans who served in the conflict. One historian calculates that about 50,000 (or approximately 17.5 percent of all soldiers from Texas sent to Korea) were of Mexican descent. But of that number (a rough estimate at best) how many called West Texas their home is unknown.[39] It may be sensibly surmised, however, that they came from the same small farm and ranch communities as had the previous (World War II) cadre of soldiers, and of course, from towns such as San Angelo, Fort Stockton, Del Rio, and Midland/Odessa.

It would be a painstaking and perhaps impossible task to compute the exact number of casualties that West Texas Tejanos sustained between the time they arrived in Korea with United Nations forces in September 1950 until the signing of the armistice in July 1953. National Archives documents, however, identify by name and county those men killed in action. The tabulation shows seven of them as having lived in the region of the Edwards Plateau and Trans-Pecos: Alfredo Paredes Charles from Val Verde County, Alberto Hernández and Tranquilino Pérez from Tom Green County, Manuel S. Uranga from Ector County, Frank Salgado Jr. and Eduardo T. Tenorio from Presidio County, and Benito Martínez of Hudspeth County.[40]

Martínez's bravery on the battlefield earned him the Medal of Honor. Born and raised in the border community of Fort Hancock in Hudspeth County, Martínez joined the military in 1951 and went to Hawaii with the Twenty-Fifth Infantry Division when the war broke out. Soon the Twenty-Fifth was fighting on the front lines in Korea. On September 6, 1952, the twenty-one-year-old Martínez and fellow soldiers manned a position at one of the bunkers acting as listening posts protecting a larger defense station behind them named Sandbag Castle. Around midnight, North Korean soldiers attacked these bunkers, and the commanding officer ordered Martínez and his fellow soldiers to retreat. But Martínez alone refused the command, opting not to surrender his position lest his larger unit at Sandbag Castle be exposed to deadly attack. From his bunker, Martínez slew several of the attackers, then retreated to a fallback position from where he maintained another defense until around 6:00 a.m. armed only with his automatic rifle and a .45 caliber pistol. Although it cost him his life, Martínez's actions had allowed his unit to counterattack and repel the aggressors. The secretary of the army presented the Medal of Honor posthumously to his mother at the Pentagon in September 1953. Elementary schools in the Fort Hancock Independent School District and in the Socorro Independent School District (of El Paso County) have been named Benito Martínez in his honor.[41]

Veterans of World War II and Korea returned to West Texas to mixed receptions. Towns held community-wide festivities honoring their World War II heroes, and in the barrios fellow Mexican Americans viewed the men who had worn the uniform with admiration, lavishing them with deserved respect. But the public welcome proved short-lived. For one thing, white society refused Tejano veterans the opportunity to acquire jobs normally reserved for white people. Of necessity, men who had risked their lives for their country returned to the kinds of jobs they had held before the war: sheepshearing, cotton picking, grubbing, dry cleaning, wool packing, dishwashing, garbage collecting, or doing pick-and-shovel work, carpentry, or service repair. Manuel Gonzales, the hero at Salerno and in other Italian campaigns, came back to Fort Davis to support his family as a stonemason.[42]

Racial prejudice lingered, most perniciously in the form of segregation, even as the country had engaged in a struggle against Nazi racist ideology. In West Texas proper, ethnic Mexicans during the war years could not eat or even get a cup of coffee in many restaurants or cafés, could not get haircuts in some towns (in McCamey, men had to journey forty-five miles to Fort Stockton to the nearest Mexican barbershop), could not find hotel accommodations, and otherwise could not mingle with white people.[43] A most disgraceful case of racial discrimination in a public place occurred in March 1945 when Senator Eugenio Prado of Mexico's Congress and the accompanying members of his group encountered rejection at a restaurant in Pecos, Texas.[44]

Even more insulting, Anglos continued wedded to the custom of not serving Mexican American servicemen. Two weeks before the attack on Pearl Harbor, two Mexican American soldiers in uniform dropped by the Dew Drop Inn in downtown San Angelo, only to be asked to leave. In July 1943, Corporal Jesse García faced the indignity of being rejected in uniform at the Fort Stockton public swimming pool with the curt explanation that "he was a Mexican." In May 1944, a drugstore in Ozona refused to serve refreshments to Private Arturo Ramírez and his wife (Ramírez was killed in France on July 10, 1944); later that year the local sheriff forced Private Tomás Garza at gunpoint to leave the counter at the same premises when Garza ordered a soda pop. The rule of not waiting on soldiers in uniform predominated throughout the state of Texas.[45]

As with the matter of scarce and low-paying jobs, then, war veterans returned to their communities to find racial prejudice and segregation lodged in thought and habit. Whites appeared intractable in conceding Mexican Americans rights for which they (Hispanics) had so courageously fought. A man from Sutton County named Sam Smith grumbled to officials that he and other white Texans had not gone overseas so that "ill-smelling Mexicans" would be pressing for integration in local theaters, schools, eating places, and swimming pools while displacing white ex-servicemen from jobs.[46] Salvador Guerrero recalled that public places in his native San Angelo still refused Mexican American clientele, even if soldiers wore military dress.[47]

Situations for Mexican Americans improved during the 1950s, albeit gradually. Even as the Korean War approached, Mexican Americans dealt with the affront of rejection. In West Texas in general, and on Highway 290 (the stretch running from about Fort Stockton, Ozona, Sonora, and Junction) in particular, restaurants customarily denied Mexican Americans service. In May 1948, a high school coach named Raymond Wheat from Marfa wrote to officials bringing to their attention the indignity his track and basketball teams had suffered by being turned away in restaurants along this route—because some of the athletes were Mexican. He complained that Latin Americans in West Texas were being "treated wrongly as second-rate Americans."[48]

Throughout the state, segregation indeed remained a standard in race relations: real estate rules prohibited Mexican Americans from buying homes in the white part of town; social norms discouraged Mexican Americans from using white barbershops, white restaurants, or white swimming pools; and school boards continued to assign Hispanic children to so-called Mexican schools (where teachers enforced the no-Spanish rule). Racism at midcentury still dictated that Mexican Americans strike a deferential pose when interacting with white people, they accept demeaning labels (such as Meskin, greaser, or beaner), and Mexican American boys not make romantic overtures toward white girls. White society in the 1950s still stigmatized Mexican Americans as intellectually inferior and considered Mexican American customs and tradition as being un-American. The political system disarmed Mexican American communities through at-large elections, the application of the poll tax, and boss rule. Anglos maintained white supremacy by force if needed; the local sheriff's department, the Texas Rangers, or the Border Patrol acted as mechanisms of control should Mexican Americans challenge white authority. Daily, entrenched patterns of discrimination reminded Mexican Americans of their status as second-class citizens.

In these postwar environments, many veterans seriously deliberated the irony of having fought for justice for others while being denied it themselves. Thus they now channeled the kind of energy they had expended on winning freedom for Europeans and Asians toward efforts to duplicate a like victory at home. They joined League of United Latin American Citizens (LULAC) councils, founded a new organization such as the American GI Forum (AGIF), and otherwise sought to make their political power known. It was in fact during the 1950s that this "GI Generation" joined the many battles that eventually toppled barriers that had long forestalled ethnic mobility. LULAC and AGIF worked side by side to end school segregation and remove hindrances that led to poor school achievement for Mexican American children, to bring down obstacles to civic participation (such as jury service), or remove completely cemented Jim Crow customs.[49] AGIF and LULAC membership in 1960 formed Viva Kennedy Clubs in an attempt to acquire a needed voice in national politics. Efforts proved successful in many ways for GI Generation activists as the 1950s closed, but old conditions lingered. Chicanos in the 1960s would challenge persisting problems, among them educational practices detrimental to student achievement, abuses by police departments (and primarily the Texas Rangers), discrimination in employment, and political disfranchisement.[50]

More remains to be told of West Texas Mexican American World War II and Korean War involvement than has been said here. At the very least, this chapter adds a regional dimension to war participation, arguing that West Texas Mexican Americans' contribution to the military record deserves greater notice and credit. Shaped by comparable experiences as their counterparts elsewhere in the state—hometown prejudice but as powerfully by the Americanization process—Mexican Americans from West Texas defended the sanctity of freedom, democracy, and egalitarianism like all others. This chapter recaps their personal valor and sacrifice in the foxholes and trenches of World War II and Korea in support of those values. Many veterans went on to engage in civil rights struggles with gallantry paralleling that demonstrated on the battlefield.

Notes

1. Salvador Guerrero, *Memorias: A West Texas Life* (Lubbock: Texas Tech University Press, 1995), 67–69.

2. For examples of such listings, search through entries (circa 1941 to 1945) in Arnoldo De León, *Apuntes San Angeleños: An Index of Newspaper Items Extracted from the San Angelo Standard Times, 1884–1984* (San Angelo: Fort Concho Museum Press, 1987). Other examples included Ballinger *Ledger*, Ballinger, Texas, July 9, 1942, 1; August 13, 1942, 1; October 22, 1942, 1; December 17, 1942, 1; June 24, 1943, 1; September 2, 1943, 1; June 1, 1944, 1.

3. Rosa Lee Wylie, *History of Van Horn and Culberson County, Texas* (Hereford, TX: Pioneer Book Publishers, 1973), 70–71.

4. María Eva Flores, "What a Difference a War Makes," in *Mexican Americans and World War II*, ed. Maggie Rivas-Rodríguez (Austin: University of Texas Press, 2005), 180; Guerrero, *Memorias*, "Jobs Galore," chap. 7.

5. Guerrero, *Memorias*, 69. In *Among the Valiant: Mexican Americans in World War II and Korea* (Alhambra, CA: Borden Publishing, 1963), 27–29, Raul Morin elaborates on the diverse cast of individuals from across the United States who responded to war service.

6. Flores, "What a Difference a War Makes," 177, 180–81.

7. Guerrero, *Memorias*, 69–71; Flores, "What a Difference a War Makes," 183.

8. Flores, "What a Difference a War Makes," 182; Maggie Rivas-Rodríguez et al., *A Legacy Greater Than Words: Stories of U.S. Latinos and Latinas of the World War II Generation* (Austin: U.S. Latino and Latina World War II Oral History Project, 2006), 45, 111.

9. Agustín "Gus" Silvas Chávez, "Mexican Americans Who Served in World War II, 1941–1945, Sonora, Texas," http://www.somosprimos.com/sp2007/spdec07.htm; personal communication with Mr. Gus (Agustín) Chávez via e-mail dated February 16, 2014. At least six sets of brothers and one set of three brothers from San Angelo fought in the war. *Men and Women in the Armed Forces from Tom Green County* (San Angelo, TX: n.d., n.p.); Guerrero, *Memorias*, 94–95. See further San Angelo *Standard-Times*, July 28, 1944, 14; January 14, 1945, 7, section 1. The Pablo González family of Fort Stockton had six members enlisted in the armed forces during the course of the war. Flores, "What a Difference a War Makes," 183.

10. Sources for this discussion are Glen Sample Ely, *Where the West Begins: Debating Texas Identity* (Lubbock: Texas Tech University Press, 2011), 90; Flores, "What a Difference a War Makes," 189, 180, 191–92; Guerrero, *Memorias*, 57–59, 70, 72, 73, 91.

11. Flores, "What a Difference a War Makes," 177.

12. Guerrero, *Memorias*, 65, 69; quote is from p. 74.

13. United States, Office of the Deputy Assistant Secretary of Defense for Military Manpower and Personnel Policy, *Hispanics in America's Defense* (Washington, DC: Office of the Deputy Assistant Secretary of Defense for Military Manpower and Personnel Policy, 1990), 27.

14. Morin, *Among the Valiant*, 27–29; Guerrero, *Memorias*, chaps. 11 to 14.

15. Del Rio *News-Herald*, July 6, 1944, 1; May 26, 2013, 1A; Chávez, "Mexican Americans Who Served In World War II, 1941–1945, Sonora, Texas." Salvador Guerrero includes some of the popular nicknames that abounded in the San Angelo barrios during his growing-up years. Guerrero, *Memorias*, 125.

16. Guerrero, *Memorias*, 72–73.

17. Flores, "What a Difference a War Makes," 181–82.

18. María Eva Flores, CDP, "The Good Life the Hard Way: The Mexican American Community of Fort Stockton, Texas" (PhD diss., Arizona State University, 2000), 252–74.

19. Cecilia Thompson, *History of Marfa and Presidio County, 1535–1946*, 2 vols. (Austin: Nortex, 1985), 2: 501.

20. Arnoldo De León, "Eva Camúñez-Tucker: Hispanic Philanthropist in the Concho Country," *Journal of Big Bend Studies* 15 (2003): 186–87.

21. Thompson, *History of Marfa and Presidio County*, 2: 501.

22. Flores, "What a Difference a War Makes," 181–82, 188.

23. Flores, "What a Difference a War Makes," 177, 183, San Angelo *Standard-Times*, March 23, 1943, 9; April 20, 1943, 2; May 8, 1945, 8 (European peace edition); Rivas-Rodríguez et al., *A Legacy Greater Than Words*, 111, 122, 263, 283; *Men and Women in the Armed Forces from Tom Green County* (San Angelo, TX: n.d., n.p.); *Men and Women in the Armed Forces from Runnels County* (S.I.: s.n., 194?); Jo-Ann E. Palmer, *How Sutton County Helped in World War II* (Sonora: Sutton County Historical Society, 2000); Wylie, *History of Van Horn and Culberson County*, 173; Clifford B. Casey, *Mirages, Mysteries, and Reality: Brewster County, Texas: The Big Bend of the Rio Grande* (Hereford, TX: Pioneer Book Publishers, 1972), 319; Thompson, *History of Marfa and Presidio County*, 2: 518, 526; Lucy Miller Jacobson and Mildred Bloys Nored, *Jeff Davis County, Texas* (Fort Davis, TX: Fort Davis Historical Society, 1993), 295; Flores, "The Good Life the Hard Way," 275–77; Alton Hughes, *Pecos: A History of the Pioneer West*, 2 vols. (Seagraves, TX: Pioneer Book Publishers, 1978), 2: 21.

24. Guerrero, *Memorias*, 72, 87. Lyrics to "Soldado Razo" in Rodolfo Acuña, *Occupied America: A History of Chicanos*, 4th ed. (New York: Longman, 2000), 265.

25. Jacobson and Nored, *Jeff Davis County*, 294–95. Quote comes from Fort Worth *Star-Telegram*, July 30, 1944, cited in ibid. Francis Trevelyan Miller, *The Complete History of World War II* (1945; Chicago: Progress Research Corp., 1949), 687; Morin, *Among the Valiant*, 61–66; Alonso S. Perales, *Are We Good Neighbors?* (New York: Arno Press, 1974), 293–96; Robert L. Wagner, *The Texas Army: A History of the 36th Division in the Italian Campaign* (Austin: [s.n.], 1972), 14; United States, Office of the Deputy Assistant Secretary of Defense for Military Manpower and Personnel Policy, *Hispanics in America's Defense*, 29.

26. Wagner, *The Texas Army*, 12; United States, Office of the Deputy Assistant Secretary of Defense for Military Manpower and Personnel Policy, *Hispanics in America's Defense*, 29.

27. The Mexican American participation in the Rio Rapido Crossing is told in Morin, *Among the Valiant*, 67–74. On Ramón G. Gutiérrez, see Del Rio *News-Herald*, July 6, 1944, 1; Del Rio *News-Herald*, May 26, 2013, 1A; Chávez, "Mexican Americans Who Served in World War II, 1941–1945, Sonora, Texas"; ancestry.com/search/db.aspx?dbid=2441 (US Department of Veterans Affairs BIRLS Death File, 1850–2010); http://texasmilitaryforcesmuseum.yuku.com/topic/1386/141st-E-Company#.UvlkX5tzbTd. Of further relevance to the story of Ramón Gutiérrez is Dave Gutiérrez, *Patriots from the Barrio: The True WWII Story of the Men Who Served in the U.S. Army's All Mexican American Combat Unit, the 36 Division 141st Combat Regiment, 2nd Battalion, Company E* (Bloomington, IN: XLIBRIS, 2014), which appeared when this chapter was in the copy-editing stage.

28. Guerrero, *Memorias*, chap. 14.

29. Among such sources would be Rivas-Rodríguez et al., *A Legacy Greater Than Words*, 45, 51, 61, 67, 123, 128, 263, 305; *Men and Women in the Armed Forces from Tom Green County* (San Angelo, TX: n.d., n.p.); *Conexión San Angelo*, San Angelo, Texas, vol. 13, #20, May 22, 2014, 6A; *Men and Women in the Armed Forces from Runnels County* (S.I.: s.n., 194?); Palmer, *How Sutton County Helped in World War II*; www.familiasdeterlingua.com (accessed February 11, 2014).

30. *La Prensa* began reporting casualties through the "Boletín" circa August 1944 and ended publishing the information around October 1945. To gain access to *La Prensa* notices, I utilized the database titled Hispanic American Newspapers, 1808–1980 (Stillwater, MN: Readex, a Division of NewsBank). I retrieved information on the Texas World War II era by entering key words such as "Del Rio" (or whatever the town being researched); then "*soldado*"; and, last "Boletín del departamento de guerra."

31. Valuable for this research was http://www.archives.gov/research/military/ww2/army-casualties/texas.html.

32. Wylie, *History of Van Horn and Culberson County*, 173; Casey, *Mirages, Mysteries, and Reality*, 319; Thompson, *History of Marfa and Presidio County*, 2: 518, 526; Jacobson and Nored, *Jeff Davis County*, 295; Flores, "The Good Life the Hard Way," 275–77; Hughes, *Pecos*, 2: 21; Jewell G. Pritchett, *From the Top of Old Hayrick: A Narrative History of Coke County* (Abilene, TX: Protchett, 1970), 175–76; Schleicher County Historical Society, *A History of Schleicher County* (San Angelo, TX: Anchor Publishing, 1979), 131–32 (has photos only).

See further, Rivas-Rodríguez et al., *A Legacy Greater Than Words*, 51, 61, 127, 128; *Men and Women in the Armed Forces from Tom Green County* (San Angelo, TX: n.d., n.p.); *Men and Women in the Armed Forces from Runnels County* (S.I.: s.n., 194?); Palmer, *How Sutton County Helped in World War II*; San Angelo *Standard-Times*, May 8, 1945, 12–13 (European peace edition).

33. San Angelo *Standard-Times*, May 8, 1945, 8, 12–13 (European peace edition); May 11, 1948, 18; Wylie, *History of Van Horn and Culberson County*, 173; Casey, *Mirages, Mysteries, and Reality*, 319; Thompson, *History of Marfa and Presidio County*, 2: 518, 526; Jacobson and Nored, *Jeff Davis County*, 295; Flores, "The Good Life the Hard Way," 275–77; Flores, "What a Difference a War Makes," 185, 194; Hughes, *Pecos*, 2: 21; Whitehead Memorial Museum, *La Hacienda: An Official Bicentennial Publication* (Del Rio, TX: The Museum, 1976), 212–13; Guerrero, *Memorias*, 96; Arnoldo De León, *San Angeleños: Mexican Americans in San Angelo, Texas* (San Angelo, TX: Fort Concho Museum Press, 1985), 58; San Angelo *Standard-Times*, October 2, 1945, 7; May 30, 1946, 11; November 12, 1947, p. 8. See further, Perales, *Are We Good Neighbors?*, 284–89; *Men and Women in the Armed Forces from Tom Green County* (San Angelo, TX: n.d., n.p.); http://www.archives.gov/research/military/ww2/army-casualties/texas.html.

34. Thompson, *History of Marfa and Presidio County*, 2: 518; Wylie, *History of Van Horn and Culberson County*, 173; *Men and Women in the Armed Forces from Tom Green County* (San Angelo, TX: n.d., n.p.); *Men and Women in the Armed Forces from Runnels County* (S.I.: s.n., 194?); Palmer, *How Sutton County Helped in World War II*.

35. The "Boletín" also listed those killed in action ("*muertos en acción*") and prisoners of war that Germany released following its defeat.

36. San Angelo *Standard-Times*, December 14, 1941, 4; June 7, 1942, 5; February 3, 1943, 16; February 12, 1943, p. 6; August 18, 1943, 5; January 2, 1944, 12, section 1; February 4, 1944, 1, 9; February 4, 1945, 10, section 2; September 23, 1945, 1; November 3, 1946, 25; Austin *American-Statesman*, Austin, Texas, August 11, 1997, A9. The following sources also list POWs: Casey, *Mirages, Mysteries, and Reality*, 319; Wylie, *History of Van Horn and Culberson County*, 173, 174. The Mexican American involvement in the fight for the Philippines is discussed in Morin, *Among the Valiant*, 40–41.

37. Guerrero, *Memorias*, 94–95; Flores, "What a Difference a War Makes," 187; Wylie, *History of Van Horn and Culberson County*, 174; Thompson, *History of Marfa and Presidio County*, 2: 518; Hughes, *Pecos*, 2: 21; Casey, *Mirages, Mysteries, and Reality*, 319; Rivas-Rodríguez et al., *A Legacy Greater Than Words*, 51, 122, 128, 305; *Men and Women in the Armed Forces from Tom Green County* (San Angelo, TX: n.d., n.p.); *Men and Women in the Armed Forces from Runnels County* (S.l.: s.n., 194?); Palmer, *How Sutton County Helped in World War II*.

38. Thompson, *History of Marfa and Presidio County*, 2: 518; Rivas-Rodríguez et al., *A Legacy Greater Than Words*, 127; Earl H. Elam, "Acculturation on the Rio Grande Frontier: The Founding of San José del Polvo and the Family of Lucía Rede Madrid Family," *Journal of Big Bend Studies* 5 (January 1993): 79–95.

39. See Alexander Mendoza and Charles David Grear, eds., *Texans and War: New Interpretations of the State's Military History* (College Station: Texas A&M University Press, 2012), 55, 67 n. 65.

40. http://www.archives.gov/research/military/korean-war/casualty-lists/tx-alpha.pdf. Also, San Angelo *Standard-Times*, December 8, 1950, 12; March 17, 1952, 7; October 15, 1952, 2.

41. Morin, *Among the Valiant*, 270–75; www.forthancockisd.net; www.sisd.net.

42. Flores, "What a Difference a War Makes," 194–95; Guerrero, *Memorias*, 97–98, 101; Jacobson and Nored, *Jeff Davis County*, 295.

43. *La Prensa*, San Antonio, Texas, "Dos casos mas de discriminación," April 29, 1944, 2. West Texas towns that practiced segregation are included in Perales, *Are We Good Neighbors?*, 213–22. See further Flores, "The Good Life the Hard Way," 250; De León, *San Angeleños*, 70–71.

44. Perales, *Are We Good Neighbors?*, 124–25, 263–65; Emilio Zamora, *Claiming Rights and Righting Wrongs in Texas: Mexican Workers and Job Politics during World War II* (College Station: Texas A&M University Press, 2009), 104–6.

45. Perales, *Are We Good Neighbors?*, 168–69, 122–23, 213–23; Flores, "What a Difference a War Makes," 192–93.

46. Cited in David Montejano, *Anglos and Mexicans in the Making of Texas, 1836–1986* (Austin: University of Texas Press, 1987), 270.

47. Guerrero, *Memorias*, 101; Flores, "What a Difference a War Makes," 196. The most notorious such case took place in the East Texas town of Richmond where Sergeant Macario García, who had won the Medal of Honor, was refused service in September 1945 while in uniform. See Michael A. Olivas, "The 'Trial of the Century' That Never Was: Staff Sgt. Macario García, the Congressional Medal of Honor, and the Oasis Café," *Indiana Law Journal* 83, no. 4 (2008).

48. Letter from Raymond Wheat to Mr. Everett Williams, identified as 180.23 in Dr. Héctor P. García Papers, Special Collections and Archives, Mary and Jeff Bell Library, Texas A&M University–Corpus Christi.

49. Marty Beard, "The Right to Learn: Desegregation in a West Texas Town," *Junior Historian* 52, no. 5 (1992): 9–12; Flores, "What a Difference a War Makes," 196–97; De León, *San Angeleños*, 73–76; Arnold García, "Memorial Day, Salute Latino Soldiers Who Shaped History," Austin *American-Statesman*, May 27, 2007, G03. For an overview of post–World War II politics in Texas, see Arnoldo De León, *Mexican American in Texas: A Brief History*, 3rd ed. (Wheeling, IL: Harlan Davidson, 2009), chap. 8.

50. De León, *Mexican Americans in Texas*, chaps. 8 and 9.

Eva Camúñez Tucker

Hispanic Philanthropist in the Concho Country

Although raised under humble circumstances, Eva Camúñez never lacked for encouragement and moral support at home. Her parents urged her to pursue an education and aspire for something above their own common station. Taking their encouragement to heart, Eva went on to become an educator, a State Department translator after World War II, a successful partner with her husband in the West Texas oil business, and ultimately a well-known philanthropist. Sharing her good fortune, she granted millions of dollars to causes ranging from religious instruction, to medicine, to social services, and to education.

Into her nineties, Eva Camúñez Tucker remains firmly committed to concerns held since an early age: the well-being and vigor of the Catholic Church, the centrality of religion to the human character, the undeniable worth of an education, the powerlessness of the disadvantaged, and even the status of such varied institutions as hospitals and museums. Her good fortune—including a healthy condition, a still unshakable religious faith, confidence in her convictions, and social acclaim and affluence—allows her to continue advancing these issues across the Concho Country.

Eva Camúñez Tucker was no newcomer to West Texas. The Camúñez family had lived in the Concho Valley for more than a hundred years; her father Reynaldo, in fact, was born in the San Angelo area in 1883 and married Josefa Lara, a young woman from Fort Stockton (in Far West Texas), in 1909. Two children issued from the marriage: Eva Camúñez, born on April 9, 1911, and Noé Camúñez, born in 1913.[1]

Reynaldo and Josefa Camúñez were the products of traditional nineteenth-century Hispanic pioneer values. They understood that familial

This chapter was originally published in the *Journal of Big Bend Studies* 15 (2003): 181–94.

love fostered strength, confidence, and a positive self-image. Moral principles grounded in adult example and the conservative codes of rural America—which called for chaperoned dances, a certain etiquette for dating, and specific expectations of female modesty—were to be instilled. A craving for learning, self-control, and tenacity were virtues to be acquired early in life.[2]

The Camúñez family also placed much value on religion. Josefa, in particular, was a devout Catholic who believed service to the church to be a Christian duty, prayer helpful to attaining life ambitions, and a religious education as fundamental as a secular one. Indeed, she enrolled Eva at age five (1916) at San Angelo's St. Peter's School, a two-room adobe, segregated Catholic learning center—"one room was for wood and chickens and the other was the school for us Mexicans," in Eva's own words—under the tutorship of the Sisters of Charity of the Incarnate Word from Mexico. At St. Peter's, the young scholar received lessons on discipline, patience, and humility, as well as on the correct usage of the Spanish language.[3]

Public school policy in San Angelo, until about the mid-1950s, called for racial separation, so that education after St. Peter's was at a segregated campus—or, as in the language of that age, the "Mexican school." Another matter during the 1920s was a rule denying Mexicans advancement into the higher grades.

But Josefa (using money from a small family inheritance) devised a clever plan to have her daughter enter the city's junior high. Off to San Antonio and parochial school went the fifteen-year-old Eva in 1926. At the Incarnate Word Academy, she received proper preparation for secondary schooling, instruction on the church's teachings, and exposure to other people's cultures, for Incarnate Word was an integrated institution. She returned to San Angelo after two years away and entered the eighth grade with the help of the determined Josefa who would not let the issue of race sidetrack a future. In 1930, Eva became the first native-born San Angelo Hispanic to graduate from high school.[4]

Not satisfied with this major accomplishment, Eva set out in pursuit of new goals. The most feasible thing to do after graduation, it appeared, was enrolling at the local commercial college and there acquiring a useful trade. Her family, after all, had little money to finance a college education. At the business school, the hand of luck intervened; it came by way of the headmistress, an empathetic, understanding, and far-seeing community activist named Mrs. W. W. Carson. Taking Eva under her wing, Mrs. Carson mentored and guided her, gave her renewed confidence, cultivated her innate intelligence, and reminded Eva of the power embedded in positive thinking.

Speaking frankly, Mrs. Carson reminded her student of the harsh realities of being "Mexican" in the 1930s: that Anglo-Americans believed Mexican-descent people to be inferior, and that not much of a career could be expected of a Mexican stenographer, since few businesses would hire her. But Mrs. Carson simultaneously reinforced the aspiring secretary's ingrained belief that an education provided the way to success in the world. The kindly instructor posed a question to the young Eva: why not consider a teaching career instead? Eva would then not only attend to humanity in general but also serve as an educator for the less privileged—namely, Mexican American children—and become a role model.

Mrs. Carson then proposed a compact. If Eva determined to pursue a college education, she would see to it that her young charge enrolled at San Angelo Junior College (SAJC, the local institution of higher learning during that era), find her the necessary financial assistance for tuition, books, and fees, and most enticing of all, place her in a teaching position upon acquiring certification. With financial support from her own mother, the hopeful educator started SAJC in 1931 and earned her teaching credentials the next year.[5]

Keeping her word, Mrs. Carson found employment for Eva in Mertzon, Texas, a rural community situated some thirty miles west of San Angelo. Instead of living up to high expectations, however, the Mertzon job was laden with problems. First, it hardly measured up to a golden nest; the pay was quite low at $60 a month. Second, the learning environment consisted of a crowded schoolroom with overaged children who had to do without enough desks, school supplies, and books. Third, Mertzon was a long way to travel without an automobile; in the early days in Mertzon, Eva commuted with sheepshearers (who owned a pickup truck) on weekends. Fourth, lodging proved difficult to find; in that era, whites did not volunteer accommodations even for the "Mexican teacher." To cope, Miss Camúñez found boarding in a Mexican American household in the town. Ultimately, the parish from Sacred Heart Church in Mertzon took her in as a tenant at a small cottage adjacent to the church. As part of a reciprocal agreement, she would teach the catechism to local Hispanic children.[6]

Adjusting to the situation as best she could, Eva worked diligently to advance the educational status of the Mexican American children, most of whom belonged to poor families who made their living as ranch and oil field hands. Where possible, she undertook efforts to improve material circumstances for her students, if not for their parents. The spiritual condition of the class was no less important to the young teacher, so that on a regular basis, she walked the children two or three blocks to Sacred

Heart Church for religious instruction. As noted above, a material motive lay behind the catechism lessons, for through them she paid for staying at the church's cottage. To help supplement the rent, her mother would come in every other weekend and clean house for the priest.[7]

After five years in Mertzon, the now veteran educator received a new offer—doing the same thing for $75—from the school district in Ballinger, another West Texas community located some thirty-five miles northeast of San Angelo. Upon arriving in Ballinger in June 1937, she realized that she had only exchanged one set of inferior surroundings for another; she would have to teach all seven grades in the same classroom, make space for more than two hundred students, and somehow acquire better equipment and learning materials. In short order, however, the school board provided her with additional rooms and another teacher. Ultimately, she won promotion to principal of the "Mexican School."

In Ballinger, she continued playing a role that no longer made her uncomfortable. As Mrs. Carson had predicted, Miss Camúñez had long become a role model for young Hispanics; additionally, the Mexican community in town recognized and respected her as a person of education and "distinction." People sought her out as a friend, a confidante, and interpreter. As had been the case in Mertzon, she acted as a "jack-of-all-trades," helping with civic matters, community festivals, and religious instruction. Further, she began to assume a close interest in the welfare of her fellow man. For example, she came to the rescue of those needing financial assistance, facing health problems, or lacking transportation to neighboring cities.[8]

By 1942, new opportunities beckoned. Teaching had been good to her, providing her with a rewarding and unforgettable experience. Education remained a priority, but she longed to test her independence, to travel, and see other parts of the country beyond West Texas—especially the big city. She would never forget that people invariably expressed heartfelt gratitude for help they received, that disadvantaged people were no less human, and that a nudge of assistance could conceivably change their luck. She would relate later in life that plain folks—with whom she shared much in common—had become for her a source of support and inspiration, that "they had made her."[9]

Newer opportunities revolved around World War II exigencies, as the government desperately needed all kinds of assistance on the home front. Wishing to try something new and wanting to contribute to the war effort, Eva applied for a job in government. Her mother and father strongly disapproved of this career choice. They believed it improper (and dangerous) for a single woman to be going off to the big city; indeed, by their standard of morality, a woman who was thirty-one years old should long ago have taken a husband and settled down to raise her family. Equally strong opposition came from Art Tucker, an independent oil producer from Ballinger with extensive oil field interests throughout West Texas, whom Eva had met about the time she left her teaching job. Tucker had marriage in mind and did not want to see his prospective bride depart for places unknown.[10]

But their objections failed to deter her, and by March 1942 she was working as a mail censor in San Antonio (at a pay lower than that of a school administrator). Her job description called for reviewing the mail—namely, that written in Spanish. Considered an excellent worker and administrator, she soon won promotion as head of her department. Subsequently, the government transferred her to Brownsville and Laredo, where she managed local offices. She was in the latter city when the war ended.[11]

Her sense of self-reliance carried over into the postwar era. After a brief visit to San Angelo, Eva Camúñez relocated in August 1945 to Washington, DC; there, she found living accommodations just five blocks away from the White House and employment as a translator of legal documents for the State Department. In the nation's capital, she developed a cosmopolitan flair, gaining insight into the world beyond Texas—mostly from her roommates, young Anglo girls from throughout the country, some of whom worked in the Pentagon. She also learned about the most modern fashions in style (people in Washington wore gloves, hats, and dress shoes), the art of choosing the proper eating places and employing the best restaurant etiquette, and about presenting an image of proper comportment.[12]

The persistent Art Tucker had, in the meantime, traveled to see her everywhere she had been since 1942, and he continued his courtship in Washington. Eva kept spurning him, emphasizing that her religious beliefs permitted nothing less than a church marriage—a matter that posed problems since Art was not Catholic. Moreover, he was an older man—fifty-one years of age compared to Eva's thirty-seven—a factor that did not sit well with her father and brother. There also existed a "race" factor; since this would obviously be a cross-cultural marriage, it presented another consideration for the Camúñez family. After years of debate, however, all concerned conceded to the marriage, and Eva returned from Washington. Art and Eva exchanged wedding vows at St. Joseph's Church in San Angelo on December 30, 1948.[13]

Marriage brought dramatic changes to the young girl who had grown up in the San Angelo barrio but had then gone on to find a new life outside West Texas. To be sure, marriage had not produced acceptance on the part of white society. In Ballinger, the Tuckers still found it difficult to find housing because of Mrs. Tucker's ethnicity,[14] although other changes did come to pass. Her material standing, for one thing, took an upward turn, as Art Tucker was a person of some wealth, and his oil business in the later 1940s showed no signs of slackening. Second, her marriage took on the likeness of a business copartnership.

The Tuckers soon found someone to rent them quarters in Ballinger, and it would be from their apartment that Eva Tucker, for the next decade, managed her husband's trucking concern while Art worked in other areas of the business. The front room of the household was turned into an improvised office; from it Eva conducted much of the company's affairs, including scheduling routes for the truckers and dispersing the payroll. Mrs. Tucker not only coordinated the Tucker enterprise effectively, but also became proficient in the new calling. Learning on the job and asking questions of the truckers, she came to master the details of the oil industry, knowing it better than Art, it came to be said. With helpful instruction from a kindly neighbor, she began dabbling in the stock market by the late 1940s, achieving proficiency in the techniques of investment. In 1958, Art Tucker bought an oil refinery in Lueders (a small town twenty-five miles north of Abilene), and the couple relocated there.[15]

Business took up much of Eva Tucker's time during the course of her marriage, but she allowed herself to indulge in some favorite causes. She participated in the religious activities of St. Ann's Catholic Church in Stamford (just down the road from their home), and got involved in the WICS (Women in Community Service) program that was active in Lueders. The organization had as its mission helping female dropouts or assisting young women in need of job training.[16]

Actually, marriage postponed Mrs. Tucker's commitment to important issues until after her retirement, which came shortly after Art Tucker's sudden death on February 24, 1975. Tucker's loss occurred on the heels of her mother's own departure from life in 1972, and it preceded Noé's capitulation to cancer in 1976. Within a matter of four years she had lost all those dear to her (Eva's father Reynaldo had passed on in 1966), a tragedy made worse as the Tuckers had been childless.[17]

Her mourning was made more difficult by the task of having to oversee the de-accession of the Tucker business, which she sold to Pride Petroleum in 1975.[18] In the early 1980s, she made the permanent move to the city of her upbringing, settling back into the old neighborhood and the house where she had come of age.

Returning to San Angelo and her modest home on Fourteenth Street not only offered comfort and familiarity but also made a statement about Mrs. Tucker's views on worldly materialism. Though the Tuckers had amassed riches, Mrs. Tucker found no redeeming satisfaction in flaunting her wealth; standing in life—in her view—derived from the spiritual and religious contentment one felt and nourished. From that unpretentious home—enclosed by a simple wire fence to keep in a few chickens—Eva Camúñez Tucker hastened her commitment to philanthropy.[19]

Much of the impulse behind her altruism could be traced to her youth. From her parents, Mrs. Tucker had learned the meaning of religion and the need to be vigilant in furthering the work of the church. She had grown up economically disadvantaged, and in fact, had seen poverty all around during her formative years in San Angelo. She had experienced prejudice and educational inequality firsthand, and struggled against the odds to achieve what others acquired as a matter of course. As a teacher for some fifteen years, she had witnessed the toll that life's travail took on the poor, noting among many things, their helplessness in emergency situations. Her philosophy of giving would be based on these personal experiences, but most directly on the advice she received from her brother as he approached death: that she should use her money in a manner that would bring the most good for humanity. As a philanthropist, therefore, Mrs. Tucker would consider herself no more than a conduit for the Lord. "I am just being a good steward. What I have belongs to the Lord. I am just giving it back to the Lord. I only want to do the most good for the most people."[20]

The Catholic Church, both locally and elsewhere, would become a major beneficiary of her charitable acts. During the late 1970s, she helped finance religious centers in the West Texas towns of Brady, Stamford, and Ballinger;[21] in the city of her birth—at the same time—she helped to establish Christ the King Retreat Center, a multipurpose facility where the bishop conducted diocesan business. In San Angelo, also, she saw in 1988 to the construction of a monastery named the Carmel of Our Lady of Grace for the Carmelite Cloistered Nuns and, in 1994, provided vast sums of money to have her own parish church of St. Joseph's remodeled and expanded. In 2002, she donated land on which Catholic Outreach Services of San Angelo built its Social Service Agency and Thrift Shop. St. John's Hospital, established in 1910 by the Sisters of Charity of the Incarnate Word, but later functioning as a private institution, likewise profited from her generosity. Mrs. Tucker contributed to the hospital's hospice program and to an expansion undertaken on its physical plant during the 1980s.[22] Until St. John's Hospital closed its inpatient acute hospital in 1999, a day surgery unit there bore Mrs. Tucker's name.

Education, particularly as it affected Hispanics ("my people," she would remark matter-of-factly), would continue to be a major consideration for Mrs. Tucker. She freely donated to projects of educational value such as tours of the nation's capital, visits to conferences on Mexican American issues, and trips to motivational sessions that might benefit Mexican Americans. A favorite cause came to be a library at Fort Concho Elementary School, located in a predominantly Mexican American neighborhood, to which Mrs. Tucker donated some $20,000 in 1988 when the San Angelo Independent School District built the new school complex. The school board gratefully named the library building and collection after her brother, Noé Camúñez, who had left a mark on San Angelo education, becoming the city's first Mexican American principal during the 1940s and 1950s.[23]

On a regular basis, she contributed funds to assist college students through the local chapters of the League of United Latin American Citizens (LULAC), the American GI Forum, and through Angelo State University (ASU). Her interest in higher education motivated her in October 1995 to contribute $150,000 to the "Up and Coming Scholars Program" at Angelo State University. The enterprise identified eighth-grade high achievers who came from financially distressed backgrounds, helped them prepare for college during their secondary school years, and then guaranteed their college tuition and fees so they could acquire their degrees.[24]

Helping those burdened by a twist of fate, a physical mishap, or advanced age also engaged her interests. She donated thousands of dollars to pursuits intended to assist those victimized by adversity, such as the West Texas Rehab Center of San Angelo and the San Angelo Day Care Nursery. In 1993, she became the first private benefactor to help the Concho Valley Home for Girls project, which came to be called the Tucker Home, at 329 Preusser Street.[25] On many occasions, she interceded financially to assist a needy family or a person in the midst of a crisis.

Artistic expression in San Angelo was also enhanced by her philanthropy. Her donations to the San Angelo Museum of Fine Arts (one of several programs offered by Fort Concho Museum, a national historic landmark in the city) helped to finance its many programs.[26] She helped maintain music as a feature of the city's elegance, contributing to the San Angelo Symphony, and through special underwriting to local organizations (among them the Association of Mexican American Students at ASU) that sponsored professional mariachi bands from out of town.

By the late 1980s, many knew of Mrs. Tucker's accomplishments. Those most touched by her goodwill expressed their gratitude in several ways.

Local organizations held special functions in appreciation of her benevolence. The city did its part to credit her role in advancing civic life: May 17, 1988, was designated by the mayor as Eva Camúñez Tucker Day, and the San Angelo Chamber of Commerce chose her in 1996 as "Citizen of the Year." Angelo State University similarly acknowledged her important role in promoting education by granting her an honorary Doctor of Law in May 1996.[27] Honors from outside the city further recognized her legacy. In 1999, the Women's Chamber of Commerce of Texas listed Mrs. Tucker as one of the state's most influential women, and the next year, the Images of Women Conference (held at Southwest Texas State University in San Marcos, Texas) recognized her as a Latina Legend.[28]

The most special distinctions for her work came from Rome, however. Religion had been an important component of her character since a youth in the 1910s, and her lifelong work to advance the spiritual and temporal condition of the church resulted in two milestones. In 1981, she became a Papal Lady when the Pope appointed her a member of the Equestrian Order of the Holy Sepulchre, a papal honor society for those providing outstanding charity to the church. Another award of great distinction, again for generosity, reached her in June 1996. The bishop of the San Angelo diocese celebrated mass wherein he bestowed, on behalf of the Pope, the Pro Ecclesia et Pontifice Award on Mrs. Tucker.[29]

The story of Mrs. Eva Camúñez Tucker is instructive in a number of ways. First, it serves as another example of how circumstances need not be barriers to success in life; she gained prominence and recognition despite immense odds. Second, historical subjects can be other than great statespersons, military figures, political activists, or feminist advocates. Some of Mrs. Tucker's most distinguished Mexican American contemporaries included Dr. Hector P. García, congressman Henry B. González, federal judge Reynaldo G. Garza, and 1930s LULAC leader Alice Dickerson Montemayor. Yet, ordinary people can improve upon the human condition via a multitude of acts. For instance, philanthropists have pursued efforts to uplift humankind by combating disease, conducting missionary work among those in need of religious enlightenment, and seeking to amend circumstances in impoverished environments. Such objectives similarly underlay Mrs. Tucker's intentions, but she held particular concerns about disadvantaged Mexican Americans in West Texas. Specifically, she hoped to encourage political solidarity among Mexican American associations and to promote interracial understandings. The last thing that one can obtain from the case of Eva Camúñez Tucker is that historical actors are not always distant, aloof types who break with their past upon finding success. To the contrary, Mrs. Tucker retains an old-fashioned allegiance to humility, ethnic pride, and American values.

Notes

1. *Los Tiempos*, a supplement of the San Angelo *Standard-Times*, December 14, 1983, 1–2.
2. Ibid.
3. San Angelo *Standard-Times*, February 12, 1989, 1E, and Verónica Salazar, "Philanthropist Says Giving Is Good Stewardship to God," undated newspaper clipping in the Eva Camúñez Tucker Papers held in the West Texas Collection in the Porter Henderson Library at Angelo State University.
4. *Los Tiempos*, December 14, 1983, 1–2; and San Angelo *Standard-Times*, February 12, 1989, 1E.
5. San Angelo *Standard-Times*, February 12, 1989, 1E; October 10, 1995, 1A; and May 7, 2000, 3E. Also, oral interview with Eva Tucker, March 26, 1993, transcript in the Eva Camúñez Tucker Papers, West Texas Collection.
6. *Los Tiempos*, December 14, 1983, 1–2; San Angelo *Standard-Times*, February 12, 1989, 1E; and Eva Tucker interview, March 26, 1993.
7. *Los Tiempos*, December 14, 1983, 1–2; San Angelo *Standard-Times*, February 12, 1989, 1E; and Eva Tucker interview, March 26, 1993.
8. *Los Tiempos*, December 14, 1983, 1–2; San Angelo *Standard-Times*, February 12, 1989, 1E.
9. San Angelo *Standard-Times*, February 12, 1989, 1E.
10. Ibid.
11. *Los Tiempos*, December 14, 1983, 1–2; San Angelo *Standard-Times*, February 12, 1989, 1E; and Eva Tucker interview, March 26, 1993.
12. San Angelo *Standard-Times*, February 12, 1989, 1E; and Eva Tucker interview, March 26, 1993.
13. Eva Tucker interview, March 26, 1993.
14. San Angelo *Standard-Times*, February 12, 1989, 1E.
15. *Los Tiempos*, December 14, 1983, 1–2; San Angelo *Standard-Times*, February 12, 1989, 1E.
16. Undated newspaper clipping in Eva Camúñez Papers, West Texas Collection.
17. *Los Tiempos*, December 14, 1983, 1–2. Salazar, "Philanthropist Says Giving Is Good Stewardship to God."
18. San Angelo *Standard-Times*, May 7, 2000, 3E.
19. Ibid., February 12, 1989, 1E; and May 7, 2000, 1E.
20. Salazar, "Philanthropist Says Giving Is Good Stewardship to God."
21. *Los Tiempos*, December 14, 1983, 1–2.
22. San Angelo *Standard-Times*, February 12, 1989, 1E; February 25, 1989, 1C; and April 3, 1994, 6E.
23. Ibid., January 13, 1988, 1C; May 20, 1988, 1C; and San Angelo *Standard-Times* undated newspaper clipping in Eva Camúñez Tucker Papers, West Texas Collection.
24. San Angelo *Standard-Times*, October 10, 1995, 1A.
25. Ibid., August 3, 1989, 6E; August 23, 1992, 1E; March 29, 1993, 1A; April 25, 1993, 1E.
26. *Compadre: The Newsletter of the Museum of Fine Art*, vol. 1, issue 2 (1988): 8.
27. San Angelo *Standard-Times*, February 16, 1996, 5A; February 18, 1996, 8A; February 24, 1996, 2A; and May 11, 1996, 8B.
28. San Angelo *Standard-Times*, November 7, 1999, 1A; and March 26, 2000, 1B.
29. *Los Tiempos*, December 14, 1983, 1–2; San Angelo *Standard-Times*, May 25, 1996, 3B; and June 10, 1996, 5A.

María Cárdenas

San Angelo Chicano-Era Activist

Many Mexican Americans got involved in the political movements of the 1960s through the early 1980s. In this highly politicized era, María Cárdenas emerged as a leading voice in the San Angelo barrios. *As an activist, she succeeded in bringing the single-member district system to San Angelo, won three terms on the city council, helped usher in Tom Green County redistricting, and in other ways improved conditions for the Mexican American community. A new generation of leaders during the 1990s and after gratefully recognized her achievements.*

They go by several names in the *barrio*. People refer to them as "*una doña*," "*una Juana Gallo*," or an Adelita. More derisively their critics call them "*una vieja*," or "*una entremetida*."[1] Every family produces such a feisty kind and every neighborhood knows one. Until very recently, however, such persons were not widely known outside Mexican American enclaves. For one thing, most restricted their activities to events within the barrio, among them church affairs, community celebrations, emergencies, and the like. Then, they kept a low profile, for a variety of reasons: perhaps a lack of education, an inability to speak English well, or a desire not to cross over into the realm of wider politics. Contemporary ethnographers find these types an absorbing subject of study, especially as many of them today have become determined voices for their neglected neighborhoods.

Whether operating behind the scenes or as public figures, these barrio activists have common leadership traits. They tend to be bold, confident, aggressive, and confrontational when necessary, and innately intelligent. Their admirers have a healthy respect for them, praise their courage, and

This chapter was originally published in Donald Willett and Stephen Curley, eds., *Invisible Texans: Women and Minorities in Texas History* (Boston: McGraw-Hill, 2005): 226–36.

trust their instincts. Their detractors, on the other hand, depict them as calculating, ambitious, cunning, and troublemaking. In the West Texas city of San Angelo (population about 90,000, according to the census of 2000), such a woman from the barrio rose to prominence during the Chicano Era of the 1960s and 1970s. Her name was María Cárdenas (1935–1993).

María Guevara was born on January 20, 1935, in Tivoli, Texas, a small farm community in Refugio County (South Texas). Typical of poor Mexican-descent people of the Depression and World War II eras, her school attendance was erratic and she never actually graduated. María spent a portion of her young life as did many youngsters then: picking cotton and working at odd jobs when they availed themselves (at the age of eight, she found part-time work as a dishwasher in a family restaurant). Her family moved to San Angelo sometime in 1945 to escape the tuberculosis epidemic then ravaging South Texas. She married in the city at age 15, and children followed quickly. Any hopes she had entertained about finishing her eighth-grade education diminished, as much of her life by the time she turned twenty-five was devoted to doing household chores and raising her six youngsters. But she always held an intellectual curiosity and an interest in the world (especially the political sphere) outside the home. She had never forgotten the inspiration of her mother ("a typical housewife," María told an interviewer, with "dreams and aspirations for the good life"), nor her counsel: "she had told her girls that marriage shackles people."[2]

The Chicano movement became the catalyst for what would become a lengthy, and ultimately, a rather productive political career. María's initial plunges into the political arena remain obscure, but by the late 1960s and early 1970s her passion for the political game roused her into expressing opinions on local controversies through letters to the editor of the San Angelo *Standard-Times*, the city's newspaper. In one such opinion, she complained about school busing, noting the discriminatory nature of a program that daily transferred Mexican American youngsters to area white schools but did not compel Anglo children to be brought to classrooms in the barrios. How could human understanding be fostered under such a skewed system of integration, she questioned?[3]

Simultaneously, she kept abreast of national, statewide, and community issues.[4] Particularly attractive to her were the politics of the nascent Raza Unida Party (RUP), a Texas third party of that period that addressed problems afflicting Mexican American communities. In late 1971, Cárdenas traveled to San Antonio to attend a meeting called by RUP leaders to decide whether the party should expand statewide (the delegates did in fact vote to do that).[5] In the fall of the next year, she journeyed to El Paso to attend

RUP's national convention, and there won recognition as the Tom Green County voting delegate.[6] The gubernatorial race of November 1972 found her in the thick of campaigning in San Angelo for Ramsey Muñiz (the RUP candidate), her sharp responses to questions and quick wit (trademarks of her later public persona) already in evidence. When one skeptical Anglo observer in the *Standard-Times* questioned the need for an ethnic party such as RUP, she answered that the likes of racists such as the letter writer required it.[7]

On an everyday basis, however, local problems and city politics interested her most. She joined grassroots neighborhood associations organized to address pervasive problems in the San Angelo barrios or to deal with stressful matters when they surfaced. One such organization she joined went by the name of the Consejo del Barrio ("neighborhood council"), whose purpose it was to guide and support people as they attempted to resolve issues with local government, business officials, or school authorities. A major problem that worried many was the danger to children who daily crossed a heavily traveled thoroughfare (actually Highway 87) in order to get to the local neighborhood school. By February 1972, Cárdenas had emerged as the state chairperson of an advisory board that represented the several Consejos del Barrio existing throughout Texas.[8]

Her involvement in city politics took a more serious turn around 1973 when her son Abel, an 18-year-old senior at Central High School in the city, entered the race for city commissioner Place 5. The young contestant had apparently learned much from his mother's activism with Raza Unida: he referred to himself as a "Chicano" (the popular term of self-reference among RUP people) and belonged to the Mexican American Youth Organization (MAYO), a strong activist group of the late 1960s and 1970s that had actually been the force behind the birth of RUP. His platform, however, said little of ethnicity but focused on municipal issues: city finances, water problems, and the need for better recreational facilities. The campaign proved unsuccessful, though it would not be young Abel's last foray into politics.[9]

Certainly, the defeat did not diminish María's zeal for politics. Community affairs continued to entice her. She dealt with neighborhood questions (one of them being the naming of the city park in the south-side barrio) and with national propositions (such as the clamor for resurrecting the defunct Bracero Program) in a straightforward manner, an approach that kept her in the limelight,[10] though it also alienated fellow leaders uncomfortable with her combative style. By the mid-1970s, life took a turn for María. Her marriage ended in divorce, she passed her General Education Development

(GED) test in 1974, and the next year she enrolled at Angelo State University (ASU) as a government major.[11] She now set her sights on loftier goals.

The year 1976 found her leading a drive designed to bring the concept of Single Member Districts (SMD) to the city of San Angelo. SMD proponents sought to divide San Angelo into six districts, one of them being the heavily Mexican American barrio in the southern section of the city. Along with several other interested leaders from throughout the city, she succeeded in her goal of acquiring 1,500 signatures for a petition that would force the SMD issue onto a Charter Amendment ballot in that year's election.[12]

Mexican Americans in San Angelo in the 1970s constituted about 25 percent of the city's total population, and while Mexican American leaders had served on the city commission since the 1960s, Cárdenas and her barrio supporters believed it high time for their section of town to have its own voice in city government. All earlier Mexican American incumbents had been elected at-large, and having to win the "favor" of Anglos in order to gain office—so Cárdenas's logic went—found themselves beholden to their political backers.

For its supporters, furthermore, in the 1970s, SMD came of age, as San Angelo appeared to lag historically in clinging to at-large representation. SMDs assured the election of one who would faithfully stand up for a district's needs, allowed for heretofore voiceless groups to gain direct representation in the city commission, and permitted constituents greater leverage in ensuring that the city extended municipal services to their neglected neighborhoods.[13] Opponents of the SMD plan countered that at-large elections mirrored the American democratic tradition because they permitted those most passionate about politics and the best qualified to win election. The SMD proposition, on the other hand, unfairly gave power to areas with traditionally low voter turnout. Single member districts further generated "turf" fights, as incumbents looked out for the good of the district and not that of the city.[14]

On April 3, 1976, the people of San Angelo approved the SMD plan that María Cárdenas and SMD proponents had so vigorously pushed. María proclaimed herself "overwhelmed" by the victory. But the process of implementation was still ahead. For one thing, SMD government would not take effect until the spring of 1978, and a panel would have to establish the district lines and work out the technical details of the new order. In June of 1976, María Cárdenas recommended to the post that then incumbent city commissioner Cato Cedillo gain membership in the SMD advisory committee.[15]

While anticipating what might unfold as a result of the election results, Cárdenas continued attending ASU and working eight-hour days and staying close to pertinent political issues. In December 1977, she attended the International Women's Year Conference held in Houston, where along with a company of other women from San Angelo, she heard support for women's causes dear to her: gender equality, the need for women's shelters and stronger laws to protect battered women, the Equal Rights Amendment, and the like.[16] She served as vice president of the Rio Vista Neighborhood Council. This lobbying group, affiliated with the local Community Action Council, acted as an intermediary with the local government bureaucracy such as the Public Housing Authority (PHA) administration.[17]

Being a part of the new concept she had just helped create was too tempting, and Cárdenas in January 1978 announced her candidacy for the City Commission District #3, the predominantly Mexican American area of San Angelo on the south side of the city. At that time she was forty-three years old, the head of a household supporting teenage children, a proud grandmother, and an ASU student still working on a degree in political science. Despite her personal goals and responsibilities, she had continued her work with the Rio Vista Neighborhood Council and had joined the Tom Green County Democratic Club and the local League of United Latin American Citizens (LULAC) council. Assets in her run for office included name recognition, an established reputation in the barrio as a fighter for neighborhood matters, and of course, voters' awareness that she had been the force behind the SMD victory. In May 1978, she brushed aside two rivals for the post and won the election for District #3. Her victory earned her the distinction of being one of the first women to win a seat in the city commission.[18] To this day, no other Mexican American woman has served in that body.

Her two-year stint (1978–80) in city government proved productive and self-satisfying. Juggling home and family duties, work, and her college education, Cárdenas dedicated herself to honing her skills in compromise and expanding her knowledge of issues that concerned the entire city and not her district alone.[19] In so doing, she won recognition and accolades from different quarters. In June 1978, for instance, she drove to Houston as a guest of US Representative Bob Krueger to attend a breakfast meeting held by Joseph Califano, the Secretary of Health, Education and Welfare. Locally, a Mexican American coalition board selected her as its chairperson to address issues relevant to Mexican Americans, though the group proved to be short-lived. Letters from constituents to the editor of the *Standard-Times* defended Cárdenas from political criticism. Appreciation dinners from grateful members of the south side barrio occasionally honored her.[20]

Respect for her ability to accomplish things mounted, but said respect flowed not from her willingness to compromise with the opposition but from her knack for forcing adversaries to bargain on the stands she took. She did so by projecting an image as a barrio person elected to articulate the needs of common folks and by employing tactics seldom used by other Mexican American politicians before her. "Dressing simply and talking directly, Cárdenas pursued her purpose by a technique that involved shrewdness, brashness, and intimidation of foes with charges of racism," a historical account of San Angelo's Mexican American community reads.[21] On one occasion, in April 1980, she alleged that "the police are trying to railroad me," as she defended herself from accusations of violating the law by not reporting an accident to which she was a party. She threatened to picket the police station if the harassment persisted and to pursue legal recourse if necessary. Her allegations attracted such media attention that the chief of police felt obliged to defend his officers for simply carrying out their duties.[22] Her reputation as a grandstanding gadfly mounted, and the 135-pound, five-foot-one María relished it.

Validation of her work and accomplishments in the city commission came in 1980 via two endorsements. First, she won reelection handily.[23] Next, the fighter from the barrio, who earned her livelihood working as a nurse's aide at a local hospital while attending ASU and suffering from chronic high blood pressure and the debilitating effects of diabetes,[24] gained wider recognition when a panel of judges picked to ascertain the top twenty-five most politically powerful people in the city listed her as among the local "power elite." The results derived from the work of a local television station reporter who, employing a sociology–political science model applied elsewhere in the country (but modified for his survey), selected a panel of fifteen citizens familiar with local matters and charged them with ranking in order of perceived power those people most effective in political, economic, and community affairs. The reporter in turn calculated the findings and determined the twenty-five most influential figures. Cárdenas made the list—she was the only woman on it. She responded modestly: "I'm honored, flabbergasted, pleased and this makes me want to go out and try to do a little bit more."[25] The San Angelo *Standard-Times* lavished praise on her singular selection: "Add the fact that she is a Mexican-American in a heavily Anglo power structure. Add to those circumstances her background as a onetime high school dropout (albeit she has gone on to become a university junior in her mid-40s) and the unique character of her position comes into focus." The newspaper went on: "There were times when [the battle over SMD system] earned her the label of an abrasive woman. She came on strong, cared little about appearances, and often raised her voice in public meetings. But when María Cárdenas won her fight, she took off the battle dress, traded it for a well-groomed exterior and began to smile more often. But the judges in the survey recognized that under the new look is still a fighter. And the combination makes her a powerful woman."[26]

Cárdenas's fighting style indeed persisted, as she still took on both Mexican Americans and Anglo-Americans whom she believed either did the minimum or nothing at all for the good of those she represented. Whenever a letter writer needed chastisement, she penned hot letters to the editor of the *Standard-Times* defending, clarifying, or explaining an issue.[27] She disdained false promises and tore into those whom she thought pseudo-representatives for Mexican Americans. In April 1981 she attended a district convention of LULAC being held in the city and there berated state and national leaders (some of them in attendance) for much talk about Mexican American problems but little action and results. "I don't want to hear more pretty speeches—I want producing," she chided those campaigning for national office.[28] In 1983 she joined an ad hoc committee of local Mexican American leaders investigating an episode of racial conflict that had occurred in the city's junior high school, and criticized the San Angelo Independent School District's failure to control this matter. Mexican American parents, she observed, felt frustrated with the "administration's inability to cope with the situation."[29] All the while, she maintained her grassroots connections. She volunteered in the community, holding in 1981, for instance, a monthly blood pressure clinic in the barrio. Politically, she worked with others toward convincing the US Department of Housing and Urban Development (HUD) to erect government-subsidized homes for the elderly in the barrio.[30]

In 1981, she also got into the politics of redistricting Tom Green County, a seemingly logical involvement given her earlier success with the SMD initiative at the city level. That year a county redistricting committee proposed a plan that Mexican American members of the committee and fellow community leaders rejected as unacceptable.[31] With the redistricting committee obstinate on its decision to move forward, Cárdenas and local attorney Roberto Soto—working for the San Angelo Texas Rural Legal Services office—called for assistance from Texas Rural Legal Aid (TRLA) in San Antonio.[32] TRLA sent attorney Raúl Noriega, the director of the Voting Rights Litigation Project, who for the duration of the dispute over county reapportionment worked closely with Soto and the other members of the community pushing for 58 percent representation in a minority district.[33] For weeks, the standoff continued with the county commission unable to develop a plan it could live with, and Soto, representing the local LULAC council and the local chapter of the American GI Forum, threatening to sue.[34] On December 4, 1981, Soto took the promised step to litigate by filing a class-action suit in federal court against the county for adopting a plan on November 16, 1981, that the plaintiffs alleged weakened the voting capacity of minorities in the city. Among the four individuals listed in the lawsuit as an aggrieved party was Abel Cárdenas Jr., Maria's oldest son and the same one who in 1973 had campaigned for a city commission post.[35] Within weeks following the lawsuit, talk of compromise surfaced, as the county commission began retreating.[36] In mid-March 1982, a United States district judge dismissed the suit in light of a settlement agreement reached by both the county commissioners and county minorities. The compromise plan established Precinct 1, with a 62 percent minority population at that time.[37]

As the above incident unfolded, María Cárdenas prepared her campaign for a third term on the city council. In April 1982, no particular issue dominated the race; Cárdenas ran on her record of four years' service facing only light opposition in a district that included approximately 12,000 inhabitants, 61 percent of them being minorities. She took the race handily with 65 percent of the vote.[38] In May, her colleagues on the city council recognized her political savvy by selecting her as mayor pro tem for the 1982–83 term.[39] The next year, Cárdenas achieved her life goal of getting a college degree when she graduated from Angelo State University as a political science major.[40]

Three terms on the city council seemed long enough for Cárdenas by 1984. Younger talent readied to replace her at the city level in case she decided to retire, and the newly created County Precinct 1 seat appeared tantalizing. She had, after all, played a part—albeit a behind-the-scenes role—in seeing the new precinct created. The position paid good money, and the possibility for doing more for the people seemed an opportunity too good to pass up. To that end, in September 1983, she formed a campaign finance committee as required by law of those persons wanting to receive financial donations from supporters. She described this step as a tentative one, as she remained undecided about campaigning, a posture she had maintained for some time.[41] A few days later, her major competitor in the upcoming race, B. C. Domínguez, announced without vacillation his own intention to run for the newly established post. A well-known figure in the barrio, Domínguez was a retired police sergeant then working as an office manager for the San Angelo representative to the state legislature. He declared that his long career as a public servant had earned widespread support across San Angelo and Tom Green County and that many had called upon him to enter the competition.[42]

In February 1984, Cárdenas made it official: she would seek the Precinct 1 opening in the scheduled May 5 primary. As of 1984, with her family grown and her college education behind, she remained as spunky at forty-nine years of age as she had ever been. Despite her status and accomplishments, she remained in the old family home and made her living running a home child-care center. But she referenced her career as an activist, touted her six-year experience on the city council, and accented her acquaintance with bureaucratic administration. As always, she would campaign as a person "of the barrio," as the gallant contender challenging the Establishment, just as she had done since the late 1960s.[43]

But her election was not to be. Within four months of her announcement, her career as an elected official and peerless activist withered. First, misfortune struck. In early April 1984, she admitted herself into a local hospital to have corrective surgery; apparently, a suture from an old operation had abscessed.[44] In the May election, she barely reached a runoff against the frontrunner, B. C. Domínguez.[45] On May 31 just two days before the runoff election, the San Angelo *Standard-Times*, as if by calculation, published a front-page story reporting Cárdenas to have been delinquent in paying property taxes (approximately $1,200) on three homes she had purchased for her children. Cárdenas hardly denied the charges and refused to give any excuse for her delinquency, other than to state the obvious: she had always worked at minimum wage jobs and had no professional career to speak of despite her newly acquired college degree, of necessity she had gone into debt to finance her schooling, and as of late had taken on the responsibility of caring for her ailing father (who had passed away earlier that month).[46] She suffered a sound defeat on June 2 at the hands of Domínguez,[47] but her loss paled in the face of continuing tribulations. The next day, June 3, Cárdenas suffered cardiac arrest (attributable to exhaustion from campaigning, the stress of the political race, or perhaps the loss of her father), and her family rushed her to the hospital where she recovered gradually during the ensuing days.[48]

What explains the loss at the polls? She and her campaign workers had been mystified by the results of the earlier election on May 5, and were as confounded now by the results of the runoff. Had she lost the support of her constituents, the ones for whom she had taken personal risks and for whom she had sacrificed, juggling a personal life with college and politics?

Not necessarily. She won only the Rio Vista box (representing the center of the south-side barrio). She placed the setback on a conspiracy by the opposition and influential clique in the city (the ones responsible for digging up her tax problems, for instance) who did not wish to see a "Mexican loudmouth" earning a cozy income by serving in a respectable position.[49] One thesis, offered soon after the defeat, still appears logical:

> Her strengths in the predominantly Mexican-American section of town turned into liabilities in a situation where her candidacy had to be broadened to incorporate newer areas. Her independence, her image as a "barrio person," her identification with "Mexican causes," her abrasive techniques in getting things done did not win new constituents. Cárdenas's old style of barrio politics—which involved door-to-door canvassing, an improvised election staff comprised primarily of her family, plus a low campaign budget—proved ineffective.[50]

Still, neither the defeat nor her health problems deflated her interest in barrio politics. During the mid-1980s, she continued attending community meetings and offering counsel (and criticism) to Mexican American organizations, and she also enjoyed discussing issues of relevance to Mexican Americans as panel or conference commentator.[51] In May 1985, she won appointment as commissioner to the local office of the Public Housing Authority, and, in that capacity, hardly made an effort to avoid controversy. In August 1986, Cárdenas took on the local powers-that-be by secretly mailing a letter to the United States Department of Housing and Urban Development (HUD) accusing high-ranking members in city politics of taking from monies earmarked for government housing and redirecting it to finance pet city projects. The accusation that the city gave higher priority to civic needs instead of programs designed to help the poor only earned her public denunciation from those identified as part of the alleged (and unfounded) intrigue.[52] The early 1990s, by which time health ailments were taking their toll, found her still making endorsements of Mexican American politicians running for one position or another.[53]

During this time, Cárdenas's work and status as a living icon did not go unrecognized. In August 1984, in recognition of her example as a role model and political activist, the Commission for Women nominated her to the Texas Women's Hall of Fame.[54] In the community, groups acknowledged her heroic status, honoring her at formal functions or inviting her to address their club or group. When the newly founded Hispanic Development Division of the San Angelo Chamber of Commerce held its inaugural "Quest for Success" awards luncheon in May 1993, María Cárdenas was one of seven luminaries recognized. By then confined to a wheelchair, she could still have the last word, as indeed she did by lavishing pride on the younger set in attendance whom she expected to continue her work.[55] Some two weeks after that memorable tribute, María Cárdenas, age fifty-eight, passed away in her home.[56]

Eulogies were not difficult to compose. She had been one of San Angelo's Chicano era's most successful activists. Beginning from about the late 1960s, she had spoken unapologetically for the city's underrepresented Mexican American barrios, either as a member of Raza Unida Party or the Democratic Party, or as an independent spokesperson. She had forged a reputation as one unafraid of confronting formidable challenges, even relishing "pit fights" with the good old boys. She had challenged conventional thinking that the voters opposed single member districts, and had triumphed. She was the only Mexican American woman to serve on the city council and the only woman on the 1980 list of twenty-five most powerful people in San Angelo. She had maintained an arduous pace of civic involvement while battling her health, contending with work, and facing financial worries and personal problems, all the while raising a family and earning a college education.[57] Her personality had made political enemies along the way, but cultivated many admirers. "Some people don't like me because I am outspoken; others like me because I *am* outspoken," she had said on one occasion.[58]

María Cárdenas's legacy to San Angelo is also impressive. Her work on the city council brought visible improvements to the district she represented via upgraded streets, city lights, and utility services, accomplishments made possible by getting her colleagues on the city council to use federal revenue sharing and community development monies for said purposes.[59] HUD housing for the elderly in San Angelo's south side is largely due to Cárdenas's insistence that public housing be built there, notwithstanding HUD's policy of discouraging the clustering of minorities in segregated areas.[60] It was María Cárdenas who also spearheaded a drive to get a pedestrian overpass built so children from the barrio attending Rio Vista Elementary School could safely cross Bryant Boulevard (Highway 87).[61] But it was the implementation of single member districts at the city level (a concept since extended to the county and to the school district) for which she is best remembered. As the eulogy in the San Angelo *Standard-Times* read on June 2, 1993: "It was that coup that earned for María Cárdenas an undisputed place in the history of San Angelo."[62]

Notes

1. No easy translation comes with these names, and in fact a literal translation can very well be corrupted by a person's body language when employing the terms, or one's intonation when uttering the words. But if English translations must be offered, then "*una doña*," or "*una Juana Gallo*" implies feistiness in women, while Adelita refers to the courageous women soldiers (*soldaderas*) who accompanied armies during the Mexican Revolution of 1910. One historian has defined a "*vieja*" as a wench (perhaps too derisive a translation), and *una entremetida* can be loosely defined as a busybody.

2. Le Kilgore, "Women in Power," *San Angelo Magazine*, 2 (February 1983): 6–7; *Los Tiempos*, a supplement to the San Angelo *Standard-Times*, April 25, 1984, 1; *Standard-Times*, May 30, 1993, 1A, 4A; obituary of Maria's father is in ibid., May 8, 1984, 2A. Also, interview with Abel Cárdenas Jr., San Angelo, Texas, November 8, 2003.

3. San Angelo *Standard-Times*, September 9, 1971, 4B. Unless otherwise noted, all citations from the *Standard-Times* come from the morning editions.

4. Ibid., April 3, 1968, 4A.

5. Ibid., November 1, 1971, 2A.

6. Ibid., September 4, 1972, 6A.

7. Ibid., September 10, 1972, 7A; and October 17, 1972, 4B.

8. San Angelo *Evening-Standard*, October 27, 1971, 12A; and February 18, 1972, 1B.

9. San Angelo *Standard-Times*, February 22, 1973, 1A; and April 5, 1973, 4D.

10. Ibid., July 6, 1974, 1A; September 15, 1974, 4A.

11. Kilgore, "Women in Power," 6–7.

12. San Angelo *Standard-Times*, April 4, 1976, 1A, 14A.

13. Ibid., March 28, 1976, 3B.

14. Ibid., March 14, 1976, 3B.

15. Ibid., June 15, 1976, 3A; and December 16, 1976, 6B.

16. Ibid., December 11, 1977, 11A; and September 3, 1977, 3A.

17. Ibid., December 15, 1977, 8A; and December 18, 1977, 3A.

18. Ibid., January 20, 1978, 1A; March 2, 1978, 1A; April 2, 1978, 1A, 12A; and May 14, 1978, 1A; San Angelo *Evening-Standard*, May 10, 1978, 3A.

19. San Angelo *Evening-Standard*, August 28, 1980, 1A, 4A.

20. San Angelo *Standard-Times*, June 27, 1978, 3A; September 13, 1979, 4A; and April 25, 1980, 2A; San Angelo *Evening-Standard*, August 28, 1979, 2A.

21. Arnoldo De León, *San Angeleños: Mexican Americans in San Angelo, Texas* (San Angelo: Fort Concho Museum Press, 1985), 117.

22. San Angelo *Evening-Standard*, April 30, 1980, 3A.

23. San Angelo *Standard-Times*, February 7, 1980, 2B; and March 30, 1980, 2C.

24. Interview with Abel Cárdenas Jr., November 8, 2003.

25. San Angelo *Evening-Standard*, August 28, 1980, 1A, 4A; June 4, 1984, 1A.

26. Editorial in San Angelo *Evening-Standard*, August 28, 1980, 1A, 4A.

27. San Angelo *Standard-Times*, August 18, 1981, 6A.

28. Ibid., April 12, 1981, 1A.

29. Ibid., February 7, 1983, 6B; February 14, 1983, 4B; and February 16, 1983, 1A.

30. San Angelo *Evening-Standard*, June 25, 1981, 1A.

31. San Angelo *Standard-Times*, October 22, 1981, 1C; and May 3, 1984, 1C.

32. San Angelo *Standard-Times*, November 6, 1981, 1A; San Angelo *Evening-Standard*, November 2, 1981, 1A; January 12, 1982, 1A.

33. San Angelo *Standard-Times*, November 3, 1981, 4B; November 6, 1981, p. 1A; and November 10, 1981, 5B.

34. Ibid., November 10, 1981, 5B; November 13, 1981, 5B; November 21, 1981, 2B; and November 26, 1981, 4C.

35. Ibid., November 21, 1981, 2B; and December 5, 1981, 1A.

36. Ibid., January 26, 1982, 1A; January 20, 1982, 1B; and January 27, 1982, 1A.

37. Ibid., March 16, 1982, 8B.

38. Ibid., February 2, 1982, 2A; March 28, 1982, 1C; and April 4, 1982, 1A.

39. Ibid., May 19, 1982, 2B.

40. Ibid., September 28, 1983, 10A; and February 3, 1984, 13A.

41. Ibid., September 28, 1983, 10A.

42. Ibid., September 30, 1983, 10A; and February 3, 1984, 13A.

43. Ibid., February 3, 1984, 13A.

44. Ibid., April 5, 1984, 2D.

45. Ibid., May 6, 1984, 1A, 9A.

46. Ibid., May 31, 1984, 1A; San Angelo *Evening-Standard*, May 31, 1984, 1A.

47. San Angelo *Standard-Times*, June 3, 1984, 1A.

48. Ibid., June 5, 1984, 11A; June 6, 1984, 2A; June 8, 1984, 15A; San Angelo *Evening-Standard*, June 12, 1984, 3A.

49. San Angelo *Standard-Times*, May 6, 1984, 9A; June 3, 1984, p. 15A. I was at the Cárdenas home on election night.

50. De León, *San Angeleños*, 118.

51. San Angelo *Standard-Times*, March 29, 1985, 4A; February 2, 1986, 1A.

52. Ibid., May 7, 1985, 7B; April 4, 1986, 1A; August 30, 1986, 1A; May 30, 1993, 4A.

53. Ibid., April 27, 1991, 2C.

54. Ibid., September 5, 1984, news clipping courtesy of *Standard-Times*.

55. Ibid., May 16, 1993, 1C; May 20, 1993, 1A, 4A.

56. Ibid., May 30, 1993, 1A, 4A; June 2, 1993, 1A, 6A.

57. Ibid., May 30, 1993, 1A, 4A.

58. Ibid., *Los Tiempos*, April 25, 1984, 1.

59. San Angelo *Standard-Times*, December 31, 1989, 7C; and December 26, 1982, 4C.

60. Ibid., May 30, 1993, 4A.

61. Ibid., May 16, 1993, 1C, 2C.

62. Ibid., June 2, 1993, 1A, 6A.

Selected Bibliography

Baeza, Abelardo. "*La Escuela de Don Clemente*: History of the Madero Ward Elementary School in Alpine, Texas, 1910–1936." *Journal of Big Bend Studies* 7 (January 1995): 41–53.

———. "*La Escuela del Barrio*: A History of Alpine's Centennial School, 1936–1969." *Journal of Big Bend Studies* 4 (January 1992): 131–45.

Braudaway, Doug. "Bracketing Bean: The Other Two Leaders of Langtry, Texas." *Journal of Big Bend Studies* 20 (2008): 61–73.

———. "Santos Garza: The Father of San Felipe Schools." *Journal of South Texas* 19 (Fall 2006): 210–20.

———. "Torres Founders of Langtry." Online publication for Val Verde County Historical Commission.

Cano, Alexander Soto. "The Mexican American Community of Knickerbocker." *West Texas Historical Association Yearbook* 79 (October 2003): 24–34.

De León, Arnoldo. "Blowout 1910 Style: A Chicano School Boycott in West Texas." *Texana* 12, no. 2 (1974): 124–40.

———. "Eva Camúñez Tucker: Hispanic Philanthropist in the Concho Country." *Journal of Big Bend Studies* 15 (2003): 181 94.

———. *Las Fiestas Patrias: Biographic Notes on the Hispanic Presence in San Angelo, Texas.* San Antonio: Caravel Press, 1978.

———. "María Cárdenas: San Angelo Chicano Era Activist." In *Invisible Texans: Women and Minorities in Texas History*, edited by Donald Willett and Stephen Curley, 226–36. Boston: McGraw-Hill, 2005.

———. "Mexican Americans in the Edwards Plateau and Trans-Pecos Region, 1900–2000: A Demographic Study." *Southwestern Historical Quarterly* 112 (October 2008): 149–70.

———. *San Angeleños: Mexican Americans in San Angelo, Texas.* San Angelo: Fort Concho Museum Press, 1985.

———. "*Los Tasinques* and the Sheep Shearers' Union of North America: A Strike in West Texas, 1934." *West Texas Historical Association Yearbook* 55 (1979): 3–16.

De León, Arnoldo, and Bruce A. Glasrud. "Bibliophiling Tejano Scholarship: A West Texas Collaboration." *West Texas Historical Association Yearbook* 80 (2004).

Duarte, Gloria. "The Education of Eva Camúñez Tucker: *El Querer es Poder*." *West Texas Historical Association Yearbook* 79 (October 2003): 106–18.

———. "Eva Camúñez's Teaching Career, 1932–1942." *West Texas Historical Association Yearbook* 85 (October 2009): 96–107.

———. "From Boxing to Painting: Lorenzo Castañeda, Jr." *Journal of Big Bend Studies* 20 (2008): 27–37.

———. "Josefa Lara Camúñez: Mexican American Businesswoman." *Journal of Big Bend Studies* 18 (2006): 121–34.

Elam, Earl H. "Acculturation on the Rio Grande Frontier: The Founding of San José del Polvo and the Family of Lucía Rede Madrid." *Journal of Big Bend Studies* 5 (January 1993): 81–95.

Esparza, Jesse J. "Schools of Their Own: The San Felipe Independent School District and Mexican American Educational Autonomy, Del Rio, Texas, 1928–1972." PhD diss., University of Houston, 2008.

Flores, María Eva, CDP. "The Good Life the Hard Way: The Mexican American Community of Fort Stockton, Texas, 1930–1945." PhD diss., Arizona State University, 2000.

———. "What a Difference a Day Makes!" In *Mexican Americans and World War II*, edited by Maggie Rivas-Rodriguez, 177–200. Austin: University of Texas Press, 2005.

Glasrud, Bruce A., and Arnoldo De León. "Tejanos in West Texas: A Selected Bibliography." *Journal of Big Bend Studies* 15 (2003).

Lindsay, Marcia. "A Study of the Hispanic Population of Tom Green County, Texas, in 1910." *Fort Concho Report* 19 (Fall 1987): 3–18.

Mendoza de Levario, Israel. *A Brief Chronicle of Presidio del Norte: Homeland of the Jumano.* Austin: La Junta Press, 2012.

Prewitt, Steven W. "'We Didn't Ask to Come to This Party': Self-Determination Collides with the Federal Government in the Public Schools of Del Rio, Texas, 1890–1971." PhD diss., University of Houston, 2000.

Primera, José C. "*Los Hermanos* Torres: Early Settlers of Pecos County." *Permian Historical Annual* 20 (1980): 89–96.

Stewart, Kenneth L., and Arnoldo De León. "Education, Literacy, and Occupational Structure in West Texas, 1860–1900." *West Texas Historical Association Yearbook* 60 (1984): 127–43.

Tinney, Ed. "I'll Keep My Children: The Life of Pioneer Educator Noé Lara Camúñez." *West Texas Historical Association Yearbook* 75 (1999): 23–31.

Villanueva, Nicholas, Jr. "Decade of Disorder: The Execution of León Martínez, Jr. and Mexican/Anglo Race Relations in Texas during the First Four Years of the Mexican Revolution." In *The Mexican Revolution: Conflict and Consolidation, 1910–1940*, edited by Douglas W. Richmond and Sam W. Haynes, 7–34. College Station: Texas A&M University Press, 2013.

Wright, Paul. "Life on Both Sides of the Tracks in Early Alpine." *West Texas Historical Association Yearbook* 73 (1997): 96–112.

———. "Population Patterns in Presidio County in 1880: Evidence from the Census." *Journal of Big Bend Studies* 7 (January 1995): 181–201.

———. "Residential Segregation in Two Early West Texas Towns." *Southwestern Historical Quarterly* 102 (January 1999): 295–320.

———. "A Tumultuous Decade: Changes in the Mexican-Origin Population of the Big Bend, 1910–1920." *Journal of Big Bend Studies* 10 (1998): 163–87.

———. "Work among Anglos and Hispanics in the Big Bend, 1910." *West Texas Historical Association Yearbook* 62 (1995): 21–35.

Index